HUMANITARIAN
CHALLENGES AND
INTERVENTION

DILEMMAS IN WORLD POLITICS

Series Editor
George A. Lopez, University of Notre Dame

Dilemmas in World Politics offers teachers and students in international relations a series of quality books on critical issues, trends, and regions in international politics. Each text examines a "real world" dilemma and is structured to cover the historical, theoretical, practical, and projected dimensions of its subject.

EDITORIAL BOARD

BOOKS IN THIS SERIES

Humanitarian Challenges and Intervention, Second Edition
Thomas G. Weiss and Cindy Collins

The European Union: Dilemmas of Regional Integration
James A. Caporaso

The United Nations in the Post–Cold War Era, Second Edition
Karen A. Mingst and Margaret P. Karns

International Futures: Choices in the Face of Uncertainty, Third Edition
Barry B. Hughes

Global Gender Issues, Second Edition
V. Spike Peterson and Anne Sisson Runyon

International Human Rights, Second Edition
Jack Donnelly

Democracy and Democratization in a Changing World, Second Edition
Georg Sørensen

Revolution and Transition in East-Central Europe, Second Edition
David S. Mason

Ethnic Conflict in World Politics
Ted Robert Gurr and Barbara Harff

Dilemmas of Development Assistance
Sarah J. Tisch and Michael B. Wallace

East Asian Dynamism, Second Edition
Steven Chan

FORTHCOMING

Dilemmas of International Trade, Second Edition
Bruce E. Moon

☐   ☐   ☐

Global Environmental Politics, Third Edition
Gareth Porter, Janet Brown, and Pamela Chasek

☐   ☐   ☐

One Land, Two Peoples, Third Edition
Deborah Gerner

☐   ☐   ☐

Russia and the World
Andrew C. Kuchins

HUMANITARIAN CHALLENGES AND INTERVENTION

SECOND EDITION

Thomas G. Weiss
THE GRADUATE CENTER, THE CITY UNIVERSITY OF NEW YORK

Cindy Collins
DEPARTMENT OF POLITICAL SCIENCE, BROWN UNIVERSITY

Westview Press
A Member of the Perseus Books Group

Dilemmas in World Politics

Copyright © 2000 by Westview Press, A Member of the Perseus Books Group

Published in 2000 in the United States of America by Westview Press, 5500 Central Avenue, Boulder, Colorado 80301–2877, and in the United Kingdom by Westview Press, 12 Hid's Copse Road, Cumnor Hill, Oxford OX2 9JJ

Find us on the World Wide Web at www.westviewpress.com

Library of Congress Cataloging-in-Publication Data
Weiss, Thomas George.
    Humanitarian challenges and intervention / Thomas G. Weiss, Cindy Collins.—2nd ed.
        p.   cm. — (Dilemmas in world politics)
    Includes bibliographical references and index.
    ISBN 0-8133-6799-9
    1. International relief.   2. War victims—Services for.   3. World politics—1989–
I. Collins, Cindy.   II. Title.   III. Series.

HV553.W425   2000
362.87'0526—dc21   00-039875

10   9   8   7   6   5   4   3   2   1

Contents

□　□　□

Illustrations

Maps

Photographs

Cartoons

□ □ □

Preface to the
Second Edition

Authors should always ask themselves whether a second edition of a book is necessary. In regard to this particular book, several colleagues who regularly have used the text in the classroom urged us to prepare a new edition, commenting that although they still found the first edition useful in their courses, it was in need of updating. Much has occurred in the years since the publication of the first edition, including the most recent *annus horribilis*, 1999. Humanitarian intervention remains at least as central to American and international politics as it was in 1995, when the first edition was written. The first humanitarian air war, waged in Kosovo, and the first full-fledged U.N. trusteeship, after the catastrophe in Timor, were sufficient to take us back to our word processors.

These two events signaled an end to "Vietmalia syndrome"—the American hesitancy to get involved militarily overseas, a long-standing consequence of the more than 50,000 fatalities in Southeast Asia (not to mention the 18 body bags from the humanitarian mission in Mogadishu). Today, the deployment of U.S. forces for humanitarian ends remains a policy option in crises around the world. As Joseph Nye wrote shortly after returning to his academic position at Harvard, following a stint in Washington as assistant secretary of defense: "Such crises raise moral concerns that the American people consistently include in their list of foreign policy interests. Policy experts may deplore such sympathies, but they are a democratic reality."[1] Students of international relations—both as students and as citizens—should be aware of the difficult issues involved in deciding whether to undertake military humanitarian action.

Thus, the central purpose of this new and expanded edition remains to synthesize for our readers the insights that we have gained through field research and analysis in recent years. The 1990s have witnessed an increasing emphasis on human rights and humanitarian values. As we go to press, events once again have demonstrated the intimate but seemingly bizarre link between the hardheaded and hardhearted application of force usually associated with "realists" in textbooks, and the supposedly softheaded and softhearted application of norms usually associated with "idealists." This last year of the millennium has confirmed a long-term trend redefining certain humanitarian norms and crises as being sufficiently intertwined with national interests to justify rigorous action on behalf of victims.

The book has the same title as its predecessor and is recognizably drawn from the earlier text. However, several organizational and substantive changes have been made. At the suggestion of many readers, "Actors" and "Arenas," previously addressed in a single chapter, are now separately discussed, in Chapters 2 and 3. The latter has been expanded to include Kosovo and updated material on the former Yugoslavia after the Dayton Accords. A more general treatment of the upheaval in the African Great Lakes has been added to an expanded treatment of genocide in Rwanda. Again at the suggestion of interested readers, the material in Chapters 3, 4, and 5 has been restructured and expanded into two new chapters focused respectively on dilemmas in the humanitarian sphere faced in the field, and those faced in policymaking at headquarters (Chapters 4 and 5). A new chapter (6) focuses on policy- and decision-making in the sphere of international peace and security, where militarized humanitarian intervention has become a tool of increasingly frequent resort during the past decade.

As our French colleagues might note, "Plus ça change, plus c'est la même chose." There are new crises and new information, but the basic decisionmaking challenges remain painfully familiar. In this regard, a passage from Albert Camus's *La peste* (The Plague) is particularly apt—a passage that even after the incredible human devastation described in this novel, many find uplifting: "He knew that the tale he had to tell could not be one of a final victory. It could be only the record of what had to be done, and what assuredly would have to be done again in the never-ending fight against terror and its onslaughts . . . by all who, while unable to be saints but refusing to bow to pestilence, strive their utmost to be healers." We hope readers will gain from our book a clearer idea of the ongoing dynamics of humanitarian action in war zones—new insights for judging not only what has been done thus far but also what might be done better in the future to help victims. If so, we will have achieved our goal.

Although this edition, like the first, is primarily a product of our own labor, we would like to acknowledge helpful suggestions made by Leo Wiegman and David McBride at Westview Press, and by the press's two anonymous readers. Sofia Heine at The Graduate Center of The City University of New York was invaluable in helping check facts and polish the final manuscript. We would be remiss if we did not repeat a few acknowl-edgments from the first edition: on the substantive side, Larry Minear, Antonio Donini, Giles Whitcomb, George Lopez, and Jennifer Knerr; and on the production side, Fred Fullerton, Richard Gann, Gregory Kazarian, Amy Langlais, and Jennifer Patrick.

Thomas G. Weiss and Cindy Collins

Acronyms

ADRA	International Adventist Development and Relief Agency
AICF	International Action Against Hunger
AIDAB	Australian International Development Assistance Bureau
AIDS	Acquired immune deficiency syndrome
BBC	British Broadcasting Corporation
CARE	Cooperative for American Relief to Everywhere
CIA	Central Intelligence Agency
CIMIC	civilian military cooperation
CIS	Commonwealth of Independent States
CISP	International Committee for the Development of Peoples
CMOCS	Civil-Military Operations Centres
COMECON	Council for Mutual Economic Assistance
CRS	Catholic Relief Services
CRS	Congressional Research Service
DHA	Department of Humanitarian Affairs [U.N.]
DRI	Direct Relief International
EC	European Community
ECHO	European Commission Humanitarian Office
ECOMOG	Economic Community of West African States Monitoring Group
ECOSOC	Economic and Social Council [U.N.]
ECOWAS	Economic Community of West African States
EU	European Union
FAO	Food and Agriculture Organization [U.N.]
GNP	gross national product
HUMPROFOR	Humanitarian Protection Force
ICJ	International Court of Justice
ICRC	International Committee of the Red Cross
ICVA	International Council for Voluntary Agencies
IDP	internally displaced person

IFOR	Implementation Force (in the former Yugoslavia)
IFRC	International Federation of Red Cross and Red Crescent Societies
IGO	intergovernmental organization
ILO	International Labor Organization
IMC	International Medical Corps
IMF	International Monetary Fund
INMED	International Medical Services for Health
IRC	International Rescue Committee
JNA	Yugoslav People's Army
KFOR	Kosovo Force
KLA	Kosovo Liberation Army
MDM	Médecins du Monde [Doctors of the World]
MRE	meal ready to eat
MSF	Médecins sans Frontières [Doctors Without Borders]
NATO	North Atlantic Treaty Organization
NGO	nongovernmental organization
NRC	Norwegian Refugee Council
OAS	Organization of American States
OAU	Organization of African Unity
OCHA	Office for the Coordination of Humanitarian Affairs [U.N.]
ODA	Overseas Development Administration [U.K.]
OFDA	Office of Foreign Disaster Assistance [U.S.]
ONUCA	U.N. Observer Group in Central America
ONUSAL	U.N. Observer Mission in El Salvador
OSCE	Organization for Security and Cooperation in Europe
Oxfam	Oxford Committee for Famine Relief
P-5	Permanent Members [U.N. Security Council]
PDD	presidential decision directive
RPF	Rwandan Patriotic Front
SCF/NZ	Save the Children Foundation/New Zealand
SPLA	Sudan People's Liberation Army
SRSG	special representative of the secretary-general [U.N.]
SST	Swedish Support Team
U.N.	United Nations
UNAMET	U.N. Administrative Mission in East Timor
UNAMIR	U.N. Assistance Mission in Rwanda
UNDP	U.N. Development Programme
UNDRO	U.N. Disaster Relief Office
UNHCR	U.N. High Commissioner for Refugees
UNICEF	U.N. Children's Emergency Fund
UNITAF	Unified Task Force [Somalia]

UNMIK	U.N. Interim Administration Mission in Kosovo
UNOSOM	U.N. Operation in Somalia (I and II)
UNPA	U.N. Protected Area
UNPROFOR	U.N. Protection Force [in the former Yugoslavia]
UNSC	U.N. Security Council
USAID	U.S. Agency for International Development
WFP	World Food Programme
WHO	World Health Organization

□   □   □

Introduction

The world of humanitarian action, as seen on television and in newspapers, is one of refugees shuffling along winding dirt roads; tent villages surrounded by barbed wire; men and young boys brandishing M16s; and food tossed from the back of a U.N. truck to reaching hands and anxious, hungry faces. Through the mass media, we know that there was a humanitarian crisis in Kosovo at the end of the 1990s; another in northern Iraq and Somalia at the beginning of the same decade; and others in Rwanda and Bosnia, in the middle. It might appear that only a handful of cases of political, social, and economic collapse have required emergency humanitarian assistance.

Beyond the media's lens, approximately fifty wars are raging around the world while you read this paragraph. These wars and others have taken the lives of over 2 million children in the past decade. Some 50 million of your global neighbors will be homeless tonight because of war and famine; millions of others are homeless because of the more subtle violence of chronic poverty. War and disease are cutting lives short. In the next fifteen minutes, someone will step on a land mine. In Sierra Leone, the average length of a man's life is 36 years; in Afghanistan, more than 25 percent of children never see their fifth birthday.[1] Every day, relief workers risk their lives to treat the needy in environments where roads are often impassable, food and medical supplies are pilfered by combatants, and pharmaceutical firms still send unusable, outdated medicine in order to be able to claim charitable tax deductions.

This is the real world of humanitarian action. Although you may feel removed from such nightmarish events, this is your world, too. Approximately one-third of the 6 billion people who share this world with you lack clean water or sanitation and are chronically hungry. A greater number of people with fewer resources and less hope gives rise to environmental degradation; massive migration; the quick spread of diseases not adequately addressed or quickly identified; and increased conflict, with its accompanying proliferation of light and conventional weapons.

1

Humanitarians provide relief and protection to victims of war. In each crisis, the needs are different. A response evaluation begins with understanding the physical, mental, and economic baseline of the population prior to the official outbreak of conflict. For example, a child in the Great Lakes region of Africa is more likely than a child from the former Yugoslavia to have been malnourished, diseased, exploited, and orphaned during peace time. This is not to say that the more vulnerable child will receive a greater share of humanitarian resources and physical protection. Political and public interests in a crisis often are the determinants of relief and protection. Many of the dilemmas of humanitarian action occur at this nexus between the resource requirements of a vulnerable population and the politics of intervention.

The challenges and dilemmas of humanitarian assistance in war zones present tortuous trade-offs to policymakers and to those working directly with victims. If you worked in such a position, would you choose to move noncombatants out of the country, lead them to food distribution points within country, or designate an area as a safe haven? Would you focus solely on delivering food and medical supplies and turn a blind eye to blatant violations of human rights, such as rape and torture? Would you throw your hands up or sit on them, claiming that the suffering of those whom you cannot see and most probably will never meet is not your problem? In contemplating your alternatives, you would have to consider the agenda of your employer as well as your own. Would dead peacekeepers cost you votes in the next election? Would donors support your using funds in crises that do not receive media attention? These and other thorny problems are addressed directly in the pages that follow.

This book describes more fully the organization and challenges of the global humanitarian safety net that is meant to catch those who become vulnerable because of man-made crises. It concerns primarily two types of **humanitarian action**—the provision of **relief** to civilian populations and the **protection** of their basic **human rights.**

The international humanitarian system comprises governmental, institutional, and individual actors. This system is often called the international humanitarian *community*. But this idealistic term hides the diversity of interests and characteristics among institutional actors—a diversity that cannot be wished away as we try to understand the nature of dilemmas in humanitarian operations and how to address them. The moral and practical reasoning that supports each actor's participation in collective humanitarian action may differ dramatically from that of others and will be reflected in the choices that each actor "sees" when deciding upon courses of action (or in some cases, inaction). For these reasons, "system" is more useful than "community" for the purpose of examining challenges.

Humanitarian tasks include gathering data about the severity of a crisis, negotiating a framework with the warring parties for providing aid, mobilizing the necessary resources, orchestrating the aid effort, delivering the goods, staffing the operation, and assuring appropriate accountability. When war becomes a barrier to providing noncombatants with relief, traditional forms of humanitarian assistance may be augmented by a military presence. Human rights action during conflicts also involves data gathering and negotiations but focuses more specifically on efforts to document and expose abuses and to mobilize international pressure and policy to halt violations against human dignity. Postconflict war crimes tribunals are also part of the humanitarian and human rights agendas.

Humanitarian action in war zones shares similarities with assistance provided after natural disasters and with noncrisis reconstruction and development projects. However, when armed conflict rages, humanitarians face challenges that are far more acute. In a war zone, for example, a relief agency responsible for emergency relief or coordination may be unable to maintain **impartiality** or political **neutrality,** equal access to all noncombatants, or adequate communications with belligerents. Impartiality means helping without discrimination as to ethnic or national criteria, religious beliefs, or political opinion. In principle, humanitarian efforts made to relieve the suffering of individuals are guided solely by the victims' needs, and priority is given to the most urgent cases of distress. Neutrality means not taking sides in hostilities or engaging at any time in controversies linked to an armed conflict. Neutrality excludes advocacy in favor of a party to the conflict and public accusation. But neutrality does not mean keeping silent in defending the victims' rights, especially when those rights are grossly disregarded by the belligerents. A dilemma emerges for humanitarians—between maintaining the principle of impartiality and neutrality when noncombatants are clearly being targeted by a warring party, and making public the violations and taking the chance that the belligerents will withdraw their **consent** for a humanitarian presence. This dilemma is often distilled to the more basic conceptual question of which form of action is more humanitarian.

THE CONCEPT OF HUMANITARIANISM

Humanitarianism is defined in most dictionaries as the concern for human well-being; and a *humanitarian* is a person who actively engages in promoting human welfare. The definitions are innocuous; the manner in which humanitarianism is expressed or the objectives for which it is used as a tool, however, are not.

Each humanitarian is free to determine what actions promote human welfare. For some, human welfare is enhanced by adhering to a certain religious or political dogma; for others, by building an irrigation system or educating women. Some humanitarians have an irresistible impulse and philosophical commitment to help wherever suffering exists; others are more discriminating and practice **triage** based on calculations of who is most likely to survive and should therefore receive priority treatment, and who must be left to chance.

Politics also pushes the limits of which resources and services are identified as humanitarian. For example, the food, telecommunications equipment, and uniforms funneled to the Nicaraguan insurgents (contras) in 1985 by the U.S. government were labeled "humanitarian." In 1995, with a U.S. trade embargo still in place against the Castro regime, a U.S. citizen received permission from Washington to donate thirty pianos to Cuba under the semantic umbrella of "humanitarian aid" after promising that the pianos would not be used for political purposes. On a less humorous note, following the 1977–1978 Ogaden War between Ethiopia and Somalia, some food-aid providers followed a path of action that roamed from humanitarian to self-serving and back to humanitarian again. The donors, motivated by organizational survival and politics, continued to provide free or heavily subsidized food to the Somali people long after famine and refugee flows had subsided. Local farmers, unable to compete with free agricultural commodities, lost the incentive to work the land and maintain self-sufficiency. Resulting cycles of famine and mass urbanization were exacerbated by war, and all of these factors contributed to the **complex emergency** in Somalia in 1992. Part of the humanitarian response to the new crisis was to deliver free food again.

A complex emergency combines internal conflicts with large-scale displacements of people and fragile or failing economic, political, and social institutions. Other symptoms include noncombatant death, starvation, or malnutrition; disease and mental illness; random and systematic violence against noncombatants; infrastructure collapse; widespread lawlessness; and interrupted food production and trade. Table I.1 illustrates the number of countries experiencing complex emergencies in 1999. The root causes of complex emergencies are a combination of political power struggles, ethnic or religious tension, economic or territorial disputes, a perceived sense of widespread injustice, and/or natural disasters such as drought or flooding. Because different actors conceive of humanitarianism as limited to the provision of emergency relief, the symptoms rather than the root causes of complex emergencies usually receive attention. Limited resources are thus allocated to relief operations instead of reconstruction and development, sometimes in the midst of external military

TABLE I.1   Complex Humanitarian Emergencies, 1999

Country	People in Need*
Afghanistan	3.9 million
Angola	more than 3 million
Azerbaijan	820,000
Bosnia and Herzegovina	1.4 million
Burundi	880,000
Colombia	750,000
Croatia	360,000
Democratic Republic of Congo (DROC)	625,000
Eritrea	400,000
Ethiopia	2 million
Federal Republic of Yugoslavia	1.6 million
Georgia	330,000
Haiti	400,000
Iraq	1.5 million
Liberia	400,000
North Korea	6.7 million
Rwanda	300,000
Sierra Leone	less than 1 million
Somalia	1 million
Sri Lanka	500,000
Sudan	4.4 million
Tajikistan	0.9 million**
Uganda	500,000

* "The number of people in need includes refugees *from* the named country, internally displaced persons (IDPs) and others requiring humanitarian aid in their home locations. These numbers represent our best estimate, based on a review of information available not only from the U.S. Committee for Refugees but also from the U.N. High Commissioner for Refugees (UNHCR), other nongovernmental organizations, and the media. Because the definitions of populations 'in need' of emergency humanitarian assistance used by the international relief community are often inconsistent and imprecise, the numbers should be treated as approximations."

** The number in need is highly questionable due to inadequate access by relief agencies, the small number of relief agencies operating in the country, and the difficulty in distinguishing economic migrants from victims of humanitarian emergencies."

Source: National Intelligence Council, *Global Humanitarian Emergencies: Trends and Projections, 1999–2000* (Washington, D.C.: National Intelligence Council, August 1999), pp. ix–xv, quotes from p. xv.

involvement. The absence of a standard definition of or principles for humanitarianism intensifies the challenges already posed by the motivations and actions of warring parties as well as by humanitarian actors.

The International Court of Justice (ICJ) missed an opportunity for clarification of what actions legitimately fall within a category of humanitarian behavior in a 1986 decision that ruled in favor of Nicaragua and
against the United States, which had laid mines in Nicaraguan territorial
waters. The ICJ, the judicial organ of the United Nations, was asked to define humanitarianism in legal terms but declined. Instead, the ICJ pointed
to the principles held by one humanitarian actor, the International Committee of the Red Cross (ICRC), to demonstrate the actions, rather than
define the concept, of what is indeed humanitarian. The principles of the
ICRC state that humanitarian aid must be given without discrimination
to all in need of assistance once belligerents have given their **consent** for
the ICRC to do so. However, the belligerents' consent to the presence of
humanitarian actors can be withdrawn if the warring parties no longer
see a political or military benefit.

The ICJ decision may lead some observers to believe, perhaps hastily,
that all activities undertaken by other actors under the rubric of humanitarian action that are *not* actions or principles condoned by the ICRC or
clones of its model are *not* truly humanitarian. The ICRC principle of independence cannot be adhered to at all times by humanitarian actors
with multiple functions and considerations, such as governments and **intergovernmental organizations (IGOs)**. The ICRC principle of independence demands that those providing assistance act without ulterior,
mainly political or military, motives and instructions. If one were to eliminate all actors whose motives include political, military, or organizational considerations in addition to their desire to relieve suffering, the
ICRC might find itself operating alone and without the resources of its
greatest benefactors—governments.

In addition to conceptual fuzziness, there have been other reasons for
cynicism and criticism of humanitarian action. Just as there is scrutiny in
the domestic arena about the legitimacy of welfare and the extent of its
abuse and waste, there are opportunists who carry that dialogue into foreign policy and humanitarian arenas. As a result, impressions of how
much the United States contributes to foreign aid or to U.N. peacekeeping
operations are distorted. For instance, a January 1995 poll found that the
average American respondent believed that 15 percent of the federal budget went to foreign aid; but the actual figure was approximately 1 percent.
An April 1995 poll showed that Americans believed that U.S. troops accounted for 40 percent of U.N. peacekeepers worldwide instead of the
actual 5 percent at that time. The perception that the American people are
calling for isolationism is also erroneous. Instead, polls indicate that the
average American is returning to universalist ideals that call for distributing among all states the responsibility for upholding principles of humanity. It is multilateral cooperation, not isolationism, that Americans

view as the best possible means for solving current conflicts with humanitarian consequences. The desire to stop being the "world's policeman" is not synonymous with the desire to withdraw from involvement altogether. A 1994 poll conducted by the Program on International Policy Attitudes revealed that only 14 percent of respondents believed that "the U.S. should not make sacrifices in an effort to help the world as a whole." And even when United Nations–bashing seemed a sport in media circles, 84 percent of respondents polled in late 1994 felt that strengthening the United Nations should be a U.S. foreign policy goal.[2]

Thus, although there is a profusion of misinformation as well as private and public debates over the efficacy and value of humanitarian action, the impulse to help remains strong and unyielding. Regardless of whether discussants are speaking positively or pejoratively, the increased attention to the mitigation of civilian suffering is indicative of a widening acceptance that humanitarian **norms** are firmly rooted in the psyche of international society. The belief that all of humanity—regardless of race, religion, age, or gender—deserves protection from unnecessary suffering is becoming a more universally accepted truth as well as a norm that occasionally guides the behavior of state-to-state and state-to-society relations.

It is worthwhile to spend a moment on the second noun in this book's title, because clarity is often absent from considerations of "intervention." This term covers the spectrum of possible actions—from making telephone calls to dispatching military forces—that are intended to alter internal affairs in another country. As such, intervention is almost synonymous with the state practice of international relations, which in the post–Cold War period has witnessed more significant outside intrusions into domestic affairs for humanitarian reasons than previously.

The history of humanitarian military intervention is the history of accessing suffering civilians without the consent of the warring parties under whose political control such victims live. Included in that history are the cross-border forays of **nongovernmental organizations (NGOs)** into Tigray and Afghanistan. Specifically what concerns us in this volume are **Chapter VII** decisions by the United Nations Security Council, which allow for the use of economic sanctions or military force to coerce a change in the behavior of belligerents. Talk-show hosts, academic conference participants, politicians, and the proverbial woman in the street are preoccupied with what the editor of *Foreign Affairs* described prematurely as the "Springtime for Interventionism."[3] These individuals are hesitating at a fork in the road about using military force in support of humanitarian objectives. One route leads back toward traditional peacekeeping and the other toward the measured application of superior military force in support of more ambitious international decisions, including the enforcement of human rights in northern Iraq, democratic processes in Haiti, and new borderlines in the Former Yugoslavia. (See Box I.1.)

The present balance of opinion, however, favors traditional peacekeeping, and the Somalia and Bosnia experiences are critical. Reflecting the residue from Vietnam, military reticence about the prospects for involvement in **humanitarian intervention** ironically joins critics who see U.S. dominance in multilateral military efforts as a continuation of American hegemony.

Two unlikely apologists for outside military forces, Alex de Waal and Rakiya Omaar, have observed: "Humanitarian intervention demands a different set of military skills. It is akin to counterinsurgency."[4] Equating humanitarian intervention with counterinsurgency causes alarm to those

---

BOX I.1   Complex Humanitarian Emergencies: Definitions

Peacemaking, also known as "conflict resolution," is action to bring hostile parties to agreement, essentially through such peaceful means as those foreseen in Chapter VII of the U.N. Charter, i.e., through negotiation, inquiry, mediation, conciliation, arbitration, judicial settlement, resort to regional agencies or arrangements, or other peaceful means. Military missions include military-to-military liaison, security assistance, preventive deployment, and show of force.

Peacekeeping is the deployment of a U.N. presence in the field, with the consent of all parties concerned, to allow contending forces that wish to stop fighting to separate with some confidence that they will not be attacked in order to create conditions conducive to a political settlement. Peacekeeping normally involves U.N. military and/or police personnel, and frequently civilians as well. Military mission mandates include monitoring existing peace arrangements.

Peace enforcement refers to actions taken when traditional peacekeeping is not sufficient to keep the peace or when the safety of peacekeeping forces is threatened by actions of one or more parties to the conflict. Peace enforcement differs from peacekeeping in that it allows forces to use measured but sufficient force to restore peaceful conditions after peace has been broken or peacekeeping forces threatened. Peace enforcement measures are usually taken without the full consent of one or more parties to the conflict. Military involvement includes application of armed forces to compel compliance, forcible separation of belligerents, restore order, guarantee/deny mobility, establish protected zones, and protect humanitarian assistance.

Peace-building refers to actions taken to forestall future eruptions between the parties to the conflict. It includes disarming warring parties, controlling and destroying weapons, repatriating refugees, training and supporting security personnel, monitoring elections, promoting human rights practices, reforming or strengthening governmental institutions, and promoting political participation. Military mission statements include activities to restore civil authority and rebuild infrastructure.

Source: Congressional Research Service, *CRS Report for Congress* (Washington, D.C.: Congressional Research Service, June 29, 1995), Appendix I.

in the U.S. Pentagon who are still recovering from the **Vietnam syndrome.** The tremendous loss of U.S. lives in Vietnam has made policymakers skittish about intervening in civil wars, especially without an exit strategy for U.S. troops prior to entering a conflict zone. Moreover, humanitarian intervention often requires a longer-term commitment to assist in postconflict nation-building. Many states are unwilling to make such a commitment. Operation Desert Storm is illustrative of the desire by states to apply overwhelming force quickly, using high-tech weaponry, and then leave the area. Although the primary objective of removing Iraq from Kuwait was accomplished, the devastation to Baghdad was left to humanitarians to remedy. The United Kingdom's military intervention in Malaysia provides an interesting contrast. There, a relatively small number of well-trained soldiers with adequate political support at home were able to accomplish their objective without resorting to excessive force or pulling out before the region was fully stabilized.

Dissenters from "military humanitarianism" include many developing countries clinging to the notion that state **sovereignty** does not permit outside intervention.[5] Sovereignty is an abstraction that theoretically gives states an equal legal status. Each state has a monopoly over the control of the means of force within its boundaries, and no other actor has a right to interfere with a state's authority over its territory and people. Developing countries cling to the sanctity of sovereignty out of fear of renewed major power bullying in the guise of protecting international peace. The Security Council's definition of what constitutes "threats" to international peace and security, on the one hand, is expanding to cover virtually any subject, and on the other hand, remains selective in application.

Developing countries are joined by others whose reasoning is less ideological and is based instead on a static interpretation of **international law.** In an anarchical world without a legitimate authority above individual states, reciprocal rules among states are required to ease the inevitable competition. The presence of outside military forces makes more problematic the tasks of an affected country's own civilian authorities. If the principle of nonintervention were abandoned, further instability and weakened democratic tendencies and institutions might follow.

International law exists only between states. It is that element that binds the members of the international system of states in their adherence to recognized values and standards. It is formulated primarily through international agreements that create rules binding upon the signatories and customary rules, which are basically state practices recognized by the community at large as laying down patterns of conduct requiring compliance. States make the laws, interpret them, and enforce them. For clarification, **international humanitarian law** seeks to regulate the conduct of hostilities during war, prohibiting certain methods of warfare and violations of human rights. A guiding principle is the requirement to protect civilians against the effects of hostilities.[6] Soldiers call these same conventions the "laws of war."

Other critics of robust intervention are civilian humanitarians working in the trenches. For them, what Oxford University's Adam Roberts has called "humanitarian war" is an oxymoron.[7] These civilian workers argue that humanitarian initiatives should be strictly consensual, premised on impartiality and neutrality. Political authorities in armed conflicts must be persuaded to meet their commitments—codified in international humanitarian law—for access to and respect of civilians. Intervention not only raises the levels of violence and complicates the lives of civilian humanitarians in the short run, argue some scholars, but also makes reconciliation more difficult in the longer run.

Yet with 1 in every 115 people on earth forced into flight from war, military involvement may sometimes be the only way to halt **genocide,** massive abuses of human rights, and starvation.[8] Genocide is the deliberate and systematic extermination of a national, racial, ethnic, or religious group. It is a crime under international law, bearing individual responsibility by belligerents and a response by the Security Council to intervene on behalf of the victims. Thus, partisans of the other route at the fork in the road are open to the option of outside military forces intervening to assist civilians trapped in wars. When consent cannot be extracted, economic and military coercion can be justified in operational and ethical terms. The difficulty is knowing precisely when to wait for consent and when to act with coercive measures. When there is sufficient political will, an effective humanitarian response may include military backup that goes far beyond the minimalist use of force in self-defense by traditional U.N. peacekeepers. Rather than suspending relief and withdrawing, the international community can use enough force to guarantee access to civilians, protect aid workers, and keep thugs at bay.

Military intervention in support of humanitarian objectives is not an end in itself. Rather, it is a last-ditch effort to create enough breathing room for the reemergence of local stability and order, which ultimately are prerequisites for the conduct of negotiations that can lead to consent about **humanitarian space** and eventually about lasting peace as well. In order to be perfectly clear about the emergence of this new basis for intervention, the Commission on Global Governance proposed "an appropriate Charter amendment permitting such intervention but restricting it to cases that constitute a violation of the security of people so gross and extreme that it requires an international response on humanitarian grounds."[9]

THE LAYOUT OF THIS BOOK

This book is structured to provide necessary building blocks for understanding the historical sources of the "humanitarian impulse." Chapter 1 outlines the evolution of humanitarian action from an idea, to its codification, to the creation of institutions to facilitate the international implementation of the idea. Chapter 2 introduces three types of external actors who make up the international humanitarian system. Chapter 3 provides up-to-date sketches of the human and political dimensions of six war zones illustrative of complex emergencies and the responses of the international humanitarian system to those crises in the post–Cold War era. You can decide whether, from crisis to crisis, any pattern of learning is emerging among the actors and if the lessons of one crisis have affected subsequent responses. Chapter 4 reflects on the choices made by combatants, noncombatants, relief workers, and soldiers as they pursue their relative interests: aggression, survival, humanitarian assistance, and protection. Chapter 5 looks at the policy choices and decisionmaking for the humanitarian sphere by those who are often sitting in offices at NGO or IGO headquarters or in government office buildings; although the physical space may be quieter than in war zones, the implications of such choices are powerful for those working at the coal face in complex emergencies. Lastly, Chapter 6 examines policy- and decisionmaking in the sphere of international peace and security, where militarized humanitarian intervention has become, on occasion, a policy option.

At the end, you may find yourself uncertain about the possibility of consistent, collective humanitarian responses. Rest assured that you have plenty of company. However, the challenges and dilemmas associated with providing relief and protection must not overshadow the reality that there are children, women, and men suffering from wars not of their making who depend upon outside sustenance for their survival. We would be surprised if most readers are not moved by the devotion and courage of the humanitarians who attempt to make a difference, and if some readers do not choose to devote part of their professional careers to helping on the front lines.

ONE

□ □ □

Evolution of the
Humanitarian Idea

Above all Nations—is Humanity.
—Creed of the Geneva Red Cross

By nightfall on June 24, 1859, the corpses of more than 40,000 Austrian and French soldiers lay scattered on a battlefield near the Italian village of Solferino. Witness to their slaughter was a young Swiss pacifist and businessman, Henri Dunant, who was in Italy seeking the assistance of French emperor Napoleon III in remedying a problem Dunant was having with his mill in Algeria. Dunant, so the story goes, had been inspired by Harriet Beecher Stowe's accounts of slavery in the United States, Florence Nightingale's service to the wounded in the Crimean War, and Elizabeth Fry's efforts at prison reform. Without hesitation, he began to assist the wounded. The carnage on the battlefield was great; the magnitude of the casualties and the lack of sufficient medical personnel, facilities, and supplies were overwhelming. Within two months, 40,000 more would be dead from war-related wounds and insufficient medical attention.

Within a week of the battle, Dunant had convinced Napoleon III to render the first official proclamation regarding the rights of those suffering from war injuries. Napoleon III ordered the release of all Austrian doctors and surgeons so that they could return to their regiments and treat their own wounded. The morally inspired and politically astute actions of Dunant following the Battle of Solferino set into motion an advancement of the idea of international humanitarian action and the necessary institutional form to help ensure the actualization of the ideal—at least, in certain circumstances. Dunant would go on to found the Red Cross in Geneva in 1864. The precedent that he set—of seeking the approval of the sovereign authority for politically neutral, humanitarian intercession on

13

behalf of the victims of war—is still the operating procedure of today's International Committee of the Red Cross. These principles were later codified in the 1864 Geneva Convention for the Amelioration of the Condition of the Wounded in Armies in the Field.

For some, Dunant's response to the Battle at Solferino marks the beginning of modern humanitarian action, even though charitable acts and religious organizations existed long before. The potency of that historical moment lies in the fortuitous convergence of four significant factors: the idea of humanitarian action, the codification of the idea through Napoleon's proclamation and the Geneva Convention, the institutionalization of the idea through the creation of the Red Cross, and the will of a powerful sovereign authority to place humanity before narrow self-interest. In studying a detailed history of humanitarian action, one can easily get lost in the number and meaning of various charters, conventions, **declarations,** and treaties and in the bureaucratic maze of institutions that seem, at times, to hinder a standard and predictable response to humanitarian crises associated with war. On a more general level, one need only remain mindful that the normative framework undergirding the written instruments and formalized institutions is the idea of humanitarian action or the humanitarian impulse, which continues to evolve and manifest itself as international norms.

The historical evolution of the humanitarian idea is represented not by a steadily progressing line but by sudden upward surges followed by temporary losses of momentum, plateaus, and sometimes backpedaling. After great losses of life resulting from war, new laws and institutions are quickly established. The greater the temporal distance from cataclysms, the slower the pace of humanitarian evolution, until events occur that again remind the world of the need for renewed restraint on inhumane behavior. This pattern cannot be explained by either idealist or realist perspectives. **Idealism** claims that war is not inevitable, that humankind is perfectible, and that state-to-state relations are moving progressively (and linearly) toward what political liberal Immanuel Kant called "perpetual peace" in the international system.[1] An idealist perspective does well in explaining the entrenchment of humanitarian ideals in largely democratic countries and the proliferation of nongovernmental humanitarian actors, but it is limited in its ability to explain the continual reemergence of war and the resistance to collective humanitarian action by states and nonstate actors.

In contrast, **realism** refutes claims of human perfectibility.[2] The motivations for behavior among individuals as well as among states are self-interest and domination. Realists do not see a linear progression toward harmony among individuals or states, or any pattern to the evolution of humanitarian ideals; any appearance of humanitarianism in the actions of states is simply a smoke screen for self-interest. A cursory glance at **Cold**

War politics seems to confirm this notion. However, realism cannot explain, for example, why Nordic countries have continually devoted a large percentage of their resources to humanitarian endeavors seemingly devoid of self-interest, or why the liberal values that were internationalized as a result of U.S. hegemony since the end of World War II continue to influence states to resist their own aggressive inclinations and to respond to the call for humanitarian assistance. This phenomenon, often referred to as embedded liberalism,[3] is mirrored in the U.S. Constitution's Bill of Rights, expressed in Roosevelt's four freedoms, and codified in the United Nations' 1948 Universal Declaration of Human Rights and the Preamble to the Charter. Humanitarianism is a reflection of embedded liberalism. It dampens unequivocal acceptance of realists' overgeneralizations of what guides states' behavior toward other states and toward suffering populations.

The pattern of humanitarian evolution is best represented by **liberal institutionalism,** a compromise between the perspectives of idealism and realism. In agreement with realism, liberal institutionalism views states as the most important actors in the international system (although not the only significant ones) and defines power capabilities and self-interest as the primary factors determining how states behave. However, according to this view, a conflict-mitigating factor emerges from transnational institutions and **regimes**—that is, from "principles, norms, rules, and decision-making procedures around which actor expectations converge in a given issue area."[4] Regimes are consequential because they foster cooperation among states. International humanitarian conventions and institutions with humanitarian agendas constrain, in various degrees, certain types of state behavior. States pursue their self-interests within successively narrower ranges of action as a result of increases in codification of international humanitarian law; increases in the number of humanitarian nonstate actors; increases in authority given to intergovernmental institutions such as the United Nations; and the embeddedness of liberal values in an expanding number of democratic societies.

In addition, turbulent conflicts that attract attention because of gross violations of basic human rights are often followed by additional augmentation to humanitarian law and by calls for changes in institutional forms and state action. For example, the atrocities of World War II prompted the Universal Declaration of Human Rights, the replacement of the League of Nations by the United Nations, and U.S. involvement in bringing the war to an end and assisting in Western Europe's reconstruction. As a result, progress in the evolution of humanitarianism took another turn upward—the range of acceptable state behavior became narrower, whereas acknowledgment of international responsibility to alleviate human suffering expanded.

THE EVOLUTION OF THE IDEA OF HUMANITARIAN ACTION

Political discourse, religion, and philosophy provide generous narratives to describe the genesis of the humanitarian impulse. In *Second Discourse,* political philosopher Jean-Jacques Rousseau (1712–1778) found the seeds for humanitarian action in the nature of humankind: "It is pity which carries us without reflection to the assistance of those we see suffer. . . . Commiseration is nothing but a sentiment that puts us in the place of him who suffers. . . . Commiseration will be all the more energetic in proportion as the Onlooking animal identifies more intimately with the suffering animal."[5]

All such social virtues as clemency, humanity, benevolence, and friendship find their origin in the virtue of pity. For Rousseau, pity stems from the intervener's identification with those in need of assistance. Rousseau might argue that if Westerners cannot "see" themselves in the hollowed and frightened faces of Rwandans or Sudanese, then the television channel will be changed, the newspaper page turned, and the aid withheld.

Grounded in Judaism, Christianity, and Islam are principles of human conduct that require a person to acknowledge his or her obligation toward the needy without consideration of self-interest or payoffs. The fourth chapter of *Proverbs* is illustrative: "Refuse no one the good on which he has a claim when it is in your power to do it for him. Say not to your neighbor, 'Go and come again, tomorrow I will give,' when you can give it at once."

Philosophy has left a trail of thought throughout history regarding obligations to intervene on humanitarian grounds.[6] Cicero (106–43 B.C.) suggested that assistance to suffering groups is a matter of justice, not morality. Some modern-day humanitarian scholars and practitioners agree with Cicero that there is a **humanitarian imperative** rather than simply a humanitarian impulse. An impulse might allow other concerns to prevail over the offering of assistance. A humanitarian imperative, subscribed to by a number of individuals and by many NGOs such as the ICRC, stifles any consideration other than providing assistance wherever it is needed, regardless of personal safety or negative potential consequences of involvement. In this we can find some explanation for varied responses by different actors in the international humanitarian system: Some are guided by the humanitarian imperative; others are sensitive, although not always responsive, to the humanitarian impulse. Another group—and this is the reason for this book—are aware that yielding to an impulse or respecting an imperative can be problematic if more harm than good results from a particular humanitarian activity.

During the Middle Ages, the belief emerged that all people are internally connected as one universal, mystical body. To current scholars, this universal body, minus the mystification, is referred to as international society. St. Thomas Aquinas (1225–1274) laid the groundwork for challenging a sovereign authority's maltreatment of people. Human rights scholar Hersch Lauterpacht has interpreted Aquinas as believing that "justification of the state is in its service to the individual; a king who is unfaithful to his duty forfeits his claim to obedience."[7] Both statements—the recognition of one bond common to all humankind, with implied rights and obligations, and the justification for compromising the integrity of the sovereign authority should that authority fail to fulfill its duty to the welfare of its people—are integral to current debates about humanitarian action.

The Age of Enlightenment in the seventeenth and eighteenth centuries brought into open public debate long-standing rumblings against religious dogma and beliefs justifying oppressive acts by religious and governmental authorities. The Age of Reason was thereby ushered in. Hugo Grotius (1583–1645), an exiled Dutch statesman who is now acknowledged as the father of international law, synthesized Aquinas's call for civil disobedience toward a malevolent king and the idea of one common humanity. Grotius's 1625 *De Jure Belli ac Pacis* (On the Rights of War and Peace) "recognized as lawful the use of force by one or more states to stop the maltreatment by a state of its own nationals when that conduct was so brutal and large-scale as to shock the conscience of the community of nations."[8] Grotius's doctrine is reflected in Chapter VII of the U.N. Charter.

Immanuel Kant (1724–1804), whose ideas influenced the formation of the League of Nations, expanded on the notion of global solidarity by linking the idea of national and international peace and security with the idea of promoting and protecting individual human dignity. To preach of democratic values and human rights within domestic politics without transferring those values to foreign politics is hypocritical, according to Kant and modern-day ethicists.

Throughout history these ideas about humanitarian action have melded and evolved. Historical contexts have determined the pace of the evolution within various societies as well as among states. With colonization of "unclaimed" lands and peoples and the Industrial Revolution came an increase in the speed of transmission and the geographical coverage of the idea of humanitarian action. And ironically it was the spread of humanitarianism and human rights that led to the demise of slavery and **imperialism.** Codification and institutionalization of the idea were largely a Western product of the late nineteenth century. The West had no monopoly on humanitarian ideas; however, it did codify its ideas and create discernible institutions for their operationalization.[9] According to many observers, there is also ample evidence of the humanitarian idea in Africa, within Native American communities, and throughout much of the non-Western world.[10] Private journals, oral histories, and traditional songs and folklore chronicle many instances of generosity in times of famine and disease. Buddhism and Hinduism accentuate the virtues of compassion and responsibility as much as do the faiths of the Western religious traditions. Islam, if anything, is even more explicit in this regard.

THE IDEA'S CODIFICATION AND INSTITUTIONALIZATION

Before World War I

The simultaneous rise of peace movements and more sophisticated war machines during the nineteenth century led Russia's minister of foreign affairs to call for a world conference to discuss international armament reduction in the interest of general peace. The work of pacifists such as Dunant and a more politically active and attentive world population, infused with information generated by capitalism and print media,[11] blended with sovereign authorities' concerns about the increasing losses in life, property, and political legitimacy incurred by war. The First Hague Conference commenced on May 18, 1899 (the czar's birthday), with twenty-six governments attending. Although no agreements to systematically disarm were reached, three **conventions,** or legally binding documents, were negotiated and signed regarding the pacific settlement of international disputes. The idea that a large number of governments could negotiate in the collective humanitarian interest became a reality, and the snowball effect of conferences and conventions surrounding humanitarianism and human rights began its roll.

U.S. president Theodore Roosevelt called for a second "Peace Conference" at The Hague, which convened on June 15, 1907. Fifty-four governments were represented at this second conclave. The three conventions signed in 1899 were revised and ten new conventions were adopted, including the Regulations for Land Warfare. More important, however, was the ability of an even greater number of states to discuss and negotiate on matters involving humanitarian concerns. The Law of The Hague sets out the rights and obligations of belligerents in the conduct of hostilities and limits the means by which one nation may do harm to another. Embodied in The Hague Conventions of 1899, which were revised in 1907, international law continued to expand with the 1954 Convention for the Protection of Cultural Property in the Event of Armed Conflict and the 1980 Convention on Prohibitions or Restrictions on the Use of Certain Conventional Weapons Which May Be Deemed to Be Excessively Injurious or to Have Indiscriminate Effects. (See Table 1.1.)

TABLE 1.1   Key International Humanitarian and Human Rights Instruments

	Instrument
1928	Convention on Asylum
1933	Convention on Political Asylum
1946	Constitution of the International Refugee Organization (UNHCR)
1948	Universal Declaration of Human Rights
1949	Geneva Convention Relative to the Protection of Civilian Persons
1950	European Convention for the Protection of Human Rights and Fundamental Freedoms with 10 Additional Protocols (1952, 3 in 1963, 1966, 1983, 1984, 1985, 1990, 1992)
1951	Convention on the Prevention and Punishment of Genocide
1952	Convention on the Political Rights of Women; Declaration of the Rights of the Child
1954	Convention Relating to the Status of Refugees; Convention on Territorial Asylum; Convention on Diplomatic Asylum
1960	Convention Relating to the Status of Stateless Persons
1967	U.N. Declaration of Territorial Asylum
1969	International Convention on the Elimination of All Forms of Racial Discrimination; OAU Convention Governing the Specific Aspects of Refugee Problems
1970	Convention on the Non-Applicability of Statutory Limitations to War Crimes
1975	Convention on the Reduction of Statelessness
1976	International Covenant of Civil and Political Rights; International Covenant of Economic, Social and Cultural Rights; International Convention on the Suppression and Punishment
1978	Additional Protocol to the 1949 Geneva Convention; American Convention on Human Rights Pact of San Jose, Costa Rica, with Additional Protocol
1979	Convention on the Elimination of All Forms of Discrimination Against Women; International Convention Against the Taking of Hostages
1980	European Agreement on Transfer of Responsibility for Refugees
1981	African Chapter on Human and Peoples' Rights
1984	Convention Against Torture and Other Cruel, Inhuman, or Degrading Treatment or Punishment
1985	Declaration of the Human Rights of Individuals Who Are Not Nationals of the Country in Which They Live
1987	European Convention for the Prevention of Torture and Inhuman or Degrading Treatment or Punishment
1990	Convention on the Rights of the Child

In the negotiations at The Hague, the customary rules of international law in interstate matters were recognized and legitimated. Provisions contained in the conventions of the two conferences were declaratory, not amendatory, of international law. Even if a state failed to ratify the conventions, it was merely rejecting the codified text. A country could not reject the principles of international law, which form the substance of the conventions, without also rejecting the basis of its own statehood.

As international law and codified texts expanded, the society of nations was expanding and expressing itself in a variety of ways other than state-to-state relations. The Hague conventions were manifestations of the "peace movement" or "internationalism" that grew in number and intensity from the 1850s onward. Other manifestations included the creation of the first truly functional international secretariats, the Expositions or World's Fairs, the establishment of Alfred Nobel's Peace Prize in 1897, endowments for international peace, and political activism by religious groups such as the Quakers and Mennonites. The world seemed to be growing smaller, thanks to technological advances in communication and transportation that facilitated a growing sense of common humanity and global responsibility. Private nongovernmental organizations increased in number to meet the challenges of providing comfort to the oppressed, domestically and internationally—as they had done since the Middle Ages—through hospitals, churches, schools, and care for the aged.[12]

World War I to World War II

The atrocities of World War I (1914–1919) led to increased codification of humanitarian law and to the creation of the League of Nations. The representatives at the 1912 International Red Cross Conference in Washington, D.C., formalized arrangements leading to standards for humane treatment of prisoners of war. Meanwhile, the balance of power in Europe was shifting, offensive military tactics were being considered, and jingoistic nationalism was spreading. Advances in technology, communication, and transportation that fostered budding international organizations also produced the military means by which humanity could be torn apart. World War I had mobilized 65 million soldiers, of whom approximately 8.5 million died and 21 million were wounded. An estimated 10 million civilians died from war-related causes—not just from armed attacks but also from starvation and disease. The creation of the League of Nations in 1919 was an effort toward collective security and global management by states repulsed by the war's human debris.[13] It is understandable, given the number of dead and dying, that the League of Nations would be cloaked in an aura of pacifism; however, the phrase *human rights* was never included in its governing legislation. With the exception of the Minorities Protection System and the endorsement of the Geneva Declaration of the Rights of the Child, the League of Nations was consumed by the regulation of state-to-state relations, with only the faintest glance of attention toward states' treatment of their own populations. Discussion of basic human rights was blocked by, among other things, the interests of states and individuals in continued imperialist holdings.

The League of Nations was incapacitated from the start. U.S. president Woodrow Wilson took the helm for drafting the League's Covenant, a kind of organizational constitution. The 66th Congress refused to ratify U.S. membership, fearing a loss of control of foreign policy. By the 1930s, Germany, Japan, and Italy had left the League; and by 1940, the Soviet Union had been expelled for invading Finland. Without any explicit mechanisms to punish transgressors and without the participation of all the great powers, the League was unable to enforce its mandates. The idealism concerning collective global security, which formed the basis of the League of Nations, was destroyed by World War II, along with much of Europe.

World War II to the End of the Cold War

Historically, new institutional responses or creations tend to follow conscience-shattering cataclysms as much as they follow transformations in the configuration of world power; and the events following World War II (1939–1945) are no exception. World War II became the next catalyst for propelling the humanitarian idea forward through increased codification of humanitarian law and the creation of the United Nations to help manage the international system. In the Charter of the United Nations—unlike the Covenant of the League of Nations—the rights of all persons and the duties of governments were explicitly, although not unambiguously, spelled out. Much of the idealism found in the Preamble to the Charter would have to lie dormant for almost fifty years, however, as Cold War politics among the great powers of the U.N. Security Council erected a seemingly insurmountable barrier to any collective response by states to human suffering and human rights violations. As history reveals, even when ideas are codified, ratified, and institutionalized, their implementation is not guaranteed.

The United Nations is a complex institution with the unenviable task of trying to maintain order in the international system of states while facilitating change for those states and people for whom the status quo is a life sentence of impoverishment or injustice. This institutional schizophrenia is evident throughout the U.N. Charter, which was signed in 1945. (See Box 1.1.) The Charter's language is ambiguous in spots and therefore a source of competing interpretations of its intentions and procedural guidelines. The Preamble begins the list of misleading texts by explicitly stating that the authors of the Charter are "We the Peoples." But the United Nations is an organization representing the interests and concerns of states. Individuals and groups have no recourse through the United Nations, nor is there a formal U.N. platform from which people can bring their concerns to the organization's attention. Although the Preamble is bathed in language supportive of human rights, equality, justice, and self-determination, other language within the Charter places a barrier between these ideals and their enforcement. Specifically, Article 2(7) prevents any state from interfering in the domestic affairs of another. This article has provided justification for noninterference in the actions of states toward their own legal subjects—for example, China's documented human rights abuses among Chinese and Tibetans. Only Chapter VII, which allows for the use of force to override the sovereignty of a targeted state, can override Article 2(7), on the grounds of grave threats to international peace and security. What is perceived as a threat is left to the subjective interpretation of U.N. Security Council members. Particularly during the Cold War, the perceived national interests of the five permanent members of the Security Council (the United States, the United Kingdom, China, France, and the Soviet Union) and the international context determined whether Chapter VII would be invoked or whether Article 2(7) would prevail. Each permanent member of the Security Council possesses veto power, and U.N. resolutions require the unanimous approval, or at least the abstention, of all five countries. Interestingly, however, since the end of the Cold War, Article 2(7) has found less support, and Chapter VII has been invoked more frequently.

The contradictions and tensions found in the text of the U.N. Charter—the primacy of the sanctity of state sovereignty versus (1) the collective defense against aggression and (2) the violation of norms for human rights and development—led to the creation of distinct and at times contradictory modes of power and concern within the U.N. system, embodied in its security, humanitarian, and development organs. Tensions between noninterference in internal affairs of sovereign states and an active concern for human dignity wherever it is at risk have played themselves out during the history of the United Nations and in international relations since World War II. The balance between the two has evolved toward a more circumspect embrace of sovereignty and a more integral relationship between sovereignty and respect for human rights and humane values. As a result, once-sacrosanct state sovereignty is no longer an acceptable justification for violations of the rights of civilians in zones of armed conflict, if it ever was. In the words of international lawyer José Alvarez, "How [a state] treats its own nationals on a range of issues is, in itself, now a proper subject of international law."[14]

Half a century of tension between the principle of sovereignty and the growing concerns with humanitarian access have led the United Nations itself to examine the need for articulating and implementing changing norms. The evolution is particularly evident in debates within the world's quintessential political forum, the General Assembly, where the political dynamics may be a more accurate barometer of world opinion than are

BOX 1.1   Key U.N. Charter Texts

PREAMBLE

WE THE PEOPLES OF THE UNITED NATIONS determined to save succeeding generations from the scourge of war, which twice in our lifetime has brought untold sorrow to mankind, and to reaffirm faith in fundamental human rights, in the dignity and worth of the human person, in the equal rights of men and women and of nations large and small, and to establish conditions under which justice and respect for the obligations arising from treaties and other sources of international law can be maintained, and to promote social progress and better standards of life in larger freedom, and for these ends to practice tolerance and live together in peace with one another as good neighbors, and to unite our strength to maintain international peace and security, and to employ international machinery for the promotion of the economic and social advancement of all peoples, have resolved to combine our efforts to accomplish these aims.

Accordingly, our respective Governments, through representatives assembled in the city of San Francisco, who have exhibited their full powers found to be in good and due form, have agreed to the present Charter of the United Nations and do hereby establish an international organization to be known as the United Nations.

ARTICLE 1

The Purposes of the United Nations are:

To maintain international peace and security, and to that end: to take effective collective measures for the prevention and removal of threats to the peace, and for the suppression of acts of aggression or other breaches of the peace, and to bring about by peaceful means, and in conformity with the principles of justice and international law, adjustment or settlement of international disputes or situations which might lead to a breach of the peace;

To develop friendly relations among nations based on respect for the principle of equal rights and self-determination of peoples, and to take other appropriate measures to strengthen universal peace;

To achieve international co-operation in solving international problems of an economic, social, cultural, or humanitarian character, and in promoting and encouraging respect for human rights and for fundamental freedoms for all without distinction as to race, sex, language, or religion; and

To be a centre for harmonizing the actions of nations in the attainment of these common ends.

ARTICLE 2(7)

Nothing contained in the present Charter shall authorize the United Nations to intervene in matters which are essentially within the domestic jurisdiction of any state or shall require the Members to submit such matters to settlement under the present Charter; but this principle shall not prejudice the application of enforcement measures under Chapter VII.

CHAPTER VI: PACIFIC SETTLEMENT OF DISPUTES

Article 33

The parties to any dispute, the continuance of which is likely to endanger the maintenance of international peace and security, shall, first of all, seek a solution by negotiations, enquiry, mediation, conciliation, arbitration, judicial settlement, resort to regional agencies or arrangements, or other peaceful means of their choice.

The Security Council shall, when it deems necessary, call upon the parties to settle their dispute by such means.

CHAPTER VII: ACTION WITH RESPECT TO THREATS TO PEACE, BREACHES OF THE PEACE, AND ACTS OF AGGRESSION

Article 39

The Security Council shall determine the existence of any threat to the peace, breach of the peace, or act of aggression and shall make recommendations, or decide what measures shall be taken in accordance with Articles 41 and 42, to maintain or restore international peace and security.

Article 40

In order to prevent an aggravation of the situation, the Security Council may, before making the recommendations or deciding upon the measures provided for in Article 39, call upon the parties concerned to comply with such provisional measures as it deems necessary or desirable. Such provisional measures shall be without prejudice to the rights, claims, or position of the parties concerned. The Security Council shall duly take account of failure to comply with such provisional measures.

Article 41

The Security Council may decide what measures not involving the use of armed force are to be employed to give effect to its decisions, and it may call upon the Members of the United Nations to apply such measures. These may include complete or partial interruption of economic relations and of rail, sea, air, postal, telegraphic, radio, and other means of communication, and the severance of diplomatic relations.

Article 42

Should the Security Council consider that measures provided for in Article 41 would be inadequate or have proved to be inadequate, it may take such action by air, sea, or land forces as may be necessary to maintain or restore international peace and security. Such action may include demonstrations, blockade, and other operations by air, sea, or land forces of Members of the United Nations.

the views of the U.N. International Court of Justice or of academics. U.N. resolutions may influence the actual application of international humanitarian law as spelled out in the Geneva conventions and protocols.

For example, in 1988, the General Assembly adopted Resolution 43/131, which recognized the rights of civilians to international assistance and the role of NGOs in humanitarian emergencies. Two years later, Resolution 45/100 reaffirmed these rights and specifically endorsed the concept of **corridors of tranquillity,** cross-border operations, and other devices to facilitate humanitarian access. In April 1991, Security Council Resolution 688 framed the plight of some 1.5 million Kurds as sufficiently threatening to international peace and security to justify outside military intervention and the creation of havens for them. Although contradictions in the U.N. Charter are just as glaring today as they were at its inception, the weight accorded state sovereignty in 1945 has lessened somewhat when measured against the recognition of basic human rights. It has been significant for the evolution of the ideals embodied in the Charter that they were further buttressed by another post–World War II instrument—the Universal Declaration of Human Rights.

The 1948 Universal Declaration, proclaimed by the General Assembly, was drafted as an ideal claiming legitimacy for the rights of individuals to human security—rights that superseded the rights of states against noninterference found in Article 2(7). Spearheaded by a U.S. delegation led by NGOs and Eleanor Roosevelt, this declaration substituted for a U.N. equivalent to the U.S. Bill of Rights; it had proven impossible to negotiate the inclusion of a legally enforceable definition of human rights in the U.N. Charter.[15] Declarations are not legally binding documents but present an ideal that all ratifiers agree is worth striving for. The Universal Declaration of Human Rights nevertheless directly challenges Article 2(7). It states that all people have "the right to life, liberty, and security of person" (Article 3); that "no one shall be subjected to torture or to cruel, inhuman or degrading treatment or punishment" (Article 5); that "everyone has the right to freedom of thought, conscience, and religion" (Article 18) and to "freedom of opinion and expression" (Article 19); and that everyone has "the right to a standard of living adequate for the health and well-being of himself and his family, including food, clothing, housing and medical care, and necessary social services" (Article 25). Moreover, "everyone is entitled to a social and international order in which the rights and freedoms set forth in [the] Declaration can be fully realized" (Article 28).

With regard to humanitarian action, the Preamble contains what is perhaps the most significant paragraph: "Member States have pledged themselves to achieve, in cooperation with the United Nations, the promotion of universal respect for the observance of human rights and fundamental freedoms." Implied is the commitment that member states should take the necessary action, in conjunction with the United Nations, to nurture and protect basic human rights, freedoms of speech and belief (positive freedoms), and freedoms from fear and want (negative freedoms). A U.N. decision respecting Article 2(7) on nonintervention might well abnegate the very same human rights enunciated in the 1948 Universal Declaration of Human Rights—the same rights that also justify humanitarian intervention in behalf of war victims.

The Universal Declaration of Human Rights contains principles that guided the French Revolution and that are considered by many scholars to represent three distinct generations of human rights: *Liberté, egalité,* and *fraternité* are codified in the Declaration, respectively, as the first generation, of civil and political rights (Articles 2–21); the second generation, of economic, social, and cultural rights (Articles 22–27); and the third generation, of solidarity rights (Article 28). The first generation protects the rights of individuals from government interference; the second generation requests governments to interfere in order to foster minimal standards of welfare; and the third generation spawns a movement toward cooperative arrangements among states, regions, and peoples. The Organization of American States (OAS) is one such regional organization. One of the OAS's first demonstrations of solidarity was its public denunciation of the military overthrow of Haitian president Jean-Bertrand Aristide in 1991.

The term *generation* can be misleading. It conjures up an image of successive stages of development of the same organism; however, the generations of human rights outlined in the Universal Declaration were conceived simultaneously and are not without controversy and incongruity. The first generation, the negative rights, are largely a product of Western beliefs that private individuals in civil society should be protected from interference by public authorities. The second generation, the positive rights, are an outgrowth of largely anticapitalist ideas about the duty of public authority to assure that minimums of food, shelter, and health care are met for all citizens. The inclusion of positive rights in the Declaration was supported by the Nordic countries but rejected by the U.S. administration under President Ronald Reagan on the grounds that these rights did not constitute basic human rights. Second-generation rights fly in the face of rights of property and minimal governmental interference in the free market, whereas the first generation places individual liberties before the collective good. The priority states give to one generation of rights over the other varies in accordance with the culture of the particular society, the nature of its economy, and the form of its government.

The Universal Declaration of Human Rights is instructive in that it points to a challenge created by the institutionalization and attempted universalization of an idea. The Universal Declaration does not specify under what conditions the rights of individuals justly supersede the rights of the collective. Moreover, it is left to philosophical debate what rights are inherent—based on the fact of being human—and what rights are constructed—based on relative cultural, political, and economic systems. How states answer these questions correlates with their opinions about humanitarian intervention. During the three years that it took to finalize the draft of the Universal Declaration, these questions were points of contention among states with different political and social cultures. The sanctity of individual human rights is relative to one's country of origin, some opponents argue; therefore, the objective of humanitarian action is to nourish and protect communities of civilians trapped in a conflict zone, not to protect the abused rights of single individuals.

Although The Hague conventions had hardly inhibited the pursuit of war aims by the Third Reich or Japan during World War II, the widespread revulsion after the war—along with the momentum from war crimes trials in Nuremberg and in Japan—led to a call for improvements in international law relating to war. Jus ad bellum is law governing the resort to war, as codified in the two Hague peace conferences of 1899 and 1907. Jus in bello is law governing the conduct of belligerents once war has commenced, and is codified in the Geneva conventions and additional protocols.

The devastation left behind by war, as we have seen, has frequently provided an impetus to the codification of international humanitarian law. The aftermath of the Battle of Solferino motivated Henri Dunant. After World War I, a series of Geneva conventions were drafted in response to various aspects of combatants' conduct in wartime. The atrocities committed against civilians in World War II propelled the international community to focus on the specific needs of noncombatants. The 1949 Geneva conventions addressed the treatment of military personnel (the first three conventions) and the obligations of belligerents to fulfill the rights and needs of victims of war (the fourth convention). Article 59 of the Fourth Geneva Convention directs that if "the whole or part of the population of an occupied territory is inadequately supplied, the Occupying Power shall agree to relief schemes on behalf of the said population and shall facilitate them by all the means at its disposal." With the passage of time and the increasing suffering among civilians as opposed to soldiers, still more codification took place. Additional Protocol I of 1977 prohibits the "starvation of civilians as a method of combat." Additional Protocol II is particularly relevant in the post–Cold War era because it applies to the "protection of victims of noninternational armed conflicts,"[16] or what most people call **civil wars.**

The Geneva conventions of 1949 are widely accepted today; in 1999, 188 states were party to the conventions, and between 148 and 155, to the two additional protocols of 1977. Although no major power has acceded to Protocol I, this international legislation nonetheless continues to influence governmental decisions—including those made by nonparties.

An Afghan man and boy use each other for support as they learn to walk with new artificial limbs. Land mines are excessively injurious and do not discriminate between combatants and noncombatants. One could argue that these weapons violate international law. UNICEF/John Isaac.

The implementation of the rights outlined in the Geneva conventions and the two additional protocols of 1977 is monitored by the ICRC, the official custodian. Critics point out the documents' limited relevance to the increasing number of lethal civil wars; 530 articles apply to the conduct of international armed conflicts, whereas only 29 apply to civil wars. This limited scope is of consequence not only because of the growing number of intrastate wars but also because civilian casualties are now the main product of armed conflict. In the U.S. Civil War, 95 percent of casualties were soldiers; in Bosnia, Rwanda, and Somalia, perhaps as many as 95 percent were noncombatants or civilians.

Currently more than a hundred conventions and covenants exist concerning humanitarian assistance and human rights. Adherence to them has been ad hoc, varying according to domestic politics and international contexts. Nonetheless, they represent the normative framework that ratifiers claim is worth universalizing. Collectively, in many respects they represent the "conscience" of the international system. Even if the international system does not actively and effectively respond to all transgressions of particular conventions, covenants, and international laws (e.g., those by Serbian and Hutu forces, as well as earlier transgressions by the white minority ruling South Africa), members of the international system feel compelled, at minimum, to take rhetorical umbrage at transgressors. Although more feeble than proponents would like, verbal commitments are a necessary, if insufficient, condition for improved behavior and better compliance with stated norms. They also are a prelude to an effective system of enforcement.

The idea of humanitarian action thus became institutionalized in the form of the United Nations and other international organizations, such as the International Court of Justice, of which all U.N. members are parties, as well as in the form of nongovernmental organizations, particularly the ICRC. Humanitarian obligations and rules of engagement are codified in the U.N. Charter, the Hague conventions, the Geneva conventions and additional protocols, and other binding conventions, such as the 1951 U.N. Refugee Convention and the 1967 protocol, which define the term **refugees** and set out minimum standards for their treatment. Each new attempt within the international system and its institutions to address humanitarian concerns by means of norm-guided conventions and declarations advances the idea of humanitarian action.

The possibilities for international military intervention vary as power relations among states change and a commitment to human rights strengthens. During the Cold War, there was a standard sequence of events in what came to be known as **peacekeeping**: First, the warring parties (normally states) would agree to a cease-fire, generally through **peacemaking** efforts; then a militarized U.N. presence would monitor the cease-fire and act as a buffer between belligerents. With the respite, negotiations about the peaceful settlement of the conflict could take place, although parties sometimes used the calm to avoid serious negotiations or to prepare for the next war. There is still no settlement in Cyprus, despite a U.N. peacekeeping presence dating from 1964; and the several peacekeeping operations that arose from four Arab-Israeli wars are likewise still in place, with no permanent peace settlement having been achieved.

Impartial "peacekeepers"—lightly armed and using force only in self-defense and as a last resort—were temporarily helpful tools of conflict management; but they were hardly the powerful enforcers originally imagined by the Charter's framers. Even with more than forty years of accumulated experience in international negotiations, the Security Council could not routinely reach peacemaking and peacekeeping agreements that satisfied the agendas of all five permanent U.N. members. Washington's and Moscow's ideological divide and power maneuvering during this period effectively prevented collective responses, with the exception of narrowly defined peacekeeping operations such as that in Korea, where U.N. action was initially approved by the Security Council (despite a boycott by the Soviet Union) and was continued by the General Assembly. Although limited in scope, peacekeeping did diffuse international tension among states. Sir Anthony Parsons, a former British ambassador to the United Nations, wrote that during the Cold War, the world organization's peacekeeping actions "help[ed] Great Powers descend a ladder from the backs of dangerously high horses that their national policies had led them to mount."[17]

The Aftermath of the Cold War

A flood of intrastate conflicts with high civilian casualties throughout the 1990s was met with seemingly improvisatory international responses.[18] To ask whether these responses have pushed the idea of humanitarian action forward is premature. There is plenty of action on the humanitarian front—an abundance of Security Council resolutions specifically addressing humanitarian and human rights concerns, the blue helmets of peacekeepers seen on the nightly news, the involvement of NATO in humanitarian operations, and relief budgets expanding and then quickly drained by demand. This frenetic action belies a paralysis of leadership and a lack of decisive, competent, and thoughtful decisionmaking in the international humanitarian system. The system appears to be responding ad hoc to events rather than constructing enduring institutions designed immediately and consistently to address the vulnerability of noncombatants during conflicts. The effectiveness of humanitarian action is being held captive by state actors unsure of whether to lead, follow, or get out of the way of collective responses to crises of inhumane proportions, and by a United Nations treading water in a sea of complex emergencies. State governments individually and the U.N. member states collectively are currently receiving the brunt of criticism for their lack of action and of vision. There is a certain irony here, as the idea of humanitarian obligations was one of the first to be taken out of Cold War storage.

State-to-state power relations began to shift shortly after Mikhail Gorbachev's 1985 ascent to power. The fall of the Berlin Wall in 1989 and the collapse of the Soviet Union in 1991 changed the landscape of international relations. The decade began with a great deal of rethinking: States had to redefine their national interests. The North Atlantic Treaty Organization (NATO) was forced to re-create itself, since its mission—to contain Soviet threats to peace—had vanished along with the Soviet Union. There was renewed hope for global cooperation in the pursuit of world peace and the defense of the defenseless according to the spirit and the letter of the U.N. Charter. This new structure of power relations among states needed new ideas, and the Security Council asked the newly elected U.N. secretary-general, Boutros Boutros-Ghali, to offer suggestions for an enhanced U.N. role in international peace and security. In response, the secretary-general wrote *An Agenda for Peace,* outlining his ideas on issues of preventive diplomacy, peacemaking, peacekeeping, and **peace-building.**

An Agenda for Peace was an attempt to integrate the concerns of states for international order with the concerns of individuals and victimized groups for justice and quality of life. The tension and contradictions found in the U.N. Charter are no less evident in *An Agenda.* The secretary-general, the secretariat, and other U.N. agencies tentatively straddle a conceptual and operational fence in their efforts at preventive diplomacy, peacemaking, peacekeeping, and peace-building. The balancing act is, as the Preamble to the Charter specifies, between respecting the fundamental sovereignty and security of states to which the United Nations is a servant, and reaffirming "faith in fundamental human rights, in the dignity and worth of the human person, in the equal rights of men and women and of nations large and small, and . . . social progress and better standards of life in larger freedom." To further the commitment to human rights, intervention in domestic affairs must have teeth. To promote social progress and better standards of life, development policies must be integrated with peace and security policies, for more often than not, problems of development and justice lie at the root of intrastate conflict. In Boutros-Ghali's vision, "The authority of the United Nations system to act . . . would rest on the consensus that social peace is as important as strategic or political peace."[19]

Since *An Agenda for Peace* was published, optimism for a unified U.N. response to human tragedies has diminished almost continuously. The accelerated demand for humanitarian assistance and for peacekeeping was unforeseen. The role of the United Nations in preventive diplomacy, as envisioned by the secretary-general—to act swiftly to contain conflicts and resolve their underlying causes rather than to deal after the fact with their consequences—was overwhelmed by an increase in the number and the intensity of internal conflicts. At the outset of the 1990s, only about 10,000 military personnel were deployed by the United Nations in ten peacekeeping operations; by December 1994, over 70,000 military and police troops were engaged in seventeen operations. A rapid decrease occurred thereafter, which has since leveled out. Only some 14,000 were engaged in U.N. service at the end of 1999—a figure that had remained virtually unchanged for three years. There were, however, another 75,000 in operations subcontracted to regional organizations. (See Figure 1.1.)

The secretary-general noted with some anguish that the 1992 peace-keeping budget of approximately US$1.69 billion had skyrocketed to $3.61 billion by 1994. The roller coaster continued in subsequent years, with the budget decreasing by half in 1996 and to less than $1 billion in 1997 and 1998. Estimates for 1999 were about $700 million; but after approvals for Kosovo and Timor, the figure seemed likely to reach $1.5 billion.[20] The linkage of military force with humanitarian objectives is not a new phenomenon; but the increasing frequency with which the two have been simultaneously implemented in recent years was not envisioned by the secretary-general in 1992: "This increased volume of activity would

FIGURE 1.1   Military and Police Personnel Deployed in U.N. Peacekeeping Operations, 1990–1999

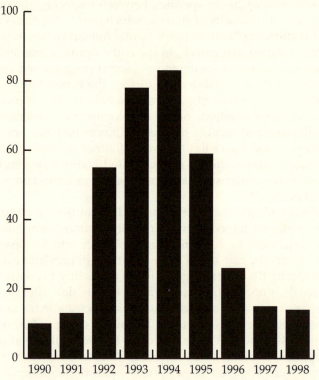

Source: United Nations.

have strained the Organization even if the nature of the activity had remained unchanged."[21]

Peacekeeping gradually metamorphosed to meet the new demands and the human consequences of war. Traditional U.N. peacekeeping missions between 1945 and 1988 normally involved separate military and diplomatic components. The purpose of the U.N. military was to interpose itself between belligerents and to monitor cease-fires after the warring parties had come to an agreement. Self-defense after an attack and as a last resort was the only legitimate cause for use of force by peacekeepers. The move away from Cold War political dynamics produced the opportunity for multidimensional peace operations combining military, civil administration, and humanitarian components with an overlay of diplomacy. The military in multidimensional peacekeeping efforts, although still operating with the consent of the parties, has more freedom to squelch violence that impedes the implementation of its mandates.

Military intervention that involves coercion in support of humanitarian objectives (Chapter VII) goes beyond peacekeeping. It focuses more on relieving the suffering of civilian populations victimized by conflict than on securing consent from belligerents. Therefore, humanitarian intervention by military forces, unlike efforts by peacekeepers, places human rights above the approval of the state. International efforts in Haiti, Somalia, the former Yugoslavia, Rwanda, Kosovo, Sierra Leone, East Timor, and northern Iraq in some respects penetrate the sanctity of sovereignty to rescue what in political theory is the source of sovereign legitimacy—the people.

By the late 1980s, multifunctional operations were being adopted from a panoply of means for countries such as El Salvador, Cambodia, and Angola; and enforcement action was approved in 1990–1991 against Iraq, for the first time in forty years. U.N. peacekeepers would assist in implementing negotiated settlements, thereby adding to the organization's menu of services, as the secretary-general outlined in 1995:

> The supervision of cease-fires, the regroupment and demobilization of forces, their reintegration into civilian life and the destruction of weapons; the design and implementation of demining programmes; the return of refugees and displaced persons; the provision of humanitarian assistance; the supervision of existing administrative structures; the establishment of new police forces; the verification of respect for human rights; the design and supervision of constitutional, judicial and electoral reforms; the observation, supervision and even organization and conduct of elections; and the coordination of support for economic rehabilitation and reconstruction.[22]

Multifunctional operations came about in direct response to the nature of the crises challenging international and individual security since 1990. These operations rely upon an international humanitarian system that is

theoretically and operationally divided among those institutions that address the root causes of complex emergencies, those that provide relief of
the symptoms, and those that employ force in the name of humanitarianism. Root causes include poverty and institutional weaknesses exacerbated by differences in the distribution of wealth and power, unresolved
ethnic and religious animosity, and in some cases, the withdrawal of **bilateral (or foreign) aid** and the removal of rivalry between the Cold
War's superpowers. In 1993, a group of representatives from the Organization of African Unity (OAU) and the United Nations as well as scholars
and military experts listed as specific root causes of African civil conflicts:
uneven economic development and gross disparities in well-being between communities within the same country, a continuation of divide-
and-rule governing strategies inherited from colonial eras, a lack of
democratic practices, a widespread sense of systematic injustice, personal
insecurity, and exogenous factors.[23]

Complex emergencies are not a new challenge for humanitarianism;
but the increased targeting of civilian populations as well as civilian humanitarian personnel and journalists during such emergencies, and the
widening range of options for dealing with these situations, are unprecedented. Unlike interstate wars, in which governments are generally willing to respect the rights of their adversary's civilian population in exchange for the respect of the rights of their own, intrastate wars, which
account for virtually all recent U.N. operations, are characterized by warring parties' blatant targeting of civilians and diversion of relief supplies
for combatants. Humanitarian action on behalf of civilians caught in the
crossfire often runs counter to the strategic military goals of belligerents.
Institutions have met the challenges of post–Cold War complex emergencies by trial and error; and regardless of intent, institutions' actions carry
negative consequences as well as positive gains for war victims.

An additional problem in responding to complex emergencies is that it
is difficult to discern who, if anyone, controls the military forces of the
belligerents and with whom peace negotiators and humanitarian groups
should establish dialogue. Even in cases where political authorities have
given humanitarian organizations permission to access vulnerable populations, local military or external mercenary groups may refuse to honor
the permission granted by supposedly higher authorities. Fighting along-
side uniformed soldiers are armed civilians and militias. For example,
Russian Cossacks joined the fight in Bosnia in solidarity with their Serbian brothers, but the Russians were not necessarily under the control of
the Bosnian Serb military command.

Humanitarians in the field are constantly confronted with operational
and ethical challenges stemming from complex emergencies, and they
must juggle resources to meet daunting demands. When displaced per-

Boy soldiers participate in a drill in Myanmar. UNICEF/4761/John Chiasson.

sons return to their homes, they find that their fields have been booby-trapped with land mines by retreating troops and cannot be plowed. In some countries, such as Cambodia, there are more land mines than people. Adult and child amputees flood temporary medical facilities in the hope of receiving prosthetics. Governments and commerce cannot function because trained personnel—not always numerous in the first place—have been executed or forced to flee. Infrastructure has been destroyed by war or simple lack of maintenance during extended armed conflict. Demobilized combatants have difficulty finding work because of shattered production infrastructures, and they are often tempted to revert to violence to achieve survival for themselves and their families. The demobilization and reintegration of combatants into civil society are further complicated because many entered the war, voluntarily or not, as children. The psychological ramifications from such early involvement in organized lawlessness affect social and political stability for years. In ethnic conflicts, lack of consensus about the ethnic composition of postconflict police and military units keeps the environment unstable and the population vulnerable to renewed fighting.

Other humanitarian challenges include parallel (or black) markets, often designed to circumvent international sanctions or simple scarcity. Black markets linger and obstruct the establishment of more formal market mechanisms and the construction of an adhered-to system of law and order. Economies have been distorted further by war and the presence of thousands of NGO and U.N. personnel, who may have been a formidable source of employment and of foreign exchange through their payments for housing, transportation, protection, and translators; but then these personnel leave. It is difficult even gradually to wean vulnerable populations away from **dependency** upon outside sources; and some observers argue that habits of dependency are virtually impossible to reverse.

In addition to the dramatically changed character of armed conflict, the costs of relief have escalated, affecting the political and humanitarian outcomes of disasters. Insurance companies require extremely high premium payments to cover relief workers who deliver food aid and medical supplies inside a war zone. If the premiums are too high, relief is limited. U.N. agencies are paying rising costs to charter trucks and airplanes from various governments for the delivery of food aid, as well as greater costs for the food itself due to the increasing number of the needy.

The changed character of intrastate conflicts requires a diversity of actors on the ground—for example, U.N. personnel coordinating policy, NGOs helping at the community level, and the military protecting the civilians who administer humanitarian relief and those who receive it. Within U.N., NGO, and military institutions, there are wide ranges of conflicting and contradictory perspectives on problems and solutions and a multiplicity of functional units. In addition to the increased number of relief and protection units, we must also factor in the continual rotation of personnel (generally, with commitments of six months or less) and the diversity of nationalities, which complicate communications and logistics. Directives for U.N. personnel emanate from headquarters in Geneva and New York. Peacekeepers often receive orders from the U.N. commander that contradict orders from their own governments. There is rarely a centralized coordinator of personnel, logistics, procurement, and administration.

Secretary-General Boutros-Ghali published in 1995 *An Agenda for Development*, a companion to *An Agenda for Peace*, at the request of countries that saw their concerns being overlooked because of the "obsession" with international security and humanitarian relief. This document attempts to draw international attention back to the root causes of conflicts, which if addressed would prevent the extensive need for humanitarian relief in the wake of war. The government of Rwanda made a similar attempt to bring the focus back to issues of economic development and justice, in calling for the termination of the presence of U.N. peacekeepers in 1996. So long as the peacekeepers remained, the government argued, the world would go on believing it was "doing something" and avoid assisting the country in long-term, sustainable development. The choice between providing relief or assisting development when funds are limited is an acute dilemma.

CHANGING LANGUAGE AND EXPECTATIONS OF STATES

A glance at field operations is but one avenue for assessing the post–Cold War changes in humanitarian action and the advancement of human rights. Another is to look at what people are writing. One will find ideas that are new, as well as old ideas framed in new language.

In most academic institutions, colloquiums, and conferences, conversations are taking place about the erosion of state sovereignty and the importance of international institutions in facilitating cooperation and advancing international norms. In the eloquent prose of Francis Deng, the U.N. secretary-general's special representative on internally displaced persons (IDPs): "Sovereignty cannot be an amoral function of authority and control; respect for fundamental human rights must be among its most basic values."[24] Debates are flourishing about tensions between territorial integrity and self-determination, nonintervention and human rights, and relief and development. Within the Security Council, humanitarian concerns have been placed more frequently and higher on the agenda. Literature promoting a more people-centered world abounds. Ideas of "global governance," including a new journal with that title, are now more abundant than they were following World War I and World War II. Visions of a "global neighborhood"—appropriately, printed on recycled paper—emanate from a culturally diverse array of scholars, contrasting with Cold War international relations literature, which was monopolized by Western (largely U.S.) minds. Old calls for a more representative Security Council are coupled with new ideas of allowing individuals and groups to petition the United Nations for consideration of key issues of concern to them. Privileges accorded to powerful states with primacy in 1945 are being scrutinized, and demands for greater transparency of action and accountability are voiced more strongly. Institutional reflection and reform are abundant at the beginning of the twenty-first century. The additional challenge for the international humanitarian system is to keep pace with the changes occurring within societies that will contribute to tomorrow's humanitarian crises.

The trends characterizing the shape of the planet at the century's beginning are unsettling. Population growth in developing countries continues to mushroom, in an inverse relationship to the resources necessary to sustain life, at the same time that technology has facilitated an increase in social contact among diverse cultures. Environmental degradation, population movements, and intrastate conflicts are partial manifestations of the crises of expanding populations, limited resources, and a rise in the volume and intensity of social contact. Transitions in state behavior are no less dynamic.

Poor countries are often unwilling or unable to provide social services and have become more willing to accede to (or less able to prevent) the transfer of some sovereign obligations to IGOs or international NGOs. In the words of Rakiya Omaar and Alex de Waal, "Increasingly, [some host] governing authorities are not fulfilling their responsibilities because they expect that international agencies will come in and do the job."[25] The altered relationship between state and society is alluded to in joking references made by foreign aid workers to the "Donor Republic of Mozambique," where the presence of more than 250 NGOs has created an alternative, nonstate source of power and authority. One NGO, World Vision International, disbursed almost $90 million in both 1994 and 1995, which made it the single largest donor in postconflict Mozambique.

Wealthy countries have acceded some sovereign authority to various intergovernmental organizations and NGOs acting as their proxies in international humanitarian efforts. Because of the transformation of world politics, none of the large or medium-sized powers has been in a position to act alone against transgressions of states against societies; yet most feel compelled by the acceptance of humanitarian norms to respond in some way, even if only to regret noninterference in other states' domestic affairs. We saw this in the case of Rwanda, where states and their representatives in the Security Council initially dodged usage of the term *genocide* to avoid Chapter VII intervention but could not ignore the crisis completely. Moreover, governments and intergovernmental organizations in the humanitarian arena, including members of the U.N. system and the European Commission Humanitarian Office (ECHO), increasingly subcontract for services to international NGOs, which often have preexisting relationships with vulnerable populations, local NGOs, and government institutions.

History has set the stage upon which, for better and for worse, the calls of the distressed are received and sometimes answered. In spite of spectacular lapses, there has been progress in the evolution of humanitarian ideals since the end of the Cold War. Political leaders are showing greater respect for international law and deeper recognition of the links between humanitarian assistance, human rights, and international peace.[26] Yet impediments to further progress and implementation of ideals continue to be found in the nature of the international humanitarian system and in the specific characteristics of each conflict.

TWO

□ □ □

Main Actors

Not inexperienced in hardships, I learn how to bring aid to the wretched.
—Virgil, *Aeneid*

The following composite snapshot in time is valuable for understanding the diversity of actors and issues in the humanitarian system. Imagine that is late 1995: A local health care worker in a Zairean refugee camp counsels a Rwandan mother about the health needs of her sick baby. He treats the infant with medical supplies donated by the U.N. International Children's Emergency Fund (UNICEF) in a tent provided by the U.N. High Commissioner for Refugees (UNHCR). The local staff are part of a medical team put together by Médecins sans Frontières (MSF, or Doctors Without Borders), a nongovernmental organization that split from the International Committee of the Red Cross (ICRC) more than three decades ago. An ICRC principle is to wait for the consent of local governments before providing assistance. MSF does not wait.

Money and politics merge a continent away, as the European Commission Humanitarian Office (ECHO), an intergovernmental organization, contemplates its annual budget and recipient list, setting aside a substantial donation to MSF. The mood is somber, however, in Washington as personnel in the U.S. Agency for International Development (USAID) worry about their jobs and their relief and development programs.

In Paris, administrators of Médecins du Monde (MDM, or Doctors of the World), a relief and development NGO founded by former MSF staff, are troubled by their increasingly successful but seemingly unethical behavior in seducing the media so as to increase donations. A full-time public relations person gives guided tours of human tragedy in Goma to raise the $200,000 per day cost of emergency relief. Médecins du Monde is also worried that a government elsewhere is relying too heavily on MDM for the care of the poor and is not taking sufficient responsibility on itself.

However, if MDM withdraws, those recovering and rebuilding from the last humanitarian crisis will become vulnerable again.

In Bosnia, a team of MSF medics treats the mentally and physically wounded in the besieged enclave of Gorazde. U.N. peacekeepers watch from a distance as the safe havens begin to fall. Meanwhile, NATO war planes sit on a runway in Italy.

Elsewhere, two journalists who covered the Rwandan massacre struggle to come to terms with what they have witnessed and continue to witness, as all humanitarians in the field must, while the rest of the world seems not to notice. "Do you think we did enough?" one journalist wonders. "Is it our fault that the world didn't react to the massacres?"[1]

The entanglement of issues and actors outlined above can frustrate analyses. Local humanitarians rely upon NGOs and the United Nations for supplies and salaries. Relief and development NGOs disagree over guiding codes of conduct in war zones. The missions of IGOs such as the United Nations are subject to the interests of states and party politics. The media have the ability to draw attention and donations toward or away from human tragedy. NGOs in the field continue to provide relief regardless of whether the safety of their mission is supported or compromised by military involvement.

Complex humanitarian emergencies require multiple responses from a variety of actors, none of whom is capable of responding alone. Yet few are willing to forfeit control of their operations to a centralized coordinating authority. This chapter outlines the barriers to cooperative and consistent humanitarian relief and protection. The following chapter provides thumbnail sketches of a number of post–Cold War cases in which emergency humanitarian operations have been or are being conducted.

Governments, including their militaries; intergovernmental organizations, such as the U.N., ECHO, and NATO; and nongovernmental organizations, such as the ICRC, CARE, MSF, and Catholic Relief Services, represent the three basic categories of actors that respond to complex humanitarian emergencies. Within each department or agency of an individual organization, there tend to be three distinct tiers of functions and authority: (1) the tier that formulates policy, (2) the tier that designs plans for implementing the policy, and (3) the tier that implements the plans. The actors within each organization and its agencies are institutionally conditioned to see the problems associated with humanitarian crises differently from actors in other organizations or in other agencies within the former's own organizational substructure.

An actor's interests, resources, organizational structure, and functions affect its behavior and ability to cooperate with other actors in a complex emergency. Actors may act in concert or in contention with one another, or somewhere in between. Conflicts of interest, competition for resources, incompatible organizational structures and cultures, and overlapping functions are the challenges that the actors themselves bring to humanitarian operations. These are discussed below.

INTERESTS

The interests of a humanitarian actor are what motivates it to respond to a plea for help. What an actor states publicly to be its motivation for responding may not be the primary explanation for its participation. Concealed motivations or hidden agendas mean that an actor may pull out of a humanitarian mission or threaten to do so if its unexpressed interests are not being served.

For example, one of Italy's contributions during the Bosnian crisis was to allow NATO the use of its airfields. However, Italy threatened to discontinue open use of its landing strips if it was not made part of the multinational contact group mediating the peace agreement in Dayton, Ohio. Humanitarian concern was mixed with a desire to play a larger diplomatic role, which Italy perceived would enhance its stature as a player in international affairs.

Others may view Washington's involvement in Somalia and its later withdrawal of troops as an example of changing priorities in U.S. interests. U.S. involvement may have served the perceived interests of decisionmakers, particularly a lame-duck president, to demonstrate proactive American leadership to the world. Somalia seemed a relatively safe arena for such posturing, at least in comparison to Bosnia. However, as the bodies of dead U.S. servicemen were dragged through the streets of Mogadishu, the interest in demonstrating leadership paled in comparison with the public relations costs. And Washington's military resources for protecting relief delivery were withdrawn.

Government Interests

A state is a legal abstraction embodied in a group of institutions called *government*, which ensure the state's control of a specified territory and its people. Primarily, the government has an interest in protecting the state against internal conflict or civil unrest and external interference in that state's affairs or territory. External conflicts that yield immense human suffering touch upon the interests of states in different ways. Voluntary participation in humanitarian operations may reflect a reasoned national or material interest in the region of conflict, such as the protection of oil reserves in Kuwait, or the preservation of European stability through peacekeeping in Kosovo; former colonial relations with the country in crisis, such as Belgium's and France's involvement in Rwanda, and Italy's in Somalia and Albania; a national identity that considers humanitarian assistance a moral responsibility, such as that of Norway; a need to acquire foreign exchange currency through payment for peacekeepers, as in the case of Bangladesh; or a desire to rekindle military honor, as in Argentina.

A government also may participate in humanitarian operations as a strategy to avoid taking stronger political and military action, particularly if the government has difficulty determining its interest in a crisis or determines that a defined political or economic interest would be jeopardized by a stronger response. Humanitarian assistance allows a government to appease a public that morally demands that its government "do something," while avoiding the commitment of military resources.

Due to the nature of democratic societies, political leaders have an interest in satisfying the will of voters and special interest groups. Governments can be shamed into involvement in humanitarian operations or constrained from involvement by public protestation, particularly if soldiers' lives are at risk. Therefore, election years, the configuration of conservatives and liberals within a government, and the influence of politically or financially powerful minorities can have an impact on the contributions that governments are willing and able to make toward humanitarian action and related peacekeeping efforts. U.S. involvement in such efforts in the Middle East since the 1960s has satisfied various economic interests as well as the Jewish lobby in the United States. The U.S. military intervention in Haiti in 1994 ameliorated the influx of Haitian refugees onto Florida's southern shoreline at the same time as it relieved political pressures brought to bear by the Black Congressional Caucus and the Haitian diaspora. Rumors of fading U.S. leadership and NATO unity were quieted by the initiation and maintenance of extensive bombing attacks against Serbs during the crisis in Kosovo.

On a more abstract level, governments also have an interest in maintaining the integrity of the international system of states, which hinges upon respect for state sovereignty and the principle of noninterference as codified in Article 2(7) of the U.N. Charter. Each time the U.N. Security Council invokes Chapter VII (the legitimate use of force) for humanitarian reasons, the legitimacy and sanctity of state sovereignty lose ground to basic human rights.

States are the most powerful actors in the humanitarian system and often the least predictable. Because the motivations for a state's involvement in a humanitarian crisis dramatically vary across time and among different governments as a result of political, economic, geographic, social, and security considerations, the other actors in the humanitarian system cannot rely upon states for consistent support or behavior.

Military Interests

Although armed forces are generally considered instruments of societies and governments, they have interests of their own. In fact, the armed forces should be considered a highly influential interest group in foreign policy making.[2] Budgets for defense must be justified, especially during times of relative peace. Armed force commanders as well as politicians with home constituencies dependent upon naval yards, military bases, and industrial defense firms may have an interest in demonstrating the continued need for new weaponry and technology and for the maintenance of troop strength—which they can do through humanitarian operations. Although there are those in Washington who prefer using Department of Defense funds for training exercises in a nonconflict arena, there are others with an interest in participating in multinational peacekeeping operations. Unilateral military actions are more expensive than joint operations. Learning to work with other military contingencies and civilian humanitarians, although an expensive lesson in the short term, may have long-term benefits for future security arrangements and the morale of the military.

As in civilian bureaucracies, in the armed forces career advancement is a primary interest of individual members. A number of U.S. enlisted soldiers involved in Somalia complained of the seeming overabundance of officers, who they believed were using the Somalia operation as a career advancement strategy. Given the relative peace among industrial democracies and the loss of the Soviet Union as an adversary, there are few opportunities for career-minded officers to demonstrate command expertise. Participation in military intervention for humanitarian reasons satisfies a field experience requirement for promotion.

Stereotypes of military personnel do not readily lend themselves to a humanitarian imaging; but there are soldiers who have a personal commitment to helping and who volunteer for duty that allows them to express their individual humanitarian impulse. A number of U.S. soldiers who volunteered to provide humanitarian assistance in hurricane-devastated Florida in 1991 also came forward for the humanitarian mission in Somalia in 1992. Although U.S. soldiers involved in Somalia spent most of their time protecting themselves and their encampments (they were not allowed to distribute food), some of them—particularly females and African Americans—volunteered to work in orphanages during their off-hours.[3]

Careful observers can recognize the efforts that militaries are making to "fit" into humanitarian operations. For example, U.S. troops do not drink off-duty when operating in Muslim cultures. Manuals in military classrooms explain the missions, operating procedures, and characteristics of

Peace process negotiations for the former Yugoslavia are in session. U.N. Archives.

nongovernmental organizations and U.N. agencies. In the field, military units can be found holding informational meetings for all humanitarian actors operating in the same area. Military forces have offered technical expertise and sheer labor power to other actors that are short on both. Bright Star '95, an operation conducted in Egypt, was the largest coalition exercise since Desert Storm, bringing together veterans of the Gulf War and of interventions in Haiti and Somalia. According to a U.S. Army commander, "We demonstrate we can work together and we can fight together."[4] The mixture of political, military, and humanitarian interests is, needless to say, not always as complementary as analysts and the actors themselves would like. Interests can clash in the field, and armed forces can turn a relief operation into a theater of military engagement.

The civil war in Liberia offers one example. The Economic Community of West African States (ECOWAS) and its military Monitoring Group (ECOMOG), with their own security concerns and economic interests in Liberia's civil strife, combined forces with a U.N. military observation effort. Also present in the field were various U.N. agencies and NGOs engaging in humanitarian activities. In one instance, the regional peacekeeping troops bombed humanitarian personnel. The United Nations itself tried to prohibit aid agencies from conducting programs in areas not controlled by the Liberian government. The political-military actors, anxious to secure a peace agreement, required the cooperation of the Liberian central authorities. The immediate humanitarian needs of those suffering from the conflict became subordinate to the peace process among the belligerents. Only those supporting the Liberian government received U.N. assistance. The logic in the discriminatory distribution of relief was that the peace agreement itself, if successful, would have positive humanitarian benefits.

IGO Interests

The United Nations is an example of an intergovernmental organization—a multistate-created institution designed to further state interests. IGOs benefit states by serving as a forum for state-to-state dialogue, by reducing the cost of information gathering, and by setting forth guidelines for reciprocal state behavior. IGOs with humanitarian agendas, such as the United Nations and its agencies, often find themselves in the impossible position of juggling the political interests of governmental elites with their own mandates to provide relief wherever there is suffering. And although IGOs theoretically represent the collective interests of all member states, the governments that are able and willing to pledge the most money to emergency budgets for individual crises have the most to say about where and how their allocations should be spent. If the budget for a crisis is exceeded, the U.N. agencies with operations in the area appeal for additional funds. If state donors' interests have changed and no additional pledges are made, U.N. agencies are forced to withdraw their relief operations.

The larger the IGO and the more diverse its functions, the greater the diversity in interests among its internal organs and member states. The United Nations includes virtually all states (188 in 1999) and performs security, economic, social, and humanitarian functions. In contrast, the European Commission Humanitarian Office includes only the fifteen members of the European Union (EU) and functions largely to disburse humanitarian aid. NATO is an IGO with restricted membership and a security function that became linked to humanitarian efforts after the end of the Cold War. The OAS, the OAU, ECOWAS, and the Commonwealth of Independent States (CIS) are examples of regional IGOs responding to regional security challenges as well as to economic, humanitarian, and social problems. The CIS has become a key player militarily in conflicts in the countries of the former Soviet Union, where there are also significant humanitarian issues. The OAS, OAU, and ECOWAS have increased their involvement in conflict resolution in recent years, partly as a result of developed countries' receding security interests in Third World conflicts

Returnees receive medical care at Zakho camp in Iraq. UNHCR/A. Hollmann.

and partly as a barrier to future "imperial" military and economic inter-vention. Of the IGOs, the United Nations and ECHO are the most rele-vant for understanding humanitarian action. Similar to governments and the armed forces, intergovernmental organizations are composed of offi-cials whose promotions and careers can be enhanced by participation in a particularly visible way. Individual interests within a bureaucracy as large as the United Nations can affect coordination between and among agencies.

NGO Interests

Nongovernmental organizations are nonstate, nonprofit, private organi-zations whose principles, mandates, functions, and accountability in re-sponding to civilians in crises defy any standard organizational form or predictable behavior. By definition, NGOs are not staffed by civil ser-vants, although there is a career progression among NGO personnel, some of whom spend their entire active careers in the voluntary sector, whereas others assume U.N. positions. Many international NGOs are un-failing defenders of single issues, such as gender equality, humanitarian assistance, development, human rights, or the environment.

Some NGOs have made the empowerment of local NGOs their primary goal. When international NGOs were expelled from Ethiopia in 1988, the local NGOs that they had supported were able to continue relief activities. But because a number of NGOs are dependent upon conditional funding from governments, the United Nations, other IGOs, and private citizens and organizations, subtle pressures bear down on NGOs to conform to the political will and interests of their supporters and may lead them to respect external, rather than internal, priorities.

A well-funded NGO, therefore, may not necessarily complement coordinated action in the field. What other humanitarian actors and war victims may need from an NGO may not coincide with the desires or interests of the NGO's main financial contributors. Noncombatants in a safe area may need a rebuilt sewage system to stop the spread of disease, but NGO donors may restrict the NGO's activity to providing food. When one considers that there may be more than 200 NGOs (the approximate number in Kigali in mid-1994 and in Bosnia in early 1996) in an area providing food and few working on water sanitation, it is easy to understand the need for a more centralized coordination of humanitarian activity. Staff experienced in field operations know the needs of the people through close work with local humanitarians and grassroots groups, but field staffs' missions can be held hostage by donors. Somalia represents an example of the need for NGO coordination. The Cooperative for American Relief to Everywhere (CARE), Catholic Relief Services, World Vision, the ICRC, World Food Programme (WFP), and the UNHCR focused largely on food distributions, which were clearly needed; but meanwhile, other programs were "comparatively underrepresented—water, sanitation, essential drugs, case-finding, public health worker outreach, surveillance, and other health interventions."[5] In addition to donor constraints, NGOs' past activities dictated their activities in Somalia, whether they were needed or not.

International NGOs have grown rapidly in number, character, and influence. In the mid-1990s, between 15,000 and 20,000 NGOs were operating in three or more countries, with funding from sources in more than one country. The large number of NGOs is one indication of the broad range of interests that they bring to humanitarian operations. The list of major international NGOs that respond regularly to complex emergencies includes Catholic Relief Services, Lutheran Federation, Oxfam, World Vision, Médecins sans Frontières, and Save the Children Federation.

The International Committee of the Red Cross is a unique NGO and worthy of special attention. Although it receives considerable funding from governments, and government representatives sit on the ICRC's board, the interests of the ICRC remain independently humanitarian. There may be political consequences as a result of its strict adherence to principles. Within the NGO community, the ICRC is the most coherent and perhaps has the most parsimonious list of interests motivating its behavior during humanitarian missions: Where there is suffering, the ICRC will respond. Its interests are operationalized with strict adherence to apolitical principles, operational neutrality, and international humanitarian law. (It is, as noted earlier, the custodian of the Geneva Conventions and additional protocols.) The national homogeneity of its Swiss staff, its internal code of conduct, and the safety of its personnel are also determinants of ICRC behavior. The ICRC philosophy is political neutrality, impartiality, and independence from the interests of other actors. The Geneva-based staff employs a steadfast patience in waiting for the approval of host-state authorities before intervening in conflict zones. Because of an unwavering dedication to principles, the ICRC plays an extraordinary role in humanitarian efforts. It has observer status with the U.N. General Assembly—giving it the right to take the floor, to place documents before governments, and to suggest items for the agenda. Since the mid-1990s, the ICRC has held private, regularly scheduled monthly meetings with the president of the Security Council (a monthly rotating position) to exchange information regarding political-military conflicts and their humanitarian consequences and to offer recommendations.

RESOURCES

The resources required for humanitarian missions include funds; medical, food, and housing supplies; transportation vehicles and communications equipment; staff experienced in relief, reconstruction, and development; diplomatic tools; and when necessary, military personnel and equipment. Simultaneously occurring humanitarian crises result in a competition for limited resources and worldwide attention. In 1998, for example, the U.N. estimated that only 54 percent of estimated needs had been met.[6]

Government Aid

Governments, through taxation, have the most dependable source of revenue to fund humanitarian operations. Although government resources also include diplomacy and the provision of troops, food, equipment, supplies, or technical expertise, the primary channel for humanitarian assistance is bilateral aid. In theory, bilateral aid is given by one government directly to another government; however, much of the aid is disbursed indirectly through U.N. agencies and NGOs. (See Figure 2.1.) Of the more than $6 billion spent on humanitarian emergencies in the peak

FIGURE 2.1   International Flow of Financial and Other Resources to
Humanitarian Operations

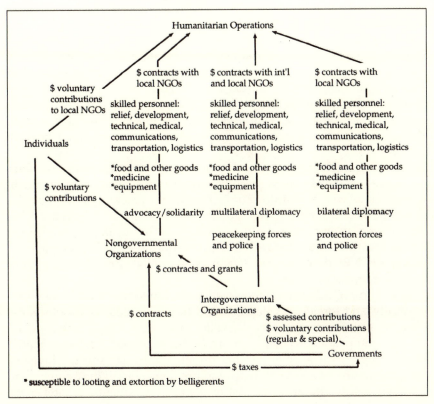

year of 1993, more than $4.5 billion originated with major donor govern-
ments.[7] "Nondonor" governments tend to be developing countries,
which generally contribute peacekeepers rather than funding to humanitarian operations.

Bilateral aid is typically limited by the political requirements and biases
of the contributing government. The political relationships of a government and its history of involvement in a region may either hinder or enhance its efforts to provide humanitarian aid. Former colonial powers
have historical and cultural links to many areas, which sometimes affect
the acceptability of their involvement to countries in crisis—sometimes
they are less acceptable, sometimes more. Because of resources, traditions,
power, and influence, the United States normally plays a major contribut-

ing role—with food, funds, experts, and logistical support. Yet Washington is often more suspect than small countries such as Sweden or Austria, whose power and leverage are considerably less and whose past efforts at manipulation have been less visible and successful.

Humanitarian or emergency aid is conceptually distinct from development assistance, although frequently both are administered through the same governmental agency. Emergency aid refers to funds earmarked for humanitarian relief for an unexpected crisis. Development assistance is budgeted by governments to foster economic and social advancement in economically less advanced countries—most often, in countries that have evoked economic or security concerns in the donor governments.

USAID is an example of a government agency charged with distributing funds for development projects abroad in the form of development assistance as well as with disbursing funds for emergency relief action. Since the end of the Cold War, governmental foreign aid in general has plummeted. Of the top twenty-one industrialized countries, the United States now ranks lowest in foreign aid donations relative to gross national product (GNP), donating only 0.09 percent of GNP; and Denmark ranks highest, with 0.87 percent.[8]

In the post–Cold War era, emergency humanitarian aid has risen dramatically, and foreign development aid has continued its long-term decline. Populations supported by relief operations may be abandoned shortly after peace agreements are struck. Some proponents for decreased development assistance argue that private enterprise and the invisible hand of the free market will reach the previous objectives of foreign aid more efficiently and at lower cost to donor governments. Whatever the logic in economically more advantaged societies, populations recovering from wars cannot rely upon the free market to pull the community out of crisis in a balanced and timely manner.

Military Resources

Armed forces receive all of their resources from their own governments. For involvement in peacekeeping operations, the United Nations reimburses each contributing government approximately $1,000 per month, per soldier. Individual governments then determine how much to pay their soldiers. The U.N. reimbursement usually leaves less-developed countries with a surplus of foreign exchange. Among the more industrialized countries of the North, $1,000 per month per soldier only covers part of the costs of peacekeeping.

Morale is also a resource to the armed forces, and there are several scenarios that deplete morale in an international operation. National contingencies tend to compare their wages with others in the field; morale can drop if one group finds its remuneration lower than that of other soldiers. Swedish troops clearing mine fields in Bosnia complained that their Nordic counterparts in NATO were receiving one-third more cash, prompting the Swedish government to allow volunteers the choice to go home rather than proceed with their activities.[9] Damage to morale also might result when troops compare their levels of risk with those of other contingents that appear positioned in less dangerous situations. Fortunately, soldiers who are placed in the most demanding situations tend to be the best trained, best equipped, and best paid.

Less-developed countries obviously are less able to provide their troops with all that is needed in a multinational peacekeeping operation, including appropriate clothing and equipment. In the middle of Croatia's winter, Pakistani troops arrived in summer uniforms. In Bihac, four Bangladeshi soldiers shared a single rifle. Bringing contingents from developing countries to the point of being functional often requires financial support from countries that are better-off.

The militaries of developed countries are comparatively rich in human capital and equipment. Their training and materiel enable them readily to render state-of-the-art aid in potable water production, bridge construction, crowd control, trauma care, and airlifting. France, for example, through Opération Turquoise in Rwanda, assisted the UNHCR in providing air traffic control, cargo handling, runway repair and security at Goma airport, water transport to the refugee camps, earthmoving at burial sites, and food; France also provided general support to UNHCR and other agencies.[10]

IGO Resources

Intergovernmental organizations receive financial resources from their member states in the form of annual dues and voluntary contributions for particular crises. An IGO such as the United Nations uses a portion of financial resources to pay for overhead and staff. Another portion is used to hire nongovernmental organizations to implement programs in the field and to pay for transportation and communication equipment rentals. Still another portion is converted into humanitarian supplies. IGOs become vulnerable if governments choose not to pay their dues, a situation that plagues the United Nations. For example, as of 1999, U.S.-accrued debt to the United Nations totaled more than $1.5 billion. As the debtor responsible for some three-quarters of U.N. arrears, Washington was perilously close to losing its vote in the General Assembly because the Charter makes such an outcome possible when arrears exceed two years' dues. Dues assessments are based roughly on a country's contribution to the world economy; but American "exceptionalism" seems once again to have overridden international law.[11]

The special financial contributions that IGOs receive for particular crises tend to reflect the perceived national interests—and some might even argue, xenophobia—of member states, rather than the actual needs of war victims. This donor bias is partially revealed in governments' responses to appeals for humanitarian assistance by the U.N. Office for the Coordination of Humanitarian Affairs (OCHA). For example, 94 percent of requested funds for the former Yugoslavia were pledged by governments, whereas only 13 percent of the funds requested for the Rwandan refugee crisis in the former Zaire were met with concrete donor pledges in spring 1995.[12] Another explanation for the reduction in U.N. contributions is that a number of governments are now funneling more humanitarian assistance through nongovernmental organizations or extending aid on a bilateral basis. By late 1995, a U.N. interagency appeal for donations to support humanitarian efforts in northern Iraq had netted only $39 million (28 percent of the $139 million needed). NGOs and other programs collected roughly $69 million for their activities in northern Iraq.[13]

Once intergovernmental organizations have pledges in hand, the manner in which the money is allocated can be determined by war victims' needs. The benefit of **multilateral aid** is that it can, in principle, dilute the political bias commonly present in bilateral aid and grant the IGO more flexibility in distributing relief and development assistance.

The European Commission Humanitarian Office is an intergovernmental organization that has grown to be one of the most generous contributors to humanitarian relief. ECHO is not field operational; it serves only as a funding channel to NGOs and U.N. agencies. ECHO's annual budgets approach $1 billion. The member states of the European Union fund ECHO in addition to their individual bilateral assistance programs. As complex emergencies have become the norm, ECHO has expanded its projects beyond the provision of food—its original focus, reflecting the massive food surpluses resulting from the common agricultural policy of the European Union. ECHO has funded water supply projects, medical aid, medical training for local personnel, nutritional supervision, mine clearance, and shelters. ECHO finances the work of the International Committee of the Red Cross and approximately thirty other nongovernmental organizations in the field.

NGO Resources

In terms of total resources in the mid-1990s, NGOs surpassed the resources of the U.N. system (excluding the International Monetary Fund [IMF] and World Bank) in the disbursement of total official development assistance. The largest NGOs have budgets of several hundred million dollars; however, most are reputed to be more responsive and manageable bureaucracies than their intergovernmental counterparts. As stated earlier, NGOs are dependent upon funds from governments and intergovernmental organizations as well as donations from private individuals and foundations. Although some NGOs vehemently refuse any government contributions or limit them to a small percentage of the overall budget, the majority of NGOs are not so discriminating about contributors to their organizational well-being.

NGO dependency on voluntary donations and on government and U.N. contracts can produce another negative effect. To maintain contribution levels, NGOs must demonstrate to donors that their presence and inputs into a humanitarian mission were valuable; there is thus an incentive for an NGO to "do it all," ignoring the inputs and ideas of local groups as well as the comparative advantages of other agencies in the field. The NGOs' creation and capture of **humanitarian space**—that is, their breadth of operational freedom—can work to disempower local institutions and professionals and lead to prolonged dependency and stunted institutional growth. This is also a danger with U.N. assistance.

Humanitarian space expands and contracts as a conflict cools down or heats up. Some international NGOs, anxious to impress their donors and at times unwilling to trust local humanitarians and coping mechanisms, can overpower local institutions and professionals. A problem occurs when indigenous humanitarians are excluded from decisionmaking and program implementation and fail to become involved in their own relief, rehabilitation, or reconstruction efforts until the powerful external actors have left the area (frequently, taking needed resources with them). Amid a frenzied scramble to win government or U.N. contracts to implement humanitarian programs, NGOs have become more market-efficient and business-wise. However, the clamor to acquire a market share in government and U.N. funding has also produced increased instances where war victims' needs were not thoughtfully assessed prior to the commencement of a relief program, or where the impact of NGO activity was not adequately monitored or evaluated for effectiveness.

NGOs can also offer noncombatants a resource that is absent from the purse of IGOs and governments. Along with providing the same types of resources to missions as the United Nations, often NGOs offer war victims advocacy and solidarity. In situations where the United Nations may be hesitant to publicly shame a warring party for human rights violations, some NGOs openly ignore the principle of political neutrality and advocate on behalf of noncombatants. In dangerous environments where the United Nations has been obliged for security reasons to shut down its field offices, NGOs have stayed and continued to provide various services as well as the comfort of their presence. NGO solidarity in Central America stimulated American public opinion against further U.S. intervention. In recent years, NGOs and the media have developed a symbiotic relationship whereby NGOs, such as Amnesty International, feed information to the press, the press moves public opinion, and public opinion (it is hoped) stimulates governments to act.

The ICRC's stature in the humanitarian community leads to a fundraising position that is enviable. Some 90 percent of the ICRC's annual budget of $800–900 million comes from states; and it has become a line item in many government budgets. Unlike the majority of NGOs, the ICRC has funds available before programs are in place and funding requirements are known. One ICRC staff member recalled, for instance, the organization's being overwhelmed with funds for conducting food distribution in the rural areas of Somalia. But not all ICRC projects are so well funded. For instance, the ICRC has been working with very limited success to gather government and U.N. support to facilitate the release of nearly 10,000 Iraqi prisoners of war who for more than fifteen years have been held in subhuman conditions in Iranian prisons.

ORGANIZATIONAL STRUCTURES AND FUNCTIONS

An actor's internal structure affects the manner in which and the speed with which it makes decisions as well as its capacity to pursue its interests. Organizational structure also affects an actor's ability and will to cooperate with other actors toward a common objective, and its flexibility in adapting to unfamiliar cultures and rapid changes on the ground. The structure and competing tendencies of large-scale bureaucracies, found within governments and the U.N. system, can prevent the formation of decisive and timely responses to calls for assistance. Multiple tiers of authority and competing interests dilute decisiveness. The policies that emerge from the bureaucratic maze are consolidated and compromised outcomes rather than clear, focused decisions that would provide more efficient and effective responses to challenges. They are "outcomes in the sense that what happens is not chosen as a solution to a problem but rather results from compromise, coalition, competition and confusion" among key officials.[14]

Negotiations among external actors over how to act collectively, or at least in the same physical territory, produce yet another layer of political outcome, rather than decision, and reduce the potency of action to an even lower common denominator than was produced in the bureaucratic process within each organization. For this reason, it is difficult for an observer of a humanitarian crisis such as that in Bosnia at the beginning of the 1990s to discern whether the inaction of humanitarian organizations was a calculated decision or bureaucratic paralysis had set in. In addition to organizational structures, the functions of various humanitarian actors may not be complementary, or they may overlap with other actors' functions. At times this produces too little, and at other times too much, assistance.

Government Organization and Functions

Government bureaucracies are hierarchical organizational structures that yield multiple seats of authority and competition for power among different internal agencies, individuals, and political parties. Government agencies have varied and often competing agendas, and individuals within a bureaucracy hardly have uniform views. Members of the Bosnian desk of the U.S. State Department resigned over the political foot-dragging in Washington while war crimes flourished unopposed by governments, except rhetorically. In June 1995, Pentagon officials with long military careers jousted with young civilian White House aides over decisionmaking and statements to the press. One day the Pentagon publicly announced that it would be transplanting 3,500 troops from Germany to Italy in preparation for a possible involvement on the ground in Bosnia. The next day, the Pentagon reduced the number to 1,500 and apologized for making statements without the approval of the White House or the NATO allies, including Italy, which was to receive the increased troop strength.[15]

In addition to internal power struggles, key information concerning a humanitarian crisis may not reach the appropriate decisionmakers before policy is formulated and action taken. Worse yet, misinformation may form as a result of multiple channels of communication. For humanitarianism, when information becomes hostage to bureaucratic haggling about power and resource allocation, high-sounding moral rhetoric flourishes and action languishes.

Military Organization and Functions

The organizational structure of armed forces is hierarchical, with a clear chain of command. Armed forces are also bureaucratic in the sense that there are organs with specialized functions and clearly defined channels of authority and responsibility. As the establishers and stabilizers of order through the use or threat of force, armed forces tend to isolate themselves from nonmembers of the armed forces in living space and by uniform; their interactions are only occasional and limited. Whereas NGO and U.N. personnel rent residential and office space within the heart of a suffering community, armed forces usually establish a barbed-wire encampment immediately upon arrival. Isolation of armed forces personnel leads to solidarity with comrades but not with nonmilitary actors, which is one reason why many European militaries are more likely than U.S. armed forces to mix with local populations. The professional culture of armed forces is therefore conditioned by an isolation-solidarity process and by a regimented lifestyle with an overwhelming emphasis on training, planning, and hierarchical discipline.

It is not surprising that soldiers are having difficulty adjusting to humanitarian functions. Armed forces are capable of a wide range of activities, trained for and practiced repeatedly during times of peace. What is lost in this continual state of practiced preparation becomes evident in a field situation where flexibility in procedure and response as well as coordination with nonmilitary (unregimented) actors are required. Soldiers' training prepares them to seek efficient functioning toward a well-defined end. Clear mission statements and well-defined standard operating procedures are essential for effective operations and maintenance of morale. Traditionally taught to identify an enemy, soldiers in peacekeeping missions frequently must practice a different mentality. Yet as a female U.S. soldier remarked after participating in Somalia, "I have a hard time with the term *humanitarian* when I'm being shot at."[16] Her lament was born of an unclear mission statement in an unfamiliar environment.

The military can become frustrated by loosely organized NGOs and volunteers who resist attempts by military personnel to "protect" them or to have their operations guided by the military's agenda or operational procedures in a hostile environment. Military personnel who were interviewed following action in Somalia stated that there were no clear agreements between military forces and NGOs, nor did many NGOs have an understanding of military capabilities. The result was unnecessary confrontations between civilian and military personnel. The military was also frustrated with U.N. agencies that refused to provide incentives for belligerents to disarm. Without a clear mandate for the forces to begin widespread disarmament and without economic incentives from the United Nations for warring parties to do so, the lives of peacekeepers were unnecessarily placed at high risk.

The military is trained to follow a regimented plan for disarmament: secure an agreement, establish and manage a cease-fire, withdraw and assemble belligerents, disarm belligerents, and disperse and rehabilitate belligerents. The military's resources, including its expertise, and its centralized command qualify it to perform multiple functions in the sequence of disarmament. Its frustration with the United Nations and NGOs stems from their not adhering to the military's standard operating procedures. In Somalia, cultures and agendas clashed, ending in the subsequent withdrawal of armed forces and government donations from the humanitarian mission.

Clearly, the expertise and resources of the military are invaluable in highly volatile environments, but the military's presence in humanitarian operations comes with a price. Armed forces involved in humanitarian operations can confuse noncombatants and belligerents alike, politicizing humanitarian efforts. As stated previously, soldiers who are professionally conditioned to operate in an environment that is cautious, hierarchical, and heavy-handed have difficulty coordinating with and understanding the organizational structure of relief and development agencies. The military is often a late arrival in humanitarian crises and an early departer. Yet while present, it has the power to take command and control away from humanitarian organizations that have developed important links of communication and services distribution with civilian victims throughout the crisis. The armed forces can be disruptive to preexisting networks for delivery of assistance, or they can be essential in assuring delivery. At times, the difference can be attributed to the personality and interpersonal skills of the military commander in the field.

IGO Organization and Functions

Being similar to governments, the United Nations and other IGOs also have problems associated with bureaucracies. The United Nations is hierarchically structured, with information gathering occurring at the base of the power structure, decisionmaking happening at the top, and strata of bureaucratic functions operating in between. The organization's multiple layers and agencies serve the political, sociocultural, economic, developmental, and humanitarian needs of member states, which are in theory equal entities (e.g., Kiribati and China are supposedly on an equal footing—which is clearly a fiction although each has one vote in the General Assembly). The United Nations employs some 60,000 people in various U.N. offices, which as Erskine Childers and Brian Urquhart have noted is about the same size as the civil service of the state of Wyoming for a population of just over half a million people. An even more striking observation about relative size was made by Foreign Minister of Australia Gareth Evans at the opening of the fiftieth session of the General Assembly: Four thousand fewer people work for the U.N. system than for the three Disney amusement parks, and more than three times as many sell McDonald's hamburgers worldwide.[17] The number of soldiers varies (80,000 in 1994, compared with only 15,000 in 1998), but the inclusion of temporary personnel would raise this figure considerably. Nonetheless, the United Nations' total budget (including that earmarked for peacekeeping) is scarcely greater than the combined budgets of the police and fire departments of

New York City. Agency infighting and contradictory agendas are as deeply rooted at the United Nations as they are in state-level decision-making. The Preamble and the 111 articles of the U.N. Charter are at odds with one another, and so are the institution's agencies. All in all, it would be erroneous to think of the U.N. system or the United Nations per se as monolithic or unified. The working-out of problems associated with being a large bureaucracy, compounded by political demands from member states, presents a unique challenge in the United Nations' provision of assistance to civilians trapped in war zones.

The United Nations performs two distinct and often conflicting functions—one political, the other technical. It facilitates the maintenance of international peace and security via the Security Council, and it provides humanitarian and development assistance through a number of organizations that belong to what is sometimes familiarly called the "U.N. family." During the Cold War, peace and security were interpreted to mean the maintenance of the status quo without engagement in the superpowers' spheres of influence. In the absence of Cold War rivalry, governments are now finding it difficult to ascertain which worldwide conflicts constitute legitimate threats to the international system of states. The Security Council has the power of self-definition—that is, whatever it determines is "aggression" or a "threat to international peace and security" is, by definition, so considered. However, the inconsistency in Security Council decisionmaking makes the United Nations vulnerable to the criticism of bias.

The United Nations has come under criticism for its handling of humanitarian crises primarily for three reasons: (1) the poor coordination among U.N. agencies and between the United Nations and external humanitarian agencies; (2) the organization's inability to link emergency relief with long-term development and to tie local groups and institutions more effectively to that process; and (3) "the difficulty of designing and implementing comprehensive programmes that combine peacemaking with measures that strengthen economic reconstruction, good governance and human rights."[18] A closer examination of the United Nations' main functions and organizational structures helps to dispel the popular image of an internally united world organization.

Peace and Security Function.   The Security Council is composed of fifteen members, five of which are permanent (the United States, Russia, China, France, and the United Kingdom). Whereas the agenda of the General Assembly is concerned with humanitarian and human rights issues as well as economic, social, legal, and financial concerns, the Security Council is the principal decisionmaker for matters regarding the maintenance of international peace and security. It is important to note, however, that "peace" and "security" are not synonymous; there are situations in which the Security Council will place security before peace, and order before justice.

The Security Council rarely addressed humanitarian issues during the Cold War, yet in recent years humanitarianism has made more and more frequent appearances on the Security Council's agenda. The mantra *humanitarian* was iterated eighteen times in the resolution approving the U.S.-led intervention in Somalia in December 1992. Intervention in the affairs of other states had formerly been reserved for situations in which one state's sovereignty was jeopardized by aggressive acts of another, such as Iraq's invasion of Kuwait. However, the Security Council's decision to protect the Kurdish population of Iraq from its own central government was based not on issues of sovereignty but on international protestation against an unjust "sovereign"—one that had violated fundamental obligations to its people. It would be naive, however, to assume that an unequivocal precedent was set by the Security Council's decision to defend the Kurds. For obvious political reasons, the council has done nothing to protect Tibetans against inhumane treatment (to the point of genocidal acts) by the Chinese government, or the Chechens against bloody retribution by the Russian army.

Humanitarian Function. The primary organizations of the United Nations that are responsible for humanitarian action include the OCHA, UNHCR, UNICEF, and WFP. Also involved are the U.N. Development Programme (UNDP), the Food and Agriculture Organization (FAO), and the World Health Organization (WHO).

The Office for the Coordination of Humanitarian Affairs, formerly the Department of Humanitarian Affairs (DHA), is a creation of the post–Cold War era. The DHA was established in response to the immense frustration of major donors over the inability of multiple U.N. agencies and NGOs to effectively coordinate humanitarian activities during the crisis in the Persian Gulf. The U.N. Disaster Relief Office (UNDRO) was the DHA's predecessor and is now subsumed within the OCHA, which was christened in January 1998.[19] One of the major functions of the OCHA is to launch consolidated appeals for funding. Though it has few funds of its own—it has a small revolving emergency fund—the OCHA is a major source of information for the international community's response to natural and human-made disasters.

The Statute of the Office of the U.N. High Commissioner for Refugees (1950) "declares that UNHCR's work is humanitarian, social and of an entirely nonpolitical character."[20] The UNHCR is guardian of the 1951 Convention Relating to the Status of Refugees and the 1967 Protocol. Its responsibilities include the protection and nurture of refugees, their

resettlement into a recipient country when appropriate, and their **repatriation** to their country of origin. The UNHCR also coordinates the actions of multiple relief organizations in the field that receive UNHCR funds to assist refugees. The UNHCR was not meant to be field-operational but to provide the financial and material assistance necessary to carry out its strategies. Other U.N. agencies and NGOs routinely contract with the UNHCR to implement programs. When an urgent problem arises, such as the massive flow of refugees out of Rwanda, the UNHCR initially draws upon financial resources held in reserve in an emergency fund. Approximately $10 million are placed in the fund annually, and no more than $4 million are allowed for one emergency. But the main operating funds are raised from donor governments for each emergency as it arises. In the mid-1990s, the commission's total budget peaked at about $1.3 billion, about $500 million of which was devoted to the former Yugoslavia and another $300 million to Rwanda. In the latter 1990s, the budget hovered between $700 million and $800 million, but the 1999 crises in Kosovo and Timor altered the picture again.

UNICEF was established in 1946 to provide immediate relief to the child victims of World War II. With headquarters in New York, at Forty-fourth Street and First Avenue, opposite the United Nations, UNICEF provides material assistance such as food, clothing, and medical supplies in emergency relief operations with an eye toward long-term development. UNICEF, like the UNHCR, draws upon an emergency fund for humanitarian crises in war zones. This fund is financed almost exclusively by voluntary contributions from governments. UNICEF also conducts various independent fund-raising activities. Many readers may remember receiving a Christmas or other greeting card produced by UNICEF or trick-or-treating for UNICEF as a child without fully understanding that the fund-raising directly supported a U.N. agency. A growing percentage (now about 25) of UNICEF's almost $1 billion budget is devoted to emergency relief.

The funding source for the UNDP's development projects is voluntary contributions from governments. The UNDP was established as the central source of funding for technical cooperation and prefeasibility projects for the U.N. system as a whole. Its annual budget is now just under $1 billion because several major funding sources have substantially decreased their contributions. The senior UNDP official in recipient countries (called the UNDP resident representative) acts during nonviolent times as the U.N. resident coordinator for all development activities by the members of the U.N. system. He or she also acts as the OCHA country representative in case of natural disasters. When war erupts, sometimes this official remains to help with the coordination of humanitarian aid. Sometimes, however, this official (usually with a background in development and

According to government sources, an estimated 230,000 East Timorese had been displaced to West Timor by the end of September 1999. In Wini Camp, pictured here, many of the displaced had only palm-frond huts for shelter. UN/UNHCR/ F. Pagetti.

with a previous career in such a specialization) is inadequately qualified to assume such responsibilities; at other times, U.N. security units force the preconflict U.N. personnel to be evacuated. In such situations, a special representative of the secretary-general (SRSG) may assume overall responsibility. Once violence is relatively under control, UNDP expertise generally focuses on reconstruction and development activities, and the UNDP's top official resumes overall coordination responsibilities.

Food insecurity following on the heels of World War II led to the establishment of the FAO in Rome. The primary activity of this organization is agricultural development. It also deals with emergency food shortages brought on by natural or human-made disasters, monitors food insecurity situations, and maintains the International Emergency Food Reserve. Its work in field operations is crucial during the reconstruction of a war-torn society, when a gap exists between the time at which conflict is resolved or contained and the first viable harvest is brought in.

The WFP, also based in Rome, is a food surplus disposal body jointly established by the United Nations and the FAO. Originally intended as a development (food for work) organization, the WFP is now a mainstay of the U.N. system's response to emergencies. Part of the WFP's funding is derived from the FAO's International Emergency Food Reserve, but the remaining portion results from voluntary contributions in kind and in cash from bilateral relief donors. With a budget of over $1 billion, the WFP primarily provides emergency food, although it still pays attention to long-term issues of chronic malnutrition. In light of the growth recently in the number and intensity of armed conflicts, the WFP now devotes about 80 percent of its resources to emergency efforts rather than to longer-term development. The WFP closely coordinates food needs with other U.N. agencies and NGOs and has become the logistics specialist for emergency aid within the U.N. system.

The World Health Organization, based in Geneva, is another U.N. agency created after World War II. Its function in humanitarian operations is to coordinate the activities of health care providers in the field. The work of WHO is integral to attending to the health needs of noncombatants during a crisis and immediately thereafter. The agency has been seeking a larger, more long-term role in providing such assistance.

NGO Organization and Functions

Nongovernmental organizations are generally structured horizontally. In other words, there are fewer tiers of authority, and those that exist are normally flat rather than top-down. Decisionmaking by consensus is more a norm in NGOs than elsewhere, particularly in smaller NGOs. NGO field operations are frequently staffed by younger volunteers, particularly as such agencies struggle to respond to more and more complex emergencies with larger numbers of victims. The age and inexperience of some NGO staff members operating in conflict areas have become problems in their own right.

The organizational structure of NGOs often affords them the ability to mobilize quickly and to be flexible in field operations as conflicts evolve. A growing number of international NGOs perform both humanitarian and development functions and are therefore working in isolated areas long before and after most U.N. agencies and protection force contingents. However, given the diversity within the NGO universe, it is necessary, yet difficult, to distinguish among genuine humanitarians, on the one hand, and charlatans or loose cannons, on the other.

NGOs can complement U.N. efforts by their links to grassroots groups and expressions of solidarity with war victims. They are a key access point for first-source information. NGOs are often assisting in on-site humanitarian efforts before U.N. agencies arrive, remain long after the United Nations has discontinued its relief operations, and frequently continue with relief and development tasks in the midst of unfriendly fire. In

Somalia, for example, the U.N. relief staff was evacuated for eleven months in 1991 due to increased hostilities, whereas Save the Children/ UK was unstaffed for only seven days.[21]

The U.N. system and states increasingly depend upon NGOs to fulfill a variety of functions in a comprehensive strategy to address humanitarian needs, from human rights monitoring to the establishment of temporary hospitals and food distribution centers, to defusing land mines. Table 2.1 captures the diversity of NGO actors and functions, and their degree of interaction with other humanitarian actors in the traumatic Somalia episode from 1990 to 1994.

Clearly, NGOs duplicate many activities of IGOs. In addition, although diplomacy is generally a function of governments and IGOs, it is not entirely outside the range of NGO capabilities. For example, an Italian Catholic NGO based in Rome—the Community of San Egidio—provided the venue and neutral mediation skills necessary to bring about a 1990 peace settlement between the Mozambican government and its challenger, Resistance Nationale Mozambique. Moreover, the advice of NGOs is sought by a number of U.N. agencies and at times by the Security Council. Article 71 of the U.N. Charter supports closer ties between IGOs and NGOs. It instructs the Economic and Social Council (ECOSOC) to "make arrangements for consultation with nongovernmental organizations which are concerned with matters within its competence."

Private advocacy NGOs typically make public statements, seek to produce documents that can be circulated among decisionmakers, and publicize widely the results of their research and monitoring. Targeting officials within governmental and intergovernmental institutions, these NGOs can be loud and theatrical or discreet and more subtle—to wit, Médecins sans Frontières or the International Committee of the Red Cross. Advocacy is a growing role, and deliberations about possible modifications of consultative status in U.N. forums are assuming growing salience. Consultative status can be useful in that it provides additional access to, and enhanced credibility in the eyes of, many governments and U.N. officials.

Unlike U.N. agencies, NGOs operate without consistent regulation. With the exception of the host government, no one can expel an NGO from an area. And because unlike U.N. agencies they have no duty to respond to a crisis, NGOs do not receive negative criticism when they choose not to be present (although their fund-raising may suffer). There is little profession-wide agreement on behavior in the field. NGOs have been known to make "deals" with belligerents that control roads and border crossings to gain access to suffering civilians. Such actions often have political ramifications. For example, during fighting in the Afghan war, a number of the 150 or so NGOs present succumbed to pressures from

TABLE 2.1   Select NGO/Relief Agency Contributions to Somalia Relief Effort, 1990–1994

Agency	Involved in Food Delivery	Other Activities	Collaborating Agencies
ADRA		Health, water, training, orphans, Somali NGOs	CARE, IRC, WFP, ICRC
Africare	Logistics adviser to NRC	Pharmaceuticals, wells	IMC
AICF/USA		Health, sanitation	UNICEF
AirServe International	Transportation	Air transportation of relief teams and supplies, including to refugees in Kenya	UNICEF, international NGOs
American Jewish World Service		Health	DRI
American Refugee Committee		Medicine, health, education, and training	UNHCR, UNICEF, OFDA
CARE	Direct feeding, monetization, transportation	Agricultural, rehabilitation, vet services, water, health, environmental sanitation	WFP, OFDA, ODA, AIDAB, EC, Austrian and Norwegian governments, international NGOs
CISP/Italy	Direct feeding	Medical, sanitation, animal husbandry	OFDA, Italian government
Concern Worldwide	Monetization, feeding centers	Immunization, latrines, schools, agricultural projects	
CRS	Direct feeding, cross-border	Agricultural, rehabilitation, water, nutrition, health	
Direct Relief International		Medical supplies/equipment	Somali NGOs
International Aid (Sweden)	Direct feeding and food supplements	Reconstruction of primary schools	
INMED		Health	ADRA
International Rescue Committee	During 1992 only	Health, sanitation/water, vet services, monetization, garbage collection, income generation	UNHCR, UNICEF, WFP, CARE, JDC, international and Somali NGOs
Mercy Corps International		Medical	World Concern
Operation USA		Medical supplies/equipment	IMC
Oxfam-America	Provided through ICRC	Water, vocational training	Somali NGOs, ICRC

(continues)

TABLE 2.1 *(continued)*

Agency	Involved in Food Delivery	Other Activities	Collaborating Agencies
Save the Children/U.S.		Health posts, irrigation, training, sanitation, agricultural rehabilitation	OFDA, UNDP, UNICEF, MSF, ICRC
Save the Children/U.K.	Direct feeding, transportation, feeding centers	Health, water, agricultural rehabilitation, NGO coordination, education, nutrition, displaced persons	ODA, EU, OFDA, Cafod, UNICEF, SCF/NZ, Redd Barna, GOAL, Caritas-Switzerland
World Vision RD	Direct feeding, supplies, local purchase	Medical training, income generation, building	CRS, GOAL, ICRC, MSF, OFDA

Source: John G. Sommer, *Hope Restored? Humanitarian Aid in Somalia, 1990–1994* (Washington, D.C.: Refugee Policy Group, November 1994), Table C-9.

Afghan leaders and Pakistani authorities on where to go and what to do. Humanitarianism in this scenario transcends apolitical behavior by strengthening the position of one of the warring parties at the expense of the other, and by doing so, possibly prolongs the conflict and exacerbates the vulnerable position of those being "helped."

As with all humanitarians, NGOs bring strengths and weaknesses to complex emergencies. Nongovernmental organizations have earned a reputation for being more flexible, forthcoming, and responsive than other members of the international humanitarian system. Their customized or "retail" efforts at the grass roots can be legitimately distinguished for the most part from the "wholesale" efforts of governments and U.N. agencies.

Yet NGOs are hardly without fault; their energy may lead to frenzy and confusion. Careful planning and evaluation are rarer than they should be: The desire to get on with the next emergency contributes to a lack of attention to institutional learning. Impatience with bureaucracy can lead to naïveté and manipulation. Independence is guarded so jealously that opportunities for collaboration are missed. In response to criticism of questionable NGO behavior in the field, NGOs are rethinking what it means to be "political" and are attempting to broaden their understanding of the inevitable political repercussions of certain humanitarian strategies.[22] Annual meetings of InterAction, a professional association of U.S. NGOs, provide workshops on democracy and development, refugee reintegration, the impacts of trade liberalization on women, sustainable energy choices, and broader issues such as advocacy, influence, and power.

Certification is now offered to NGOs that agree to guiding principles of behavior in the field. In particular, the Sphere Project has spelled out minimal standards for agencies responding to complex emergencies.[23] Given the complexity of recent humanitarian actions, NGOs are also forming permanent and temporary NGO coalitions to achieve efficiency in the division of labor and costs in certain field operations. Of the NGOs, the ICRC has gained a reputation for efficiency and effectiveness in the functions it performs.

The ICRC pallet of humanitarianism includes but is not limited to the building and staffing of hospitals and health posts for the war wounded, delivery of food and medical supplies, and working toward humanizing the treatment of prisoners of war. Although traditionally it has chosen limited spheres in which to work—it addresses specific needs, such as a hospital here or food distribution there, rather than broad, countrywide operations—in recent years the ICRC has been called upon by U.N. agencies and governments to expand its operations because of its logistical expertise and well-deserved reputation for professionalism. In fact, a former head of a major U.N. agency—James Ingram, the onetime executive director of the World Food Programme—has even proposed that the ICRC be expanded and "internationalized" (that is, lose its purely Swiss character) to provide in a more centralized fashion the types of help in war zones that are presently delivered by the host of U.N. agencies and NGOs described earlier.[24]

Currently, there is an identity crisis of sorts within the ICRC. Since 1997, it has convened an annual high-level workshop in Wolfsberg and also commissioned outside consultants to analyze the institution; this effort is referred to generally as the "avenir project." Some members of the organization believe that the strictly humanitarian agenda of the ICRC is being compromised by its association with the peace and security operations of governments and the United Nations; these critics call for a return to the essence of the ICRC—politically impartial, neutral humanitarianism. For others, it is unrealistic and impossible to keep the humanitarian sphere from colliding and merging with that of politics. For example, even the ICRC resorted to hiring armed guards in "technicals" (pickup trucks with mounted machine guns) for protection in Somalia. It is virtually impossible to insulate humanitarian efforts within the same arena as military and political activities, such as in the former Yugoslavia. Indeed, the ICRC is having difficulty maintaining an appearance of political neutrality; the introduction of outside peacekeeping forces has often cast an unwelcome hue upon ICRC activities in spite of protestations to the contrary by ICRC staff.[25]

The ICRC is one organizational component of the International Red Cross and Red Crescent Movement. Other organizations under the movement's umbrella include the International Federation of Red Cross and Red Crescent Societies (IFRC) and National Red Cross or Red Crescent Societies, which exist in almost all countries. The fundamental principles of the movement must be stringently followed by ICRC member organizations. Although various ICRC personnel may desire changes in ICRC behavior, the power of the movement pulls it back to adherence to principles. As noted earlier, MSF was formed by ICRC personnel who refused to abide by the movement's principle requiring the consent of the warring parties.

It is worth emphasizing that some nongovernmental organizations have contributed more to international agenda-setting than have many IGOs or governments. For example, at the San Francisco Conference in April 1945, NGOs acted as consultants to the U.S. delegation and played a pivotal role in securing the inclusion of human rights language in the final draft of the U.N. Charter; and they continued in 1948, with the formulation and subsequent ratification of the Universal Declaration of Human Rights. In fact, NGOs have spurred action since the middle of the nineteenth century at each stage in the evolution of the human rights regime.

There is disagreement about the precise NGO influence on governmental responses to civil wars. There is inconsistency sometimes even within individual organizations, and certainly within the entire group, about the extent to which the best responses by governments should be political, military, humanitarian, or some combination. Yet NGO efforts can be pertinent for the timing and shape of international responses to internal conflicts. In the United States, for example, they helped contribute to a supportive climate for President George Bush's decisions to override Iraqi sovereignty on behalf of the Kurds and to respond to the **anarchy** of Somalia's lapsed sovereignty. Nongovernmental organizations were unable to move the Clinton administration to acknowledge genocide and act in Rwanda in April and May 1994; but they eventually were able to get the Pentagon to help with refugee camps in Zaire and Tanzania. For three years, many American NGOs encouraged a robust enough military invasion to restore the elected government of Reverend Jean-Bertrand Aristide in Haiti. In France, NGOs have launched and sustained an activist humanitarian policy, *le devoir* (the duty) or even *le droit d'ingérence* (the right to interfere), which became the official policy of the Mitterrand government and its visible Minister of Humanitarian Action, Bernard Kouchner, and that survives both of their departures.[26] In 1999 Kouchner was appointed special representative of the U.N. secretary-general to manage the postconflict environment in Kosovo.

Summary of Actors

A review of actors' interests, resources, and organizational structures and functions clarifies why there is a collective action problem associated with humanitarian operations. Collective action, according to Charles Tilly, "is about power and politics; it inevitably raises questions of right and wrong, justice and injustice, hope and hopelessness; the very setting of the problem is likely to include judgments about who has the right to act, and what good it does."[27] Indeed, the process of collective action in humanitarian crises is extremely complicated. As Figure 2.1 shows, the potential for overlap, duplication, waste, and confusion is great. Without attention to the components of collective action for each actor of the humanitarian system, it is easier to place the blame for failed humanitarian missions entirely upon the culture of the combatants, as some have done with crises in Africa, or upon one institution, such as the United Nations.

Local Humanitarians

The humanitarian picture would not be complete without acknowledgment of the role that local groups and individuals play in relieving human suffering. This is particularly the case during the early stages of forced migration movements, when U.N. agencies and NGOs have not yet received in-country the resources necessary to meet the needs of distressed groups. Local resources are often mobilized more quickly, prove more appropriate and cost-effective, and have greater staying power than those brought in by external actors. By ignoring the capacity and will of local individuals and groups, external actors fall into the conceptual and operational trap of considering suffering populations solely as objects of assistance rather than as subjects of their own survival and recovery—an unfortunate but frequent occurrence in humanitarian operations.

The first safety net for vulnerable populations is the people or victims themselves. In the early stages of the Rwandan crisis, when the slaughter of Tutsis flooded the country, moderate Hutus risked their lives to harbor Tutsi families. A Somali woman, realizing that looters did not steal cooked food, set up a soup kitchen to feed the starving. The ICRC augmented her efforts, contributing both food and staff, and used her soup kitchen as a model for nationwide duplication. By the time U.N. agencies and Western donor governments turned their attention to the more than 1 million refugees who had made their way into Jordan following the invasion of Kuwait, the refugees' needs were already being met—first, by locals who donated bread and tomatoes from their own tables; and later, by local NGOs that set up tents and gathered donated food from locals. The Jordanian government committed some $55 million of its own resources to purchase for the refugees food, shelter, and transportation until the international humanitarian system was able to respond. In the former Yugoslavia, 95 percent of refugees pouring into Serbia, Montenegro, and Croatia in 1992 found food and shelter in private homes, initially without consideration of the refugees' ethnic background. In 1999, when UNHCR had planned for only 100,000 internally displaced ethnic Albanians in Kosovo rather than the 800,000 who fled within a few short weeks, the refugees were cared for largely by individual host families in Albania and Macedonia.

In addition, concerned individuals and groups safely outside a conflict area have formed solidarity with the suffering and acted, often without formal organizational structure or guidance, in response to their own humanitarian impulse. West Europeans rented buses and drove through mined areas and sniper fire to rescue children in Bosnia. A Rhode Island firefighter entered that country to organize emergency fire-fighting efforts in besieged areas. In Africa, countless individuals from around the world have volunteered their health care skills. Human rights and election monitors in Central America are often volunteers from abroad who have taken temporary leaves of absence from their jobs to respond to the human needs of strangers and perhaps to a personal need to do something. The next chapter outlines in greater detail the efforts of such individuals and groups in several war zones of the post–Cold War era.

THREE

□   □   □

Key Post–Cold War Arenas

There is no such thing as fighting on the winning side; one fights to find out which is the winning side.

—G. K. Chesterton, 1910

The human and political dimensions of humanitarian emergencies in Central America, northern Iraq, the former Yugoslavia, Kosovo, Somalia, and Rwanda and the Great Lakes region of Africa illustrate the challenges that humanitarian action faces in a post–Cold War world. Some of these crises are more acute than others, but in their varying geographic spread and severity, they provide a diverse analytical sample for readers. Many of the factors that affect institutional actor decisionmaking are linked to the contexts in which humanitarian operations are carried out. These factors include topography; weather (season); the number of warring parties; the existence of a regional hegemon; the condition of the area's infrastructure (particularly roads, ports, airfields, and communications); the number of local and international NGOs and U.N. agencies established in the area before the crisis; the presence of the ICRC; the enforcement of economic or military sanctions; the availability of local resources (human and otherwise); the military and political objectives of belligerents; the proliferation of small arms and light weapons in the region; the ease with which belligerents can extract and sell national resources during the conflict; and the territorial scope of the conflict.

CENTRAL AMERICA

The countries of Central America—Guatemala, Belize, Honduras, El Salvador, Nicaragua, Costa Rica, and Panama—cover an area of only 228,000 square miles (some 40,000 square miles smaller than the state of Texas).

MAP 3.1   Central America

One explanation for the turbulent history of most Central American countries is encapsulated in the well-worn regional lament "So far from God, so close to the United States." U.S. economic and military involvement is tightly woven into the historical fabric of Central American countries—from the United Fruit Company's establishment of banana plantations in Guatemala in the late 1880s (whence the phrase *banana republic*), to the military invasion of Panama a century later. The cry for humanitarian action in Nicaragua, El Salvador, and Guatemala in the 1980s is best understood through an analysis of the economic and political conditions that formed the basis for violent civil strife.

The 1960s were a period of economic and agricultural modernization for most of Central America. **Import substitution** and a Central American common market produced high growth rates for economic elites and pushed those living on the margins of society farther below the poverty level. In El Salvador, for example, the landless rural labor force rose from 12 percent in 1960 to 41 percent in 1975. As small, family-owned farms were consumed by powerful elites and modern agricultural machinery reduced the need for manual laborers, wages fell and widespread malnourishment and massive urban in-migration ensued.

In response to government neglect of social and development needs, scores of Peace Corps volunteers joined ranks with nongovernmental and religious groups, most notably the Roman Catholic Church, in providing assistance. Health and education services and development projects were implemented by the Peace Corps and development NGOs. The local clergy of the Roman Catholic church, having embraced **liberation theology,** became increasingly involved in the establishment of Christian communities, peasant associations, production and savings cooperatives, and women's groups. It also purposefully began training selected indigenous people—those deemed capable of articulating the needs and desires of all politically and economically marginalized people—for leadership positions. The creation of organizational structures and leadership in opposition to government and military oppression permanently altered the social fabric of many Central American countries. The voice of organized dissent grew louder.

The political elites and the military responded with violence rather than political reform. Torture, rape, assassination, and arbitrary arrest of community organizers, Catholic clergy, popular organizations, and reformist political parties became the strategy for dealing with political and social unrest. In the absence of democratic means of political participation, revolutionary politics became operative, with Cuba as the model. The Reagan administration grouped all movements geared toward **distributive justice** together under the rubric of "communist"; every revolutionary movement looked like Cuba and smelled of the Soviet Union. This image of a communist monolith led to covert U.S. support of conservative Central American regimes and insurgent groups deemed complementary to U.S. national and business interests. Legitimation was won by force, not consensus. Even in cases where elections were held and civilians took office, the military regimes, strengthened by U.S. financing and training, often held sway over the principles of democracy and popular representation.

The turning point from submission to revolution in El Salvador, Nicaragua, and Guatemala was linked with the people's frustration over access to political power blocked by political and military elites and by blatant violations of human rights, both individual and collective. In El Salvador, a coalition party of civilian reformist parties and the National Democratic Union (allied with the Salvadoran Community Party), in opposition to military rule, won the 1972 presidential election, but the military prevented their taking office. In the same year, in Nicaragua, a tremendous earthquake struck the capital of Managua, killing more than 10,000 people and leaving some 40,000 others homeless. The Somoza

¿Dónde están? (Where are they?) In countries of Latin America that had strong military regimes, citizens who spoke out for democratic and human rights frequently would "disappear." U.N. Photo Archives/Rob Brouwer.

regime, in control of Nicaraguan politics and economics since the mid-1930s, diverted humanitarian assistance from abroad for personal gain. In Guatemala, the CIA-assisted overthrow of democratically elected President Jacobo Arbenz in 1954 led to twelve years of military rule, followed by a civilian government subordinate to a military intent on applying repressive counterinsurgency measures. Human rights violations soared.

In all three cases, the regimes in power made no distinction between noncombatants and combatants in repressing dissent and nascent insurgent movements—noncombatants were deemed to be supporting revolutionaries by providing them food and shelter. Menaced by death and destruction, from 1981 to 1993 more than 1.8 million people from El Salvador, Nicaragua, and Guatemala were forced to flee the country or were internally displaced—a small enough number in absolute terms, but 10 percent of the total population. Every country harbored refugees, and every economy was disrupted by the region's collective and cumulative disarray.

U.S. foreign policy toward the region met with substantial opposition in many other Latin American countries—which feared future, direct military intervention—and in the European Community (EC). In early 1983, Mexico, Venezuela, Panama, and Colombia began the Contadora peace process, which excluded the United States. As one commentator noted, "Although Contadora was designed in large measure to structure the process of diplomatic bargaining between the U.S. and Sandinista Nicaragua, it had the effect of restricting Washington's freedom of maneuver in Central America."[1] European governments overtly advanced their opposition to Washington's foreign policy in Central America by funding humanitarian assistance, implemented by NGOs, on behalf of those parties not supported by the United States. Nordic governments, in particular, gave substantial economic and political support to the Sandinista government in Nicaragua (whereas U.S. "humanitarian" and military assistance went to the contras) and to the revolutionary coalition fighting the military regime in El Salvador (in contrast, U.S. public and private help was channeled mainly to the government). In 1988, the EC as a whole supplemented the Contadora political initiatives with an economic aid package.

As the governing regimes and guerrillas in El Salvador, Nicaragua, and Guatemala made few clear distinctions between combatants and noncombatants, all civilians were suspect. Fear of violence permeated rural communities, urban centers, universities, and virtually all social organizations. Actual and anticipated violations of basic human rights prompted thousands of noncombatants to seek refuge in neighboring countries, such as Honduras, Costa Rica, and Mexico; others moved farther up into the mountains, or toward international relief sites for internally displaced persons. Movement across borders affected the social and political fabric of recipient countries; movement into the mountains made the delivery of relief assistance impossible; and movement to internal relief sites led belligerents to their targets.

Much of the terrain in Central America is rugged. Populations, particularly ethnic minorities, were often scattered and isolated. Indigenous populations familiar with cultural and institutional prejudices were suspicious of external institutions, even those offering assistance. Government neglect of transportation and communication systems led to further isolation of vulnerable groups. The most valuable organizations for the provision of relief and protection, given the geographic difficulties and the suspicion of outsiders, were religious groups that had been present throughout the long periods of terror. These groups were instrumental in creating proactive organizational forms in support of political and economic justice.

Church-related groups were not only the choice of noncombatants for administering humanitarian assistance; they were also the choice of private donors. One ecumenical organization operating in El Salvador received a total of about $65 million in relief donations, compared to USAID's spending of $75 million during the same ten-year period.[2]

Guatemala was less dependent on outside sources for financial support of its conflict than were El Salvador and Nicaragua, which received bilateral assistance from a number of governments with interests, both national and humanitarian, in support of a particular warring faction. The military in El Salvador was dependent on Washington. The Sandinistas in Nicaragua received assistance from the East European Council for Mutual Economic Assistance (COMECON) and from Western Europe, particularly the Nordic countries. Their assistance was a counterresponse to massive financial assistance from USAID and military training of the former Somoza National Guard, in exile and popularly known as the contra rebels. The United States also imposed a trade embargo on Nicaragua, which delayed humanitarian supplies being delivered to the Sandinistas and stimulated overall economic hardship, thereby undermining the new Sandinista government and its development efforts.

The United Nations had spent much of the 1970s and early 1980s on the sidelines. The UNHCR was not present prior to the massive refugee problem and had no mandate to lend assistance to internally displaced persons, an increasingly acute need. Its strength came primarily during the repatriation phase, when the UNHCR implemented quick impact projects to ease noncombatants back into the communities that they had fled. The UNDP had virtually no experience with complex emergencies, and its development-related efforts were increasingly inadequate to the nature of the real tasks at hand. Of all the U.N. agencies, only UNICEF had a significant in-country presence prior to the widespread disruption of warfare, including access to remote regions.

Intermediate NGOs—those receiving bilateral aid from governments or the United Nations to implement projects—had severe logistical problems reaching isolated populations because of the often impossible terrain and harassment by the military. External NGOs concentrated their work in urban areas, relying upon church groups to provide assistance to those who were either geographically out of reach or fearful of being identified and targeted by combatants at a concentrated distribution point for food and medical assistance. One could argue, however, that the NGO function with ultimately the greatest humanitarian impact had little to do with delivering assistance in-country. That function was advocacy on an international scale—NGOs lobbying governments and policymakers, encouraging media attention, and activating public opinion against human rights abuses in Central America. Church groups also assisted in creating solidarity between suffering communities and those in developed countries by establishing **sister-city programs.** The ICRC, given its mandate not to operate in an area without the approval of the warring parties, which was elusive, was often paralyzed in the polarized terrain of Central America. Although its efforts paid off after ten years in

Nicaragua, its access was limited in El Salvador and nonexistent in Guatemala.

The Esquipulas Accords of 1987 were the culmination of a lengthy negotiating process that had begun with Contadora and had continued under the auspices of Costa Rican president Oscar Arias Sánchez, who was awarded the Nobel Peace Prize in 1987 for his efforts. Signed by combatants, it called for "cease-fires, national dialogues, amnesty, an end to external support for insurgent movements, democratization, and free elections."³

The United Nations Observer Group in Central America (ONUCA, 1989–1992) was present in Costa Rica, Nicaragua, Honduras, El Salvador, and Guatemala, monitoring cease-fires and elections. The United Nations Observer Mission in El Salvador (ONUSAL, July 1991–1995) provided military and human rights observers and police monitors. Both ONUCA and ONUSAL were composed partially of military, police, and civilians. Humanitarians were able to work expeditiously and effectively. In this case, at least, the end of Moscow and Washington's rivalry had permitted a page to be turned on armed conflict and, once repatriation and reintegration had occurred, enabled reconstruction and development to begin. By 1995, some 70,000 Nicaraguans, 32,000 Salvadorians, and 15,000 Guatemalans had voluntarily returned to their countries. In July 1999, some 22,000 Guatemalan refugees were finally given formal legal status as Mexican citizens; simultaneously, UNHCR formally ended all aid to the communities of Guatemalan refugees in Mexico.

Most humanitarian assistance extended to Central America these days is for natural rather than human-made disasters. The response of the international system, as in the 1980s, comes with no guarantees of follow-through: Almost nine months after Hurricane Mitch devastated Nicaragua in 1998, only $167 million of $1.8 billion in promised international aid had been received.⁴

NORTHERN IRAQ AND THE GULF CRISIS

The Gulf War was the first international emergency to be addressed in the post–Cold War world and the first to be televised live each evening. From a humanitarian perspective, the Gulf crisis actually consisted of three distinct crises. The first occurred as some 850,000 third-country nationals and 300,000 Palestinians from both Iraq and Kuwait fled, primarily to Jordan, in August 1990. The second crisis was the clash between Iraqi forces and the U.S.-led allied coalition. On January 17, 1991, and in pursuit of Security Council Resolution 678—which had authorized the use of "all necessary means," including the use of Chapter VII military force—the

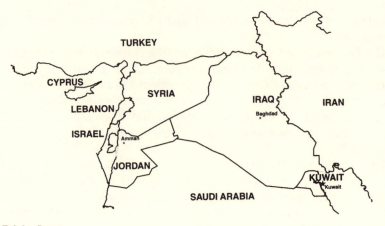

MAP 3.2   Iraq

United States and its allies began an air war against Iraqi forces. This en-
tailed civilian deaths and considerable damage to the country's infrastructure, but it was considered necessary to reverse Iraqi aggression.

The third crisis, which is the principal focus of our attention, took place
after the cease-fire on February 27 and the relinquishment of Kuwait after
Saddam Hussein's defeat.[5] Popular insurrections against the Iraqi government exploded in the north and in the south, and Iraq's Republican
Guard responded with brutal force. Some 1.5 million Iraqi Kurds fled to
the Turkish border and into Iran.[6] Within one month's time, that number
would reach nearly 2.5 million. The focus here is on the plight of the Kurdish population that sought protection in northern Iraq and received it
through Operation Provide Comfort. The troop composition of that militarized humanitarian effort, without the consent of the sovereign authority, initially included elite units from the United States, the United Kingdom, France, and the Netherlands.

The Kurds are a substantial ethnic minority in Iraq, historically found
in the northern mountainous region bordering Turkey. They constitute
between 20 and 25 percent of the total Iraqi population. Since the creation
of the Iraqi state in 1920, the Kurds have been fighting unsuccessfully for
some form of political and territorial autonomy. Although Baghdad's constitution allows for political pluralism, certain opposition groups, such as
the Kurds, have been violently repressed and prevented from participating in political life. The fate of the Kurds has been, in fact, similar in all of
the countries where they reside in substantial numbers—including
Turkey and Iran.

Saddam Hussein, who in 1979 became president of Iraq as well as the
primary wielder of military power and economic control over oil rev-

enues, continued the practice of violent repression of opposition parties, including the documented gassing of civilian populations. Although the U.N. Commission on Human Rights was aware of Iraq's gassing of Kurds, human rights violations were largely ignored for political reasons: Hussein supplied the Western world with oil and received in return the means to build a large military complex. In 1980, Iraq's invasion of Iran— a rogue state after its fundamentalist regime assumed power in 1979— permitted continued support for Hussein by much of the world throughout the 1980s. However, Hussein's unsatiated quest for regional supremacy led to Iraq's invasion of Kuwait in August 1990. Within moments, Hussein successfully shattered any state-level solidarity that he had created with the West in the preceding decades. The allied coalition, led by the United States and its 500,000 troops in the Gulf (Operation Desert Storm), acted swiftly to restore the status quo in the region.

Operation Provide Comfort resulted from Security Council Resolution 688 of April 5, 1991, which insisted "that Iraq allow immediate access by international humanitarian organizations to all those in need of assistance in all parts of Iraq." The operation also established a **no-fly zone** and banned Iraqi military personnel from the protected area. This resolution is seen by many bullish observers to be a significant precedent in the steady progression toward more frequent and robust humanitarian intervention. Operation Provide Comfort is illustrative of an unusually successful working relationship between the military forces that furnished protection and the NGOs that administered relief. The NGOs attended regular briefings held by commanders and had access to military telecommunications and transportation. The NGOs perceived the military as an ally in their efforts to assist a persecuted minority group. The NGOs also appreciated the fact that many of the military personnel involved in the operation were drawn from reserve and national guard units, with special competence in civil administration and engineering. The professional cultural divide that has stymied NGO-military relations in many joint relief ventures seemingly had narrowed. In addition, there was a clear, long-term political commitment by donor governments to maintain a ring of protection around the Kurds. It also did not hurt the operation that the party most likely to try breaking through the protection force had lost the war and was in no position to resist demands from the allied coalition. In contrast, the violation by Bosnian Serb forces of the so-called safe areas in Bosnia exemplified the difficulties inherent in protecting civilians when the conflict is still hot and the political will weak.

Inside the protection zone, after Western military units had retreated and eventually returned to their countries of origin, a hammer remained poised over the no-fly zone in the form of NATO aircraft. Inside the zone, order was facilitated by some 500 U.N. security guards. Donning blue baseball caps and brandishing only pistols, these security guards gave the illusion of a U.N. presence without luring the United Nations into a situation where it did not have the genuine consent of the sovereign. At the time of this writing, the Kurds are still highly vulnerable and under the continued protection of NATO, while civilians elsewhere in Iraq continue to suffer from seemingly indiscriminate bombing and almost a decade of various levels of economic **sanctions.** In December 1995, a published study by the FAO stated that Iraqi children were suffering severe malnutrition and that U.N. economic sanctions against Iraq had been responsible for the deaths of more than 560,000 children since the end of the Gulf War in 1991. At present, there is little available data to determine the humanitarian catastrophe caused by the 1999 bombings, which were initiated to force Iraq to comply with United Nations–led weapons inspections. This is a clear illustration of how the agendas of the United Nations' humanitarian and human rights agencies confront the security and political agendas of the Security Council.

The success of Operation Provide Comfort in addressing the third humanitarian crisis offers a sharp contrast to the melee that occurred in the coordination of humanitarian action in the first and second crises of the Gulf War. It was the failure of the United Nations as a system, especially in the first two crises, that led to the creation of the U.N. Department of Humanitarian Affairs, which later became the Office for the Coordination of Humanitarian Affairs. More particularly, U.N. organizations were unable to effectively coordinate their activities. UNICEF, UNHCR, WFP, UNDRO, UNDP, and WHO acted more as autonomous entities than as parts of what is deemed a "system." Mandates of organizations overlapped and contradicted one another, causing some activities to be overfunded and others to be relatively ignored. The UNHCR was designated the **lead agency,** responsible for coordinating the activities of other U.N. organizations as well as NGO activities and for ensuring that information was shared among actors.

In the field, response time was delayed as command and control of relief operations were directed from U.N. headquarters elsewhere. Different time zones between headquarters and the field made communications difficult. In addition, there was no single contact point in Geneva empowered to provide guidance or to make or authorize decisions. In other instances, junior staff in the field were wielding more authority than their experience qualified them to do. The level of inexperience in confronting emergency situations and in dealing with military personnel and strategy frustrated cooperation between those in the field providing relief and those rendering protection. In addition, U.N. agencies, with the exception of UNICEF, had difficulty in accelerating their procurement procedures to accommodate a quickly paced emergency. Roughly two months after refugees had begun appearing in Iran, the United Nations was able to provide only about 10 percent of the blankets and tents that were needed. Moreover, U.N. humanitarian aid seemed constrained by the political agendas of strong bilateral donor governments. As the minister of foreign affairs in Baghdad lamented: "Political considerations and interests were the prime motivation for the aid that was given, articulated, and implemented by the international community through the Gulf crisis. We welcome serious humanitarian and development activities and collaboration. However, if all the U.N. has to offer is what we have been receiving, I do not believe there is a humanitarian role for the United Nations in Iraq."[7]

SOMALIA

Somalia's history is generously peppered with colonial and Cold War interference in its government and military institutions and thereby its social cohesiveness. After more than two decades of authoritarian rule intent upon destroying the traditional clan system and authority of elders, 1991 ushered in the collapse of the functioning government, a civil war, drought, and strengthened warlords. Historic interference, a failed state, and famine proved a deadly brew for Somalia's 6 million inhabitants.

Since 1969, when General Mohammed Siad Barre's government eliminated Somalia's nascent democracy, four waves of light weapons have flooded the country and facilitated the development of a militarized society.[8] The first occurred upon Barre's assumption of power, when he established a military alliance with the Soviet Union and received the first inundation of weapons, along with military advisers. The second wave of weapons entered Somalia after his failed attempt to claim the Ogaden region of Ethiopia (1977–1978). Some 500,000 Ogaden refugees and guerrillas fled into Somalia at that time, bringing with them the modern weapons they had received through U.S. support of Ethiopia. Both the Soviet Union and the United States changed partners during the Ogaden War. By 1978, Moscow was supporting and supplying Ethiopia, and Washington had begun to provide Siad Barre's regime with the third wave of weapons (totaling $200 million in military aid in ten years) as well as economic aid (nearly $500 million). After a coalition of warlords successfully ousted Siad Barre in January 1991, the coalition fragmented, and each warlord began his bid for territorial control.

Before a U.N.-brokered cease-fire began in March 1992, a year of intense fighting had laid waste to much of Somalia's infrastructure, and a fourth wave of weapons had begun to flow into the country through various channels—an influx that continues to this day. At one point, a Greek freighter was caught delivering weapons to Somalia from Serbia. The

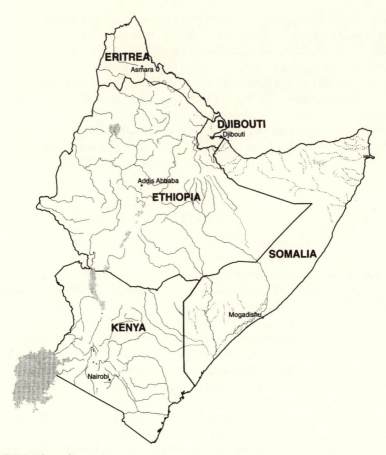

MAP 3.3   Somalia

Serbs were in need of cash because of U.N. economic sanctions and had a surplus of weapons to sell from its Cold War stockpiles. Somalia's factions needed weapons because their Cold War supply was running low. They were receiving plenty of cash not only from wealthy local traders and Somalis living abroad but also—most surprisingly—from international relief agencies working in Somalia. From relief staff, militias collected payments for office and house rentals (house rents for modest accommodations often were $10,000 to $12,000 per month); armed escorts (approximately $2,000 per month per escort to protect workers, often from the escort's own faction); and transportation vehicles used in food distribution ($300 per day for "technical" cars, a $150 fee for landing a plane, a $10,000 fee for every boat brought into port). Militias also utilized and sold food and goods stolen from U.N. agencies and NGOs. An estimated 40 to 80 percent of the nearly 60,000 metric tons of emergency food rations per month that arrived Somalia in 1992 never reached the victims of the civil war and famine.[9]

In 1992, the ICRC estimated that 95 percent of Somalis were suffering from malnutrition. This figure excluded about 350,000 who had already died from severe malnutrition and disease and more than 1 million who had become refugees and were living in squalid relief camps in Ethiopia, Kenya, Djibouti, Yemen, and Saudi Arabia. An average of 1,000 were dying each day in December 1992, when President George Bush, following a U.N. Security Council request authorizing the use of force to protect humanitarian relief efforts, committed almost 35,000 U.S. troops to the region. France, Belgium, Saudi Arabia, Canada, Pakistan, and others also deployed troops. What was dubbed Operation Restore Hope in the United States and the Unified Task Force (UNITAF) by the United Nations took form. The strongest critics of humanitarian efforts in Somalia cite the excessive and unnecessary delay in U.N. response from the time Secretary-General Javier Pérez de Cuéllar called it "the most serious humanitarian crisis of our day" in January 1991 to Security Council Resolution 794 on December 3, 1992, authorizing UNITAF.

Still riding high from success in the Gulf crisis and moved by the media coverage of thousands of Somalis starving in the midst of a civil war (what many observers label the **CNN effect**), the United Nations began diplomatic and peacekeeping efforts to produce a cease-fire, which it achieved between the two main factions in March 1992. However, there were no peacekeepers in place to monitor the cease-fire. Although in late April 1992 UNOSOM I (the first U.N. Operation in Somalia) authorized the presence of fifty U.N. observers to monitor the cease-fire, the observers did not arrive until four months after the cease-fire took effect. In late August, Security Council Resolution 775 authorized a security force to protect the delivery of humanitarian aid, but the 500 peacekeepers (the SRSG in Mogadishu had requested 7,000) did not arrive until mid-September. When the peacekeepers arrived, they were unable to move beyond the port. This was just one example of what Mohamed Sahnoun, the special representative on the ground, called "missed opportunities."[10] Three months later, UNITAF was authorized, and U.S. resolve to lead in protecting the delivery of relief aid brought 24,000 U.S. troops onto the beaches of Somalia and 12,000 from elsewhere to ensure access to civilians in the short term.

By May 1993, responsibility for U.S.-led Operation Restore Hope had been passed on to the United Nations through UNOSOM II—the first armed Chapter VII humanitarian operation under U.N. command and control. Starvation had been brought under control, and thousands of lives had been saved. The theft of relief supplies had declined, and warlords were gathering to talk of national reconciliation. However, the killing of twenty-four Pakistani Blue Helmets by faction members on June 5, 1993 led to Security Council Resolution 837, allowing force to be used in order to arrest and detain those responsible. Operation Restore Hope was transformed into a hunt for Aidid, the faction leader believed responsible for ordering the deaths of the peacekeepers. General Mohamed Farah Aidid eluded capture, and Washington's resolve to remain in Somalia withered because of its inability to capture one man, the downing of two U.S. helicopters in October 1993, and the deaths of eighteen U.S. soldiers (which included the unseemly dragging of a dead Ranger's body through the streets of Mogadishu). The Clinton administration, prodded by an anxious Congress, called for U.S. troop withdrawal. U.N. Security Council Resolution 954 ordered the complete withdrawal of all peacekeepers by March 1995. Interestingly, in June 1995 Aidid nonviolently stepped down as the leader of his faction, and the new leader asked for the return of U.N. assistance in the reconstruction and development of Somalia. Critics of forceful intervention pointed to this as proof of the futility of military involvement against the will of the local parties. In January 1996, Aidid regained his position as warlord and was himself calling for the United Nations to assist in rebuilding Somalia. Upon his death in 1998, his son, a former U.S. Marine, took his place. Interclan violence continues in Somalia to this day, as does human suffering.

In addition to criticism of the Security Council's delay in authorizing an effective multilateral response to the Somali crisis—Secretary-General Boutros-Ghali publicly drew attention to Yugoslavia's higher visibility as a "rich man's war"—the United Nations in general has been accused of basic incompetence. Even more critical from the point of view of humanitarian action, U.N. staff were absent, because of security and insurance regulations. Only the ICRC and four well-respected NGOs (the International Medical Corps, Save the Children/UK, MSF, and SOS) remained in Somalia despite the danger to personnel—in fact, they increased their staff as the United Nations withdrew. NGOs took on roles normally assumed by U.N. agencies, whose security regulations required their evacuation. According to Jeffrey Clark, "Save the Children/UK, a relatively small private relief agency, delivered more food to Somalia in 1992 than did UNICEF," and while the UNDP "left untapped $68 million budgeted for Somalia *for lack of a signature* from the nonexistent Somali government," the ICRC used 50 percent of its worldwide emergency relief budget to establish massive feeding programs (much of the funding came directly from USAID).[11] Defenders of the UNDP's nonuse of funds state that the money had been budgeted for development, not relief.

The United Nations, in an effort to bring about a peaceful settlement, went through several special representatives. The violent warlords Aidid and Mahdi were invited to New York for U.N.-sponsored peace talks (other clan leaders and elders were excluded). Political legitimacy by default was conferred on those in the urban areas who attempted to rule by force, and was largely withheld from those in the rural areas who led by relative consensus.

THE FORMER YUGOSLAVIA

There is now a considerable scholarly literature examining the sources of violent ethnic conflict in the former Yugoslavia: Some scholars go back centuries, looking for root causes in the cultural differences among ethnic groups, such as those involving religion (the uneasy coexistence of Catholic, Orthodox, and Muslim groups); others point to the beginning of the twentieth century; and still others claim that the collision between strong and manipulated nationalism in Serbia and independence movements in Croatia and Slovenia in the late 1980s had more to do with the

MAP 3.4   The former Yugoslavia

country's economic tailspin than with revenge for past ethnic grievances. In this narrative, we review the chronology of more recent political and military events and how they affected the vulnerability of noncombatants and the response of the international humanitarian system in Croatia and Bosnia-Herzegovina.

In June 1990, Communist party rule in Yugoslavia collapsed, setting into motion Croatia's and Slovenia's assertions of greater political autonomy. Serbia adamantly opposed this development, given that these lands were relatively prosperous economically and that 12 percent of the population of Croatia were ethnic Serbs. Moreover, Serbia had benefited the most from democratic centralism and thus stood to lose the most from a change in authority.

On June 25, 1991, Croatia and Slovenia each declared their independence, to the regret not only of Serbia but also of the international community at large. Armed conflict soon broke out between Serbs and Croats. Maintaining the integrity of Yugoslavia became the overwhelming international security objective, as most foreign states feared that a demonstration effect might unleash a similar, violent fragmentation of the Soviet Union. The European Community quickly became involved in peace negotiations. By January 15, 1992, Croatia and Slovenia had been formally recognized by the EC, and the Soviet Union had ceased to exist. Unsuccessful in its attempt to broker a cease-fire between Croats and Serbs in Croatia, the EC asked for assistance from the United Nations.

In September 1991, the U.N. Security Council had invoked Chapter VII and passed Resolution 713, imposing an arms embargo against all parties to the conflict in the former Yugoslavia. In December 1991, Resolution 724 was passed, calling for the presence of a peacekeeping force in Croatia once a cease-fire had been negotiated. The U.N. Protection Force (UNPROFOR) for the former Yugoslavia was established in four protected areas of the Krajina region, in Croatia. They were to be completely demilitarized, and Croatian refugees were to be permitted to return to their homes. Although a firm cease-fire had not been reached and there was no peace to keep, troop deployment was authorized in February 1992 by Resolution 743, and peacekeeping began in Croatia. Although the secretary-general estimated that $600 million were needed for the operation to be effective, the Security Council permanent members authorized only $250 million. UNPROFOR was set into motion half-funded, halfheartedly, and with its role and authorized range of behavior unclear. A "model" for future actions in the former Yugoslavia was set in place that would prove particularly problematic for the international humanitarian system.

As the conflict in Croatia waxed and waned, the February 1992 referendum in favor of independence in Bosnia-Herzegovina pushed another thorny political problem before the European Community. Of the 4.4 million people in Bosnia in 1991, 44 percent were Muslims, 31 percent were Serbs, 17 percent were Croats, and the remaining 8 percent were self-described "Yugoslavs." The Serbs had boycotted the referendum. Without any effective guarantees for minorities in place, the United States and the EC recognized Bosnia in April 1992, at Germany's insistence. U.N. recognition in May 1992 was followed by increased ethnic violence by Bosnian Serbs toward Muslims, including the use of **ethnic cleansing**— violence and incentives to ensure that no non-Serb remained in areas under the control of the Serbs.

The international response included everything except the robust use of military force. In Lawrence Freedman's words, the Security Council "experimented with about every available form of coercion short of war."[12] Economic sanctions were imposed on Serbia in retaliation for its assistance to Bosnian Serbs, and humanitarian relief operations ran in tandem with diplomatic attempts to settle the conflicts peacefully. Absent a cease-fire agreement signed by all fighting parties, the United Nations initially declined to send peacekeepers into Bosnia. From the outset of the conflict in Bosnia, the Bosnian Serbs showed no special consideration for U.N. protected areas (UNPAs) or for noncombatants. The war was about territory, and the best way to gain territory was to eliminate the presence of non-Serbs in whatever manner was most effective. The means to that end included blocking relief supplies to Muslim populations, systematizing the rape of Muslim women and young girls, shelling civilian populations, and practicing widespread and indiscriminate torture and murder.

UNPROFOR troops, in accordance with Resolution 770, were eventually deployed specifically to assist in the delivery of humanitarian aid within Bosnia, of which only an estimated 25 percent was getting through. France, Britain, Canada, Spain, Pakistan, and former COMECON countries provided the troops at the outset, by special arrangement with NATO but under a U.N. umbrella. Although authorized to use force to protect humanitarian personnel, especially the members of their own forces, the military commanders on the ground were reluctant to do so, for fear of provoking further Serbian aggression. The United States and its European allies disagreed over the use of force to bring about Serbian compliance with no-fly zones and relief delivery. Violations by all warring parties, but particularly by the Serbs, of the 1949 Geneva conventions, additional protocols, and numerous other codified and customary norms were obvious and abundant. In the absence of consensus over the use of force against transgressors, the international system focused on humanitarian relief, diplomatic negotiations, and hope—not a particularly effective strategy but certainly the one with fewest risks for external actors. It was particularly distressing for humanitarians that their actions had served as "a palliative, an alibi, an excuse," according to José-Maria

Mediluce, the UNHCR's first special envoy, who subsequently became a member of the European Parliament.[13]

Security Council Resolution 795, passed in December 1992, placed peacekeepers on the northern border of Macedonia to prevent the conflict from spilling over into that territory. The conflict seemed to feed on all humanitarian and political efforts to ease it, including the arms embargo imposed on all parties to the conflict. Article 51 of the U.N. Charter, invoked during the Gulf crisis, legitimates the "inherent right of individual or collective self-defense if an armed attack occurs against a Member of the United Nations." Yet there was no collective agreement from the major powers to help Bosnia formulate a collective self-defense. And given the disparity in the distribution of existing resources of the former Yugoslav People's Army (JNA)—about 85 percent went to Serbia—the enforcement of the arms embargo against Bosnia as well as against Serbia and Croatia amounted to collective intervention in behalf of the Serbs.

A tenuous winter cease-fire negotiated by former President Jimmy Carter unraveled in spring 1995. In the last week of May, the Serbs resumed heavy bombing of Sarajevo, which resulted in NATO's bombing of Serbian munitions storage sites near the Serbs' political headquarters in Pale. This was the strongest response by the Western alliance since the war had begun. Both NATO and U.N. commanders approved the bombing. French soldiers were the most vulnerable on the ground, numbering 3,800. France declared that if its troops did not receive significant reinforcement from NATO and the United Nations, they would be withdrawn. A few hours after the first NATO bombing, the Serbs commenced heavy shelling of five of the six so-called U.N. safe areas. Within three days, 325 peacekeepers had been taken hostage by Serb forces; and some had been chained to poles and placed in strategic locations as human shields against further U.N./NATO military action.

As a result, the line between peacekeepers and combatants became further blurred. French soldiers had come under attack immediately after NATO planes bombed the munitions site near the Serb-appointed capital of Pale. As reported by the commander of the French U.N. peacekeepers, his soldiers had radioed to headquarters that the Serbs were ordering them to surrender. "One of my lieutenants called me and said they were under fire and requested my instructions. As a peacekeeper, it was not easy to know how to respond. I told them to refrain from firing back but not to surrender." When the Serbs increased their fire and the lieutenant called his commander again for instructions, he responded: "I had never faced this kind of decision. We are deployed here as peacekeepers, not as fighting soldiers. I knew I had no way of getting them out and no way of protecting them. I said to myself, My men are going to die if they start shooting back. And for what? For peace? So I ordered them to surrender."[14] The frustration of the French reflects the inherent contradiction between their action-oriented military training and their impossible peace-keeping mission in Bosnia.

The response of the United States, Britain, France, Germany, and Russia—the contact group, which formed in 1994 to facilitate diplomacy by the major powers—was to agree to what on paper appeared to be a more robust military presence. The 22,000 peacekeepers in Bosnia were to be reinforced with 12,500 soldiers from France, Britain, and the Netherlands as part of a rapid reaction force with heavy artillery, tanks, and helicopter air support. In addition, the peacekeepers would be given more aggressive rules of engagement.

The buzz phrase *Mogadishu line* began to circulate. It alluded to the American-led intervention in Somalia, in which U.N. peacekeepers metamorphosed from protectors of humanitarian relief into partial combatants. Military force was heightened. Following Serb retaliation against NATO, the U.N. operation was flooded with an increased troop presence on the ground: The rapid reaction force represented a 50 percent increase in troop strength in Bosnia.

The decisions to increase the military peacekeeping presence was made by NATO. The U.N. secretary-general was informed of the decision to

Danziger, © *Christian Science Monitor.*

augment troops and equipment and to reposition troops already in place in Bosnia. The command and control of the U.N. peacekeeping operation at this point strayed from the humanitarian planning of the UNHCR and into the strategic military planning of NATO. And what was the Serb response to this flexing of military might? Within one month, safe areas designed for the protection of Muslim noncombatants began to fall to Serb forces, starting with Srebrenica, the first safe area established in 1993. Some 40,000 Muslims had lived in Srebrenica. Women, children, and the elderly were evacuated, forced to leave everyone else behind, including husbands, brothers, and sons of fighting age, as the Serbs entered the city. One week later, only 20,000 of Srebrenica's residents could be accounted for. The promise by the international humanitarian system—that if the residents stayed and waited out the war, they would be protected—had obviously been broken. As the residents left the city, they passed corpses hanging from trees and lying in the streets and listened to more stories of rape and torture, tragedies that the United Nations was supposed to have prevented by the establishment of the safe areas and an international tribunal to prosecute war criminals. Ironically, perhaps the most unsafe areas in the Balkans turned out to be the U.N. safe areas.

A turning point was reached after the fall of Srebrenica and Zepa, when NATO decided to use airpower to deter further attacks. Croatia then took the opportunity to launch an offensive against the Serbs. The Tudjman government immediately mobilized soldiers and prepared to return to full-scale war to recover the Krajina and other areas in western Bosnia under Serbian control. Croatia's long coastline provided means for circumventing the arms embargo and smuggling in heavy weaponry for its army of 100,000.

In only a few days, the Croatian Army overran Knin, the capital of the self-styled breakaway republic, and recovered most of the Krajina, which had been occupied for almost four years. The West talked, but Croatia acted. NATO's bluster had at least served to tie down the Serbs in Bosnia so that they could not come to the aid of their coethnics in Croatia. In an ironic twist, the largest refugee flow of the war—indeed, the largest in Europe since the Soviet crushing of the Hungarian uprising in 1956—resulted from a successful Croatian military campaign. (This sad record was later broken in Kosovo, in 1999.) An estimated 125,000 to 150,000 refugees and 50,000 soldiers were of Serbian origin. They fled into Serbia itself and toward Serbian-dominated Bosnia. The so-called UNPAs were finally "protected"—but by Croatian rather than U.N. soldiers.

In late August 1995, Serbian shells killed thirty-seven people in the same Sarajevo marketplace where an earlier Serb attack that left twice as many dead had led to the first NATO air strikes in February 1994. The Western response this time was much swifter and firmer. The efforts against Bosnian Serbs involved artillery from both the rapid reaction force and sixty NATO war planes. The explanation for the largest military efforts since the founding of the Western alliance in 1949 was twofold: Serbs were on the defensive after being trounced by Croatia in the Krajina, and their leadership was in disarray; and U.N. soldiers had abandoned the exposed areas in eastern Bosnia, removing the risk of blue helmet casualties due to Western military strikes.

From the beginning of the war, the West's vacillation over the use of military force had led to unfavorable comparisons of the United Nations to its ineffective predecessor, the League of Nations. Jamasheed K.A. Manker, about to retire after two years as Pakistan's chief representative to the United Nations, stated: "This is not the League of Nations. That would be an exaggeration." But he also noted the similarities between the international community's performance in the 1930s and its response to the current clash "between a weak multiethnic democracy and a militarily strong fascist regime prepared to use force ruthlessly."[15] Slobodan Milosevic clearly understood that the West was willing to tolerate the worst atrocities in Europe since the Nazi era and that it was not going to force him or his proxies to retreat from the ethnically pure areas that created a basis for a Greater Serbia. Fred Cuny, a veteran of many humanitarian tragedies who was later murdered during a humanitarian mission to war-torn Chechnya, commented on the international community's impotence and misplaced neutrality from his perspective in Sarajevo: "If the U.N. had been around in 1939, we would all be speaking German."

Much of the media attention and rhetoric within national legislative bodies about how to deal with the former Yugoslavia centered on the failure of the United Nations. However, as one NGO executive stated, "It's particularly hard to find fault with the U.N.'s humanitarian organizations when their failure is more a function of the lack of political support than of their own decisions."[16] In the absence of political consensus among the member states that hold the largest market share on the use of force and resources, humanitarian assistance during an escalating conflict can at best be a Band-Aid, sporadically applied and easily removed.

The UNHCR had been the designated lead U.N. agency for all of the former Yugoslavia. The complexity and volatility of the environment there were unfamiliar and overwhelming to most humanitarian workers. Because the former Yugoslavia had not hosted any Western IGOs or NGOs prior to the conflict, there was little accumulated understanding of local cultures and problems, and few "Yugoslav hands," in these institutions.

By late 1993, an estimated 200,000 persons had been killed or reported missing in the former Yugoslavia. Bosnia-Herzegovina yielded the largest number of internally displaced persons, with approximately 2.7 million homeless and dependent on international assistance. There was never a guarantee that those who sat at the negotiating table could "deliver" to the peace process either those combatants in the field intent upon the vision of a Greater Serbia or those simply looking for gains in material wealth or a feeling of personal **empowerment** through the subjugation of others. This fact was manifested in the field. Commanders of peacekeeping troops in Bosnia, in their efforts to assist the delivery of humanitarian relief, had to negotiate not only with Serb political and military authorities in Belgrade, Pale, and Sarajevo, but also with Serb and Bosnian Serb officials in the field and at roadblocks. Locally, military and especially **paramilitary** elements called the shots, regardless of what the higher authorities had agreed to.

Military contingents were unfamiliar with this new type of conflict and their new role of protecting humanitarian relief. Military strategy for protection forces changed frequently and without warning. Troops were not equipped to wage war. Front lines were constantly shifting. Oral agreements from belligerents were unreliable. At one point in 1995, U.N. peacekeeping uniforms were stolen and donned by Bosnian Serbs in their efforts to capture a U.N. outpost guarding a safe area. The United Nations in Geneva and New York was humiliated, and so were the troops on the ground, who were impotent to respond in kind to blatant violations of human rights and international law.

What should the international humanitarian system do when political authorities do not respect the norms and rules of behavior to which most others adhere? In the case of the former Yugoslavia, international resolve weakened, and attention turned more toward protecting the peacekeepers than protecting noncombatants—as witnessed by derisory comments in Bosnia suggesting that the word *self* be inserted before *protection* in UNPROFOR. Since summer 1994, the subject of peacekeeper withdrawal from the former Yugoslavia had been a staple on the agenda of the Security Council. In September 1995, the secretary-general proposed that the operation should be a "multinational" (that is, "NATO") effort rather than a U.N. one.

Before peace talks began at Wright-Patterson Air Force Base in November 1995, some 50,000 peacekeeping and policy personnel from thirty-six countries were operating in the former Yugoslavia at a total cost of about $2 billion annually. The majority were in Bosnia, protecting themselves and the approximately 3,000 humanitarians in the region, who were providing life-sustaining assistance to at least 1 million refugees and 3 million internally displaced persons. The UNHCR alone was spending nearly $500 million annually.

When a peace agreement was signed, on December 14, 1995, the three-and-a-half-year war had left some 200,000 people dead, 30,000 people missing, and another 2.7 million homeless, of whom 60 percent were internally displaced. The country was divided into two regions, one under the control of the Bosnian Serbs (49 percent) and the other under the control of a Muslim-Croat federation (51 percent), with Sarajevo reunited and ruled by the Muslim-led government. The long process of rehabilitation and reconstruction was hampered by the presence of roughly 6 million land mines, of which only 30 percent had been mapped. UNPROFOR was replaced by a peace implementation force (IFOR) under NATO command. War crimes investigations and judicial hearings were given high priority on the postconflict agenda. However, due to the logistical difficulty of locating and detaining the accused, successful prosecutions to-date have been few.

KOSOVO

In the early 1990s, questions of NATO's role in the post–Cold War world dominated international security debates. The majority of allies believed then that NATO would be a tool employed under the auspices of the United Nations or the Organization for Security and Cooperation in Europe (OSCE). In 1999, however, NATO conducted a 78-day air campaign inside Serbia proper, without U.N. or OSCE oversight or legitimation, to end what it deemed a humanitarian catastrophe in Kosovo. By sidestepping potential debate in the U.N. Security Council, NATO muted Chinese and Russian interests in the Balkans. Although NATO acknowledged during its April 1999 Washington, D.C. summit that the "UNSC has the primary responsibility for the maintenance of international peace and security," it simultaneously asserted the right to defend its proclaimed values of democracy, human rights, and the rule of law. As the new millennium begins, the United States might well view Kosovo as a precedent for acting outside of the U.N. Security Council; however, other NATO allies, such as Germany and France, see Kosovo as unique.[17] This first "humanitarian war," both supporters and detractors agree,[18] is unusual enough to justify separate treatment here, although it occurred as part of a general struggle for national self-determination among the constituents of the Yugoslav federation.

In addition to the unprecedented role of NATO, some observers also recognize the Kosovo crisis as the first "Internet war."[19] Scholars, politicians, humanitarians, journalists, and other interested individuals were able to learn about the crisis in real time from a variety of perspectives. In addition to humanitarian information provided by the United Nations and NGO Web sites, one could find an annotated list of news articles from around the world on the BBC site; information about military forces and operations at the site of the American Federation of Scientists; the position of the American government, outlined by the U.S. Information Agency; the daily activity of the International Criminal Tribunal for the former Yugoslavia, described by the tribunal's officials; the official position on Kosovo, supplied by the Yugoslav government; and perspectives from the Balkans Muslim community at a site sponsored by the California Technical Institute. Web sites not only provided information but facilitated donations to war and humanitarian efforts and encouraged political activism. Learning about the history and real-time activities of a humanitarian crisis was possible with just a few keystrokes.

Although there is a long history of ethnic tension in the Balkans, this story of the current Kosovo crisis begins in 1974 when Yugoslav President Joseph Tito gave Kosovo considerable autonomy through a new constitution. For the next fifteen years, Kosovars—90 percent of whom are ethnic Albanians and the other 10 percent, minorities, of which Serbs constituted the largest group—lived and worked more or less under self-rule.

In 1989, Yugoslav President Slobodan Milosevic abolished the Kosovo constitution and established direct rule over the region by Serbia. Ethnic Albanians were expelled from the Kosovo parliament, state bureaucracies, and state-owned industries. Ethnic Albanian physicians and teachers were removed from their positions in state-run medical facilities and schools.

A philosophy of nonviolence governed the response of most ethnic Albanians from 1989 to 1998. During that time, Kosovar Albanians created a parallel civil society, which included an unofficial government, medical facilities, and educational institutions funded primarily by voluntary donations from Albanians living and working abroad. A small minority of Kosovars, however, were disillusioned with the nonviolent approach, and in 1993 they founded the Kosovo Liberation Army (KLA).

The popularity of the KLA began to grow after the 1995 Dayton Accords. Most Kosovar Albanians prior to the accords had believed that their plight would be addressed in the Bosnian peace plan—a belief encouraged by the fact that the U.S. had already threatened Milosevic with military intervention in Kosovo and Serbia proper in 1992. Unfortunately for Albanians, Kosovo was never mentioned in the Dayton Accords. Some believe that the omission was deliberate, a concession to appease Milosevic.

In February 1998, war erupted between the Serbs and Kosovars. In response to sporadic attacks by the KLA against Serb police stations, Milosevic used armor and artillery to destroy villages and terrorize the ethnic Albanian population. The North Atlantic Council met in September and unanimously voted to demand a halt to Serb violence. NATO concluded a cease-fire arrangement on October 13, 1998, which was to be enforced by threats of NATO air strikes and overseen by some 2,000 unarmed monitors from the OSCE. Milosevic would be allowed to keep 20,000 military, paramilitary, and police troops in Kosovo. Five more months of Serb aggression against Kosovar Albanians would pass before the actual commencement of NATO air strikes. The delay was due to lack of consensus among NATO's nineteen members as to when force would be used.

Serb and KLA fighting renewed in December 1998, followed by an unconscionable massacre of ethnic Albanians in Racak in January. A February peace conference at Rambouillet, France, sponsored by the Contact Group that had originally formed for the Bosnian crisis, was ineffective. Ethnic Albanians agreed conditionally to the terms, pending approval by popular referendum, but the Serbs refused to sign. Milosevic immediately began to mass tanks and infantry in Kosovo.

A report issued by Physicians for Human Rights provides evidence that between the failure of the Rambouillet conference and the forceful expulsion of Kosovar Albanians to neighboring countries, nearly one-third of the refugees suffered human rights violations, such as killing, beating, torture, sexual assault, and looting. Over 100 medical clinics, pharmacies, and hospitals had been destroyed, and ethnic Albanian doctors had been specifically targeted. According to the report's authors, "There was a systematic attack on facilities that are supposed to provide relief from suffering."[20]

On March 24, 1999, again acting without U.N. Security Council approval, NATO began a bombing campaign in Kosovo and Serbia proper. The objectives, according to NATO press releases, were to prevent a humanitarian catastrophe and to force Milosevic to accept the terms of the Rambouillet conference and withdraw Yugoslav forces from Kosovo. Following internal NATO meetings prior to the bombing, UNHCR had been notified that it should mobilize the humanitarian resources necessary to care for the movement of some 100,000 refugees. UNHCR had already established a field office in Belgrade in 1993, to care for Serbian refugees moving out of Croatia and Bosnia. The NATO warning led to UNHCR's stockpiling of emergency supplies at its Belgrade office. Little attention was given to providing supplies to Albania and Macedonia; and within weeks, 800,000 Kosovars, rather than the expected 100,000, became refugees or internally displaced persons in need of immediate assistance.[21]

In military and political terms, the NATO bombing campaign was largely a success. Mishaps included the May bombing of the Chinese embassy in Serbia, which was blamed on the CIA's use of outdated maps. Chinese in Beijing and around the world demonstrated in protest, and Chinese President Jiang Zemin threatened to veto any future Security Council resolution regarding the Kosovo crisis. Unintended but expected collateral damage also included the deaths of ethnic Albanians, who were either mistaken for Serbian troops or mingled among them, as well as the deaths of Serbian noncombatants.

The 78-day air campaign, which was preceded by eleven months of military planning, was a model of escalation theory and high-tech, low-risk, attrition warfare. At first, bombing targets were specifically those that had military significance to the Serbian regime. One month later, mass media facilities were hit. As time passed, the intensity of the bombing ratcheted upward until the lights went out in Belgrade, figuratively and literally. In addition to the bombing, Serbia also suffered from the EU Council's embargo on the sale and delivery of crude oil and other products and the freezing of Yugoslav assets abroad.

Many analysts are of the opinion that the conflict was won by the systematic erosion of Serbia's economic structure. The U.S. Department of Defense estimates that Serbia lost 70 percent of its bridges and all of its oil refinery facilities. The European Union estimates that the reconstruction of Serbia will cost $30 billion; the Yugoslav government puts the estimate at nearly $100 billion.

In addition to the destruction to Serbia's economic infrastructure are humanitarian concerns. The Yugoslav government cites deaths; maiming; lost jobs; water, soil, and air pollution caused by depleted uranium used in NATO bombs; destruction of protected nature parks and biodiversity; negative effects on the food chain; and destruction of historic monuments. Yugoslavia's claims against NATO include violations of humanitarian law, the Hague Rules, the Geneva Convention and Protocol I, the Declaration of Human Rights, and internationally recognized environmental protection principles.[22]

On June 3, 1999, the Serbian parliament voted to approve the NATO-imposed peace plan, which contained ten points. The three most pressing were those cited in the Rambouillet peace agreement: (1) the immediate and verifiable end of violence and repression in Kosovo; (2) the verifiable withdrawal from Kosovo of all military, police, and paramilitary forces according to a rapid timetable; and (3) an international security presence with substantial NATO participation under unified command and control. The crisis, which was never referred to as a war between NATO and Yugoslavia, officially ended on June 9.

On June 10, 1999, U.N. Security Council Resolution 1244 was passed (without the threatened China veto), creating the U.N. Interim Administration Mission in Kosovo (UNMIK) with four components: (1) interim civil administration (U.N.-led); humanitarian affairs (UNHCR-led); reconstruction (EU-led); and institution building (OSCE-led). On June 12, NATO deployed the Kosovo Force (KFOR) to conduct aerial assessments to locate internally displaced persons for humanitarian agencies, and to locate mass grave sites for the International Criminal Tribunal for Former Yugoslavia. On June 13, for the first time in three months, a 23-truck, multi-agency convoy made its way into Kosovo with MREs (meals ready to eat), pallets of bottled water, wheat flour, blankets, tents, plastic sheeting, and personal hygiene kits. By June 16, Yugoslav forces had withdrawn entirely. Ten days later, the first contingent of international police arrived from the U.N. mission in Bosnia. The following day, more than 60 nations and dozens of international aid agencies pledged $2 billion to help feed and house the returning ethnic Albanian refugees. Within six weeks, some 600,000 refugees had returned to Kosovo.

Immediately prior to the February 1999 escalation in Serb violence, the largest humanitarian concerns were vulnerability caused by overcrowded housing, reduced health care provision, and disruption of the education system. The Mother Teresa Society, a local NGO that had become established well before the crisis and that was recognized by Serbian authorities, organized relief for internally displaced persons (IDPs). The Society responded well to the overall emergency, and it became the best source of information regarding the whereabouts of IDPs.

During crisis escalation, the international humanitarian system was caught off guard by the unexpectedly large number of IDPs and refugees who appeared within a short time. Under the direction of UNHCR, NATO managed the airlift of relief supplies as well as over 60,000 refugees to all 19 NATO countries; off-loaded and provided storage of aid cargoes; and provided information regarding the numbers and locations of IDPs.[23] NATO also assisted in the construction of refugee camps in Macedonia and Albania.

In addition to establishing refugee camps and distributing food and other goods, relief workers were required to pay particular attention to the number of child IDPs and refugees. Kosovo has the highest birthrate in Europe—21.2 births per 1,000 inhabitants. Children make up roughly 50 percent of the Kosovar population.[24] Health concerns for children fleeing violence include diarrhea and dehydration, malnutrition, vulnerability to disease, and degradation of short- and long-term mental wellness. The separation of children from their parents and other family members is also of grave concern. Moreover, humanitarian programming and planning must be sensitive to the fact that the needs of children vary considerably, according to age. For smaller children, basic needs may be unintentionally ignored due to a parent's state of depression; for older children, the loss of community and structure to their lives can lead to depression, lethargy, or the decision to become active in the fighting.[25]

Although the overall response to the Kosovo crisis is deemed to have been a success by those who monitored the war's conclusion through the

These children are living in a KFOR-guarded camp that houses about 5,000 Roma civilians. UN/UNHCR/P. Deloche.

media, it has left humanitarians with tremendous unease for several reasons:

1. An estimated 500 to 1,000 civilians died from NATO bombings inside Serbia. NATO defended its air campaign, stating that such "collateral damage" was unintended and unavoidable. The objective of "turning out the lights on Belgrade," according to U.S. White House spokesman Joe Lockhart, required the targeting not only of military bunkers, barracks, and ammunition depots but also of factories, bridges, television stations, and power plants inside a densely populated city. The bombing of Serbia is reminiscent of the bombing of Baghdad. The Geneva Conventions explicitly prohibit the bombing of civilian buildings or even dual civilian/military sites if the "incidental loss of civilian life . . . would be excessive in relation to the concrete and direct military advantage" of the attack.

2. The United Nations was unable to coordinate a substantial portion of humanitarian assistance because most of the resources were provided bilaterally through some 350 NGOs working in the Balkans. For example,

the efforts of Catholic Relief Services (CRS) were funded by the U.S. Office for Disaster Assistance. The effects of an uncoordinated relief program included:

A. distribution of inappropriate and costly foodstuffs as food assistance to refugees, including potentially lethal breast-milk substitutes and nutritionally inadequate, low-protein biscuits;
B. controversial air drops of food into Kosovo, which were criticized as unnecessary;
C. lack of general information on the health and nutritional problems of the affected population and how best to deal with them, particularly for refugees living with host families;
D. great disparities in rations delivered to refugees depending not on need but on location; and
E. lack of transparency and accountability due to unacceptably low reporting requirements for millions of dollars spent.[26]

3. As the emergency humanitarian crisis eased for ethnic Albanians, it increased for Kosovar Serb refugees, who were terrorized and expelled by ethnic Albanians upon their return home. Romas, or gypsies, were also targeted and terrorized, not only in Kosovo but where they were "protected," in refugee camps. As of the end of July 1999, some 5,000 Romas were still in refugee camps or with relatives in Macedonia because Kosovar Albanians were accusing them of collaborating with Serbian authorities.[27] Milosevic bears much of the responsibility for the intense, ethnicity-based violations of human rights perpetrated by Kosovar Albanians. The ultranationalist campaign of Milosevic, based upon what Shashi Tharoor refers to as "invented nationalism," provoked a backlash in the form of a pan-Albanian nationalist movement and its attempt to unite Albanian people in the Balkan states of Serbia, Albania, Macedonia, and Montenegro.[28] It is difficult for humanitarians to watch those whom they have assisted become violent toward others and thereby produce another wave of vulnerable refugees.

4. There is still no control over private groups' donations of useless items, often for tax deductions, to crisis areas. The delivery of such items often absorbs transportation resources that could have been devoted to necessary humanitarian items. The World Health Organization reported that 65 percent of the drugs and medical supplies received in refugee camps in Albania were useless because they were outdated or would soon expire. Another 32 percent were brands with which Albanian workers were unfamiliar and that they therefore could not administer.[29]

5. As Sadako Ogato, the U.N. High Commissioner for Refugees, stated in July 1999, there seemingly is a double standard in aid donations—one

for Europeans and one for Africans. By mid-1999, UNHCR had received only 25 percent of its requests, totaling $165 million, for aid to sub-Saharan Africans, while commitments for Kosovo refugees alone had topped some $265 million. Another $2 billion had been pledged to feed and house the Kosovars upon their return.[30] The disparity in pledges is accentuated by the disparity in need: The U.N. subcommittee on nutrition noted that refugees and IDPs from Kosovo were not experiencing any problems due to deviations from nutritional standards for their weight and height. In sub-Saharan Africa, 5 to 10 percent of wasting in the population is considered usual. In Kosovo there were no diseases or public health problems of epidemic proportions, nor was there significant incidence of malnutrition. In eastern and southern Africa, some 6 million children have been left orphaned by AIDS—70 percent of the world's AIDS orphans. Malaria is on the rise. All humanitarian programs in the Great Lakes region are jeopardized by the lack of funding to remedy malnutrition.[31] Although there is great satisfaction in knowing that the needs of the Kosovar Albanians were met, whether in refugee camps or with host families, the contrast in assistance given to Africa is unsettling.

RWANDA AND THE AFRICAN GREAT LAKES

Article 8 of the 1951 U.N. Convention on the Prevention and Punishment of the Crime of Genocide mandates that "competent organs of the United Nations . . . take such action under the Charter of the United Nations as they consider appropriate for the prevention and suppression of acts of genocide." Perhaps a key word missing from this article is the word *timely*—action must be taken swiftly when the crime against humanity is a massive, fast-rolling wave of genocide. Rwanda is another example of too little, too late from the international political and humanitarian systems. Moreover, the chaotic aftermath suggested how difficult it is to halt the spread of violence within a region at war with itself.

In April 1994, the president of Rwanda, Juvenal Habyarimana, was killed when his plane was shot down. The life of the president of Burundi was also taken. Rwanda and Burundi had both been trapped in regular cycles of conflict since the eve of their independence from Belgium. Ethnic tension had been exacerbated by the governance structures established in Rwanda by Germany (the colonial power there before World War I) and Belgium (U.N. trustee in Rwanda from its original mandate by the League of Nations until 1962), in which the Tutsi minority had always been granted special privileges and authority. Due in part to the country's weak political institutions and heightened impoverishment, the death of Habyarimana unleashed a sweeping massacre, of a speed and a magni-

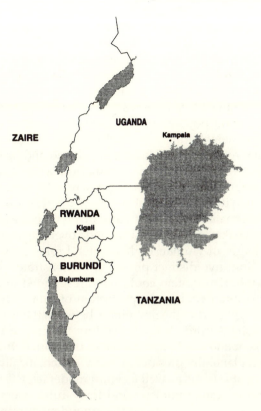

MAP 3.5   Rwanda and the African Great Lakes

tude not witnessed since World War II. The Czech Republic—at the time, a nonpermanent member of the Security Council—pleaded with the permanent members to declare the actions of belligerents in Rwanda "genocide." In contrast, the U.S. State Department issued instructions to its officials to avoid this term. By acknowledging genocide, the international community would have been obliged to respond according to the provisions of the 1951 Genocide Convention. Consequently, the Security Council determined that genocide was not rampant in Rwanda—only isolated "acts of genocide."

Were national interests indeed at work, and could they have been a barrier to an immediate response from the U.N. Security Council during the initial stages of the conflict? In May 1995, the U.S.-based Human Rights Watch accused France, Zaire, South Africa, China, and the Seychelles of violating the 1994 arms embargo by assisting the former Rwandan government in rebuilding its military forces. According to the *New York Times*,

"The human rights group's report, based on a four-month investigation in Central Africa, said that former Rwandan Government and army officials have rebuilt their military infrastructure and created a force of 50,000 men in about a dozen refugee camps, primarily in eastern Zaire."[32]

In the absence of peace **enforcement** measures, new records for the size and speed of human suffering were set. At least 500,000 persons died (15 percent of the prewar population), and hundreds of thousands of Rwandans poured into neighboring Zaire and Tanzania, where camps were established so that refugees could be adequately fed and medically treated. Almost 50 percent of the prewar population were displaced by the tragedy. The magnitude of human flight across Rwanda's borders was unprecedented. Within forty-eight hours of the death of the Rwandan president, an estimated 250,000 refugees made their way into Tanzania. An additional 500,000 poured out of Rwanda over the next few weeks.

Holly Burkhalter of Human Rights Watch broke the time line of the Rwanda crisis into five distinct phases to demonstrate where the international humanitarian system could have responded in a more timely fashion if the commitment to the protection of human life and dignity had been present.[33] During the first phase, between the August 1993 signing of the Arusha Accords formally ending the civil war between the Hutu government and Tutsi opposition and the April 6, 1994, downing of Habyarimana's plane, the president's party systematically began killing political opponents (Tutsis as well as Hutu moderates). On one occasion, a moderate Hutu cabinet minister and forty Tutsis were murdered by government soldiers. U.N. troops on the ground monitoring the so-called peace process—the U.N. Assistance Mission in Rwanda (UNAMIR)—did not respond. As Alison des Forges, a longtime Rwanda watcher, noted, "When they saw they could get away with that kind of violence in Kigali with no reaction from the U.N. troops who were supposed to be responsible for security, it encouraged them to go ahead with the larger operation."[34]

The second phase began on April 6, 1994, immediately after the president's death, which was believed to have been planned by his own army. Prime Minister Agathe Uwilingiyimana, a moderate Hutu, fled to her compound for safety, where she and three of ten Belgian UNAMIR peacekeepers were killed by a mob of militia and presidential guards. The seven remaining Belgian peacekeepers laid down their weapons, as their mandate instructed them not to become involved in combat if unnecessary. The mob mercilessly tortured the soldiers and then murdered and dismembered them. After these events, Belgium ordered the return of its 450 soldiers, who had formed the critical nucleus of UNAMIR. Within three and one-half months, between 500,000 and 1 million people were massacred in a frenzied wave of genocide. The statistics are highly variable and inconsistent but in any case appalling.

Those still hiding in schools, churches, and homes of compassionate Hutus became more vulnerable after the April 21 Security Council resolution to reduce the UNAMIR presence to only 250 men, marking the third phase of the crisis. For those doing the killing, the resolution demonstrated a total lack of international resolve and hence a green light for continuation of genocide. Two weeks later, Washington made its intentions clear regarding participation in peacekeeping when President Bill Clinton signed Presidential Decision Directive 25 (PDD 25). The United States would not become involved unless American interests could be advanced at an acceptable risk; and at least seventeen conditions had to be fulfilled to indicate an acceptable risk. Somalia-like interventions were to be avoided; the Mogadishu line was not to be approached. As one senior government official quipped in an off-the-record comment: "It is almost as if the Hutus had read it [PDD 25]."

Phase four began with mass refugee outflow and France's deployment of troops on June 23. Although France has been accused of bias toward the Hutus—France had armed and trained the government troops responsible for the genocide—the French did save thousands of lives and did not interfere with the assumption of power by the Tutsi-led Rwandan Patriotic Front (RPF). However, Opération Turquoise also protected fleeing militarized and politicized Hutus and allowed them to operate a radio station for a month that continued to broadcast encouragement for the slaughter of Tutsis.

During the fifth phase, in mid-July, after the genocide was over and the RPF had announced the formation of a national government, the Clinton administration finally acted. The Rwandan embassy in Washington was closed, and assets of Rwandans in the United States were frozen. Throughout the prior four phases, Washington had treated the crisis in Rwanda more as an embarrassing irritation than as a pressing humanitarian and human rights disaster.

During the most violent periods of massive slaughter, U.N. agency personnel, who had established offices in Rwanda, were evacuated; but the ICRC and MSF managed to maintain a symbolic presence. As in Somalia, evacuation by the United Nations reduced aid, and withdrawal of its physical presence caused more panic in an already terrorized population. Moving U.N. personnel into the UNAMIR compound until the violence subsided was apparently never an option. A follow-up critique of U.N. performance rang with similar criticism of U.N. operations in other complex emergencies: "Institutional confusion and lack of clarity on the roles of, and relationship between, the humanitarian-development and political-military arms of the U.N. . . . the slow pace of deployment, lack of visible action, and the negative implications of this for . . . overall recovery . . . point to the need for stronger linkages and synergy between the various U.N. components."[35]

By the end of 1995, there were several hundred U.N. humanitarian personnel working in Rwanda and refugee camps and nearly 1,000 NGO staff members. The tally for humanitarian assistance was enormous—for a country with only 8 million people, estimates vary between $1 and $2 billion of emergency aid in 1994 alone, or between 2 and 4 percent of total overseas development assistance.

The RPF was in control of the government but initially without the means to pay salaries to government workers and the military. The World Bank withheld over $240 million of frozen project funds from the new government until it paid over $5 million of arrears in loan reimbursements (attributed to the old regime) and presented a balanced budget and a stabilization plan. The European Union withheld funds until the World Bank was satisfied with the government's actions. Without proper funding during the rehabilitation phase, the government relied on coercion rather than consensus and incentives to bring about compliance with its policies.

Refugee camps and relief workers in Zaire, Tanzania, and Burundi waged an on-and-off battle with cholera as well as with Hutu terrorists and various militias. To intimidate the refugee population, relief workers were terrorized first. OAU and RPF soldiers took control of the camps, ostensibly with the intent of eradicating Hutu terrorism. Due to the confusion engendered by events and by the many warring factions, it is virtually impossible to locate the source of human rights violations at any given moment.

The UNHCR, UNICEF, and the WFP struggled to mobilize and distribute resources in environments convulsed by violence. The UNHCR took responsibility primarily for the refugee camps, while the DHA took responsibility for the internally displaced within Rwanda. The DHA in its coordinating function worked to bring together the operations of the U.N. and NGO communities by providing information on the evolution of the crisis. Although it lacked resources of its own to make a real difference, a friendly government established under DHA control the Swedish Support Team (SST). The SST made available to the DHA and NGOs its staff; vehicles; state-of-the-art communications; office, food, and medical supplies; and other support.[36]

After the French troops left, UNAMIR returned to Rwanda. The 2,500 French legionnaires operating under Chapter VII were replaced by more than twice as many Chapter VI U.N. soldiers. This revived operation also facilitated U.N. and NGO activities for a time by providing security and logistics support. In August 1994, UNAMIR personnel transported more than 14,000 metric tons of relief supplies and produced and distributed more than 7 million gallons of potable water to refugees in and around Goma, Zaire. UNAMIR established humanitarian liaisons within DHA offices. The DHA responded in kind by ensuring the attendance of humanitarian personnel at UNAMIR briefings.

In summer 1995, the new government had come full circle and was demanding the reduction of U.N. soldiers. These demands reflected its impatience with sizable expenditures on peacekeeping and virtually none on rehabilitation. As UNAMIR had pulled out in 1994 at the outset of violence, the RPF reasoned that UNAMIR would do so again.

As of early 1996, the humanitarian and political crises plaguing Rwandans had not abated, although the emergency inside Rwanda had passed. As violence within the country decreased, violence in refugee camps for Rwandans in Burundi, Tanzania, and Zaire rose. Because of fighting among Hutus and Tutsis in Burundi, some 15,000 Rwandan refugees fled their camp in Burundi for Tanzania. They were followed a few days later by an additional 16,000 Rwandan and Burundi asylum-seekers. The U.N. Tribunal for Rwanda began the process of handing down indictments, although many suspects were living as refugees. According to a U.N. prosecutor: "Time is of the essence. 1996 must be the year of massive investigations because justice must be done swiftly."[37] The tribunal's first indictment and sentencing of a Hutu guilty of genocide occurred in August 1999. Some observers believe such cases should be prosecuted in Rwanda, despite the international legal complications.[38]

However, what happened in Rwanda was not an isolated event. In neighboring Burundi, a slow-motion genocide took place as perhaps 150,000 persons died and nearly a million were displaced. Other countries in East and Central Africa responded to a military coup d'état in Burundi in July 1996 with regional economic sanctions. In neighboring Zaire, meanwhile, the failure to separate refugees from Hutu war criminals led to the reconstitution and restoration of their power base with the help of humanitarians. This tinderbox exploded and came to haunt aid workers who had not quite recovered from the "well-fed dead" of Bosnia—the victims of conflict whom aid workers had helped keep alive but whom they could not protect from subsequent violence.

By the end of 1995, or about a year and a half after the genocide in Rwanda, three times as much international support (roughly $1.5 billion) had been spent on refugees outside Rwanda, including the perpetrators of genocide or *genocidaires*, as on survivors within Rwanda. The international emphasis on refugees backfired. The new government in Kigali, led by Paul Kagamé, was furious not only because of the imbalance in aid disbursements but also because aid had contributed to the restoration of

As part of their treatment for psychological trauma, Rwandan boys act out the killings they witnessed. Some 90 percent of surveyed Rwandan children reported that they had witnessed the murder of a parent or an acquaintance. This type of treatment is generally underfunded, as psychological trauma is invisible. UNICEF/Betty Press.

the power base of the Hutu militias, the *Interahamwe*. Preparations began by the government against the Hutu insurgents. The Kagamé government decided that the camps had to be isolated or dismantled entirely in order to protect itself and Tutsi survivors.[39]

In an already convoluted situation with substantial humanitarian suffering, yet another variable appears, the unpredictable despot of Zaire, President Mobutu. After a corrupt reign of a quarter of a century, the tottering regime ironically contributed to its own disappearance. They delivered weapons to the Hutu *Interahamwe* and simultaneously decided in the autumn of 1996 to expel from Kivu province in Zaire ethnic Tutsis who had been settled there for as long as 200 years (called *Banyamulenge*).

The subsequent uprising by the *Banyamulenge* provided the Tutsi-dominated government of Rwanda with the occasion to support their ethnic brethren by invading neighboring Zaire and forcibly repatriating some 700,000 Hutu refugees. This combined effort destroyed the power base of the *Interahamwe* and permitted the ethnic Tutsi to remain in control of the buffer zone along the border. The Rwandan government characterized this war as a battle for its own survival, but other African states saw the effort more as an attempt to expand Rwanda's influence and power.

At the same time, the Tutsi-backed military rebellion in Kivu permitted the longtime guerrilla leader Laurent Kabila to overthrow Mobutu and install himself as the president of the renamed Democratic Republic of Congo. Instead of returning to Rwanda, an estimated 300,000 refugees, including many armed Hutu militiamen, chose to take their chances and remain in the jungles of Zaire. Although the numbers are impossible to verify, as many as 100,000 of these refugees died of starvation or were killed by Kabila's troops.[40]

In spring 1994, practically all U.N. member states chose military inaction in the face of the genocide in Rwanda; but it is unclear that a half-hearted international military intervention in fall 1996 would have been humanitarian. Canada proposed to send one such military mission to Kivu in order to stabilize the area and protect the refugee camps—an objective supported at the time by many civilian aid agencies. But the mission was not intended to disarm the *Interahamwe* or repatriate Rwandan refugees. The military operation was not approved, but it is far from evident that freezing the untenable situation on the ground would have been better or would have involved less suffering than bringing the situation to a head.

In the words of John Prendergast and David Smock, "When Rwanda sneezes, the Congo and Burundi catch a cold."[41] The legacy of genocide and the feeble international response to it thus hangs heavily over the entire region. Insurgencies, ethnic ties, economic links, and humanitarian suffering continue across borders. Regular cycles of violence suggest that peace and reconciliation are distant dreams, absent a comprehensive political strategy. Humanitarians workers as well as analysts are likely to find employment in the region for the foreseeable future.

A CONTEXTUAL COMPARISON

The similarities and differences among the contexts of each complex emergency deserve attention because ultimately they color the effectiveness of action and the quality of the dilemmas faced by humanitarians. Such variations are vital to an appreciation of the complexity of humanitarian action.

Humanitarian assistance during the various wars in Central America in the 1980s was delivered largely by NGOs, particularly religious organizations, that remained in the region to address development and political issues throughout nearly two decades of conflict between militarized governments and opposition groups. The objective of belligerents was to control civilian populations, not exterminate them. The conflicts varied in intensity over time. The role of the United Nations was largely that of managing refugee camps and coordinating repatriation and peace processes. Cold War politics had assisted in strengthening military institutions and power at the expense of civilian institutions, and had kept international institutions out of the United States' backyard—as the conflict in Afghanistan had done for the Soviet Union prior to Mikhail Gorbachev's new thinking and the change in superpower relations. This is a characteristic common also to the conflicts in Iraq and Somalia.

The humanitarian operation in northern Iraq to protect the Kurdish minority was one of three crises within what is referred to as the Gulf crisis. The United Nations initially was conspicuously absent in northern Iraq, was unable to respond to the concerns of countries hosting refugees, and floundered severely in coordinating relief efforts. The succor provided to Kurds in the safe havens in northern Iraq was handled largely by NGOs (some of which had been in the area before the conflict). The protection of the Kurds within encampments was eventually the responsibility of U.N. security guards, not peacekeepers. Elite troops from NATO offered initial protection, and they were followed later by air forces that monitored the no-fly zone over the protected region. The commitment by the U.S.-led coalition in the Gulf crisis has remained strong. The government of Saddam Hussein, whose objective was to beat the Kurds into political submission, was defeated soundly; its supine position did not allow for violations of Kurdish protection. However, the humanitarian needs of the population in Baghdad after the bombings in 1991 and in 1999 were largely ignored, and when not ignored, were said to be the responsibility of Hussein. The bombings in Belgrade during the Kosovo crisis also can be construed as violations of international humanitarian law.

The crisis in the former Yugoslavia will linger in various degrees for years. The official Balkan peace plan signed in December 1995 cannot erase overnight the pain experienced firsthand by millions. As of 2000, thousands were still missing from the war, including 7,000 Muslim men from the fallen safe haven of Srebrenica in mid-1995. The Bosnian Serbs' objective of removing non-Serbs from desired territory set the pattern for Muslim and Croatian forces' behavior once the balance of power shifted in fall 1995 with a Croatian offensive. Refugees were pushed about the Balkans, always one step ahead (if they were fortunate) of military offensives. There were no NGOs in the area prior to the conflict, Yugoslavia traditionally having attracted more tourism than developmental aid. Weapons were plentiful to the Serbs in the region because of the Cold War manufacture of weapons in Yugoslavia and the seizure by Serbia and by Bosnian Serbs of the vast bulk of hardware from the JNA after the country's breakup. The Bosnian Serbs had shown no respect for international law or the decisions of the Security Council. Due to a lack of concerted will among the major powers before the balance of Yugoslav military forces shifted in favor of the Croats in mid-1995, there was no incentive for the Serbs to choose peace over force. Humanitarian action, a massive U.N. peacekeeping effort, and cautious NATO airpower were insufficient to reverse the hunger of the Serbian political elite for new territory or its willingness to resort to war crimes to attain its objectives.

Although the pattern of Milosevic's behavior was evident—to promote and continue gross violations of human rights until met with opposing force—Serb aggression against ethnic Albanians in Kosovo was largely ignored by the international system until reports of massacres made the headlines. Kosovo is also an important study in the politics of humanitarian funding. Not only did Kosovars receive an overwhelming abundance of available resources, they were visited by more movie actors and politicians (and therefore had more media attention) than any people suffering humanitarian crisis in recent history. But even as such attention stimulates increased donations, it also interferes with relief operations. For example, "Hillary Clinton's visit [to one camp] was such a security nightmare that they ended up corraling off a small corner of the camp just for her, like a special exhibit of refugees."[42] Kosovo is also an important case in that it forces one to contemplate, given the postconflict Kosovar violence against Serbs and gypsies, the correct course of humanitarian, military, and political action when issues of individual and group survival underpin all social encounters within an ethnically diverse community.

The objective of belligerents in Somalia was to accumulate and consolidate territorial control and power over populations. Somalia is a failed state—that is, it has no functioning national government. Early warning signs of the complex emergency went unheeded. The stronger warring factions showed little respect for either the U.S.-led or U.N. military presence when there appeared to be no incentive for doing so. The humanitarian impulse to assist the vulnerable was helpful in the short term but was severely weakened after the death of eighteen U.S. soldiers, which brought humiliation on U.S. political and military leaders. The availability of weapons contributed to the deterioration of the state and the withdrawal of assistance. Its most important impact, however, was the destruction of civil society. Sean Devereux, an Anglo-Irish UNICEF aid worker who was later gunned down in the streets of Kismayu, noted in a letter home the story of a Somali fight over two camels: "At the end of three days more than thirty people had been killed. If it had not been for the guns, there would have been a few broken bones and some black eyes."[43]

Genocide was the objective of the Hutu-led Rwandan government in 1994. Systematic planning to carry out genocide had actually occurred long before the death of Rwanda's president in April. Early warning signals of the complex emergency were not addressed, as had happened in Somalia. The focus of major donor governments and permanent members of the Security Council was not on humanitarian assistance and the protection of human rights but on peacekeeping, which included a resolution to reduce, not increase, the UNAMIR force in the area before massive genocide began. Subsequently, the international humanitarian system responded remarkably well—but only after the number of deaths and displaced persons had broken previous records in terms of speed and magnitude. Indeed, the episode calls into question the capacity of the U.N. to conduct a successful humanitarian intervention: Even in the face of a tragedy that clearly violated the Genocide Convention, decisionmaking was fragmented, material and political resources lacking, and strategic direction from powerful member states absent.

Although Rwanda was the most publicized part of the area's troubles, the entire subregion of Africa could be categorized as a humanitarian disaster zone. Aid workers had their hands full in Burundi and what was Zaire became but once again the Congo. Insurgencies in Rwanda and Burundi are being played out on Congolese soil. Here the erosion of central state authority during 30 years of corrupt rule by the Mobutu regime reached a logical conclusion in a scramble for power and wealth among the Kabila government and the 50 opposition groups that signed one cease-fire in the summer of 1999. Virtually all neighboring states are involved in supporting one of the insurgents or Kinshasa. Humanitarian action will be required indefinitely unless a comprehensive strategy for peace is agreed on by African and outside powers. "African solutions to African problems" have not advanced security; a line drawn on the map from the Horn to Angola would trace a path of ongoing, continuous civil wars, even with the involvement of virtually all neighboring countries.

FOUR

□ □ □

Choices and Challenges
in the Field

Make a habit of two things—to help, or at least to do no harm.
—Hippocrates, *Epidemics*

Most of the choices of soldiers involved in humanitarian operations are made for them in the form of rules of engagement and military doctrine. Warring parties, noncombatants, and relief workers base many of their respective choices of action on the existing, volatile context of the conflict. Often choices are based on available resources or on resistance to particular actions from other actors. Each actor's motivations and financial and material resources may increase or diminish as the environment changes. This chapter is largely about the choices that combatants, noncombatants, and field-level relief workers make in response to shifts in the conflict. Each shift affects the combatants' objective to win politically, militarily, or economically; noncombatants' efforts to survive; and relief workers' attempts to alleviate human suffering. The choices of these actors, who are directly influenced by activities inside the war zone, are different from policy choices made by governments and the institutional elites posted at the headquarters of international and nongovernmental organizations. Policy choices of these actors will be addressed in the next chapter.

COMBATANTS

The dilemmas and challenges of humanitarian intervention facing policy-makers and humanitarians would not be so pressing if combatants adhered to international humanitarian and human rights laws. The incredible number of civilian deaths—an estimated 90 percent of all contemporary war casualties—and the increasing number of deaths of relief workers throughout the 1990s are evidence that international humanitarian and human rights laws are either being deliberately and flagrantly ignored or increasingly violated due to changing circumstances. A number of new factors do appear to be preventing some combatants from adhering to international norms protecting the lives and livelihoods of noncombatants.[1]

First, the methods of warfare in this decade have made it difficult to discriminate between combatants and noncombatants and to limit the numbers of dead, maimed, and homeless. Air campaigns using sophisticated bombs can mean more civilian deaths than ground-based campaigns. The use of semi-automatic firearms instead of single-shot rifles results in the indiscriminate spraying of 30 to 35 rounds of ammunition per minute; a good aim is irrelevant. Land mines kill more noncombatants working in their fields, gathering firewood, or playing children's games than they do combatants. More than 110 million land mines are planted across the globe, impeding the safe delivery of emergency relief and of postconflict developmental aid. Warring parties can purchase one land mine from a global stockpile of some 100 million land mines for as little as $3, whereas the cost to the international humanitarian system for removing one land mine is between $300 and $1,000.

Second, the conflicts of the 1990s have occurred largely *within* countries rather than between them. Ideology- and ethnicity-based conflicts are highly personalized and engender long-term instability. Unlike wars between states, intrastate wars require that the opposing sides learn to live and work together after the conflict's end, even though many continue to carry bitterness and personalized hatred. Some scholars even debate whether a postconflict, multicultural society is a rational objective for ethnicity-based conflicts, suggesting that permanent partition may be a more sensible solution.

Third, many of the conflicts, particularly those in Africa and in countries such as Afghanistan, have raged for years. The oxymoron "permanent emergency" captures this tragic reality. The longer a combatant and others touched by a conflict are exposed to horrible images of war and unbearable living conditions, the greater their chances of developing combat stress disorder—a syndrome that renders its victims unable to maintain self-discipline. The long-term chaos of one's surroundings becomes internalized.

Fourth, the conflicts of the 1990s were not necessarily fought by governments versus rebel forces. Included in the mix were militias, private mercenaries, common criminals, and organized criminals, all of whom had access to inexpensive small arms and light weapons, and many of whom were motivated more by economic gain than by political or ideological objectives. With such motivations, international humanitarian and human rights laws are seldom a consideration.

The increased proliferation of small arms and light weapons has become an international security focus within the U.N. General Assembly and elsewhere. Small arms and light weapons are transferred globally in great quantities and with relative ease. The ready availability of these weapons is credited with inflaming societal tensions to the point of armed confrontation; undermining good governance; encouraging human rights violations; increasing the incidence of murder, suicide, injury, psychosocial trauma, assault, robbery, and rape; frustrating development and peace initiatives; and altering communities' social and economic dynamics for generations to come.[2]

Compounding the harm done to noncombatants by small arms proliferation are the effects on relief personnel and relief assets. From 1992 to 1997, 160 U.N. civilian staff members were killed, and many others were held hostage or injured. Of the deaths, only 10 percent were adequately investigated and resulted in a trial. Not until January 15, 1999 did the 1994 Convention on the Safety of United Nations and Associated Personnel receive the necessary number of government ratifications to enter into force.[3]

International initiatives to reduce small arms proliferation began with the 1995 United Nations Panel of Government Experts on Small Arms and Light Weapons (GA 50/70B of 12 December 1995). The recommendations of the panel's 1997 report were endorsed by the secretary-general and adopted by the General Assembly on January 8, 1998.[4] Other initiatives include efforts to establish guidelines for disarmament and for international arms transfers as well to halt the illicit arms trade. Regional efforts include the Organization of American States' "The Inter-American Convention Against the Illicit Manufacturing of and Trafficking in Firearms, Ammunition, Explosives, and Other Related Material," endorsed on November 13, 1997, as well as similar initiatives by the European Union and West Africa. International coalitions of concerned NGOs, encouraged by the success of the land mine campaign, are also working toward controlling the availability of arms and reducing the demand, under the banners of organizations such as the International NGO Action Network on Small Arms, formed in 1998.

NONCOMBATANTS

What kinds of choices do noncombatants have when they become targets or pawns of war? Among other things, they are exposed to possible death, injury, torture, starvation, malnutrition, disease, homelessness, severe psychological trauma, suicide, rape, and family separation.

A "booby-trap" mine in Kosovo in late 1999. There was good reason to fear that the number of land mine victims would increase as returning Kosovars resumed their work in the fields and began to collect firewood for the winter. UN/UNHCR/R. Chalasani.

War scatters people in many directions. Those who can demonstrate a well-founded fear of being persecuted, who manage to avoid the dangers en route to an international border, and who are not turned back by border guards fall into the category of refugees. The rights of refugees are codified in the 1951 Convention Relating to the Status of Refugees and the 1967 Protocol. Article 33 of the convention prohibits a contracting or host state from expelling or returning a refugee *(refoulement)* to the "frontiers of territories where his life or freedom would be threatened." The U.N. High Commissioner for Refugees has the duty to supervise the application of the provisions of the convention and protocol.

Despite the obvious political and technical problems of gathering data in war zones, the most reliable and available indicator of suffering usually has been refugees, because physical displacement is prima facie evidence of vulnerability. (See Figure 4.1.) However, refugees have been diminishing in number, whereas the number of displaced persons seeking

FIGURE 4.1   Global Number of Refugees, 1960–2000

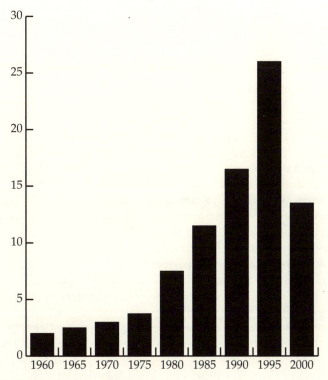

Source: U.N. High Commissioner for Refugees.

refuge within their own countries has increased dramatically. The number of refugees at the end of the century had fallen to about 13.5 million; but the number of internally displaced persons, or IDPs, was considerably larger (at least 17 to 18 million, by conservative estimates), and could conceivably be twice that of refugees. When IDPs were first counted in 1982, there were only 1 million; at that time, there were just over 10 million refugees.

In common parlance, journalists and the proverbial woman on the street tend to think of refugees rather indiscriminately as those who have been forced to flee their homes, whether or not they have left their home country. The distinction matters, however, because those who have crossed a border benefit from the convention and protocol as well as the ministrations of the UNHCR.[5] Those displaced within a country—indeed, many persons who do not move at all but remain in a war zone—often are at least as vulnerable. But they receive less attention and can call upon no special international agency, even though the General Assembly has called upon the UNHCR to help those in "refugee-like situations." Although the lot of refugees is hardly attractive, they may actually be better off than those who stayed behind, whose existence and rights depend on the very political authorities who caused the war and displacement in the first place. Indeed, many regimes intentionally deny protection and assistance to IDPs and other victims as a way of manipulating outside humanitarian agencies into providing food and medicine that can be diverted for military purposes.

What are examples of painful choices made by noncombatants, be they refugees or IDPs? When Burundi soldiers went from village to village, shooting anyone suspected of being a rebel sympathizer, some villagers chose to lie down in the fields during the day and sleep in their homes at night. Others went to the mountains. Eventually hunger overtook both groups and they chose to go to an NGO's food distribution center rather than starve. Soldiers waiting at the distribution center summarily shot anyone who showed signs of malnutrition. If someone had been in hiding, the soldiers reasoned, that person must be a rebel sympathizer. In El Salvador, internally displaced persons congregating to receive assistance from the ICRC were bombed and strafed with bullets by the Salvadoran Air Force. In Guatemala, indigenous peoples preferred to remain hungry in the mountains rather than risk violence at the food relief sites.

In Southern Sudan, rebels bomb feeding centers and other humanitarian targets by day and conduct slave raids at night. Those ineligible for slavery due to their age or other handicaps are often left behind in the village, which is then set afire.

In Sierra Leone, rebels give children the choice of shooting their parents, relatives, and childhood friends or dying themselves. Girls as young as 7, who are captured during rebel raids, are made sex slaves and are later given the choice of being "promoted" to guerrilla fighters. Rebel youths ask victims if they prefer short sleeves or long sleeves, giving them the opportunity to choose between having their arms brutally amputated at the elbow or at the wrist.

In Afghanistan, a woman who has no man in her home, often due to war, must choose between starving to death or being punished by the Taliban for going out onto the street to shop without a male escort.

In the Great Lakes region of the Congo, new mothers choose to feed their newborns with HIV-laden breast milk rather than visit a feeding center to obtain regular supplies of powdered milk. An estimated 25 percent of the region's population is infected with the AIDS virus.

In the Balkans, young boys choose between fighting with the older males or accompanying the women to a refugee or IDP camp. Estimates of male child soldiers are often determined by subtracting the number of

War games in the divided city of Mostar (Bosnia-Herzegovina). The psychological effects of armed conflict on children can be devastating and may haunt them through life, particularly when they have been attacked by neighbors and friends, as happened in Rwanda and the former Yugoslavia. UNICEF/Lemoyne.

young boys who wander into relief camps from their estimated number in the prewar population. The error in this calculation is the number of young boys who are targeted and killed by belligerents.

In Kenya's camps, women obtain food for their children in exchange for sexual favors. Rape also awaits women who wander outside the camp for firewood to cook and provide warmth for their families. A 1998 study of three Kenyan camps revealed a rape rate that was 75 percent higher than that in the normal population. After the United States agreed to assist the UNHCR in purchasing firewood, the rape rate dropped dramatically.

Noncombatants, including orphaned children, make choices every moment about food, water, shelter, family, and community. If an international relief organization is delivering food and medicine, noncombatants must choose between satisfying basic health needs and maintaining physical security. Physical security often depends upon direct military intervention by a third party or a coalition of willing governments. Without such intervention, noncombatants may use the same sources as militias and criminals to purchase small arms for self-defense. Within a relatively short period of time, an environment caught up in conflict can become saturated with weapons held by a variety of actors. A U.S. official with extensive experience in Africa, for example, noted that in 1991, Burundi was

Afghan refugees occupy a Hawai refugee village. UNHCR/H. J. Davies.

a society without arms: "No one had arms outside of the military. And it had always been this way, more or less. . . . One of the most dramatic changes for me now is the presence of weapons."[6] Postconflict disarmament and long-term political stability are extremely difficult if not impossible to achieve when all of society has become militarized. And if postconflict development funds are insufficient, then communities may experience an upsurge in armed criminal activity after political conflict ceases.

RELIEF WORKERS

Relief workers in the field make their choices by considering the resources at hand, the directives of their donors, the mandates of their agencies, and the contexts in which they are attempting to provide assistance to noncombatants. A number of today's relief workers are short on experience in making tortuous choices. Many seasoned humanitarians have left the profession due to combatants' increased targeting of relief workers. Mid-October 1999 was a tragic but unfortunately not atypical week for U.N. workers. Valentin Krumov, a Bulgarian living in New York, arrived in Kosovo and was mobbed and then shot by ethnic Albanians on his first day working for the U.N. Mission in Kosovo (UNMIK); they thought he was a Serb. The next day in Burundi, Luis Zúñiga, a Chilean who was the UNICEF representative there, and Saskia von Meijenfeldt, a Dutch employee of the WFP, were murdered. Such deaths are not unusual. Since 1992, 180 civilian U.N. employees (more than half, local recruits, and the others, expatriates) have been murdered on the job in such places as Rwanda, Afghanistan, Tajikistan, Timor, Sudan, and Angola; 80 more were detained without charges or missing at that time. Clearly, humanitarian service is not for the fainthearted.

Professional training also is lacking among the younger corps because their home office, given the reduction in donations in recent years, had to choose between professional development and relief supplies. Inadequate attention to institutional learning has led to poor training, lack of professionalism, and burnout. Ian McAllister, an experienced observer of relief aid and NGO behavior, also notes in an interview an anti-intellectual attitude in those who are responsible for preparing new relief workers for the field.

Decisions that field workers must make include choosing between drawing noncombatants to permanent food centers or keeping food distribution mobile and hoping that noncombatants find it. They choose between giving money, food, and equipment to belligerents in exchange for access to noncombatants or refusing relief diversion that might fuel the war further. Field workers decide when a refugee camp is full and they must turn away noncombatants. Worst of all, when supplies are limited, field workers must choose which of the noncombatants have the best chance to survive if given food and medical treatment. Although efforts are under way to combine delivery and protection,[7] they must also decide when to turn a blind eye to individual human rights violations so that they can continue to provide humanitarian assistance to a group.

In recent years, field workers have struggled with how to separate combatants from noncombatants as they enter refugee camps. When they fail, they must struggle to regain control of the camps from belligerents who use them as a base to rearm and find fresh recruits. Although policies established at the headquarters of IGOs and NGOs provide unequivocal guidelines for how relief workers should document and screen new arrivals to refugee camps, massive surges in population movements do not always allow workers time to strictly follow these guidelines.

Once refugee camps are established, relief workers observe the internal political dynamics of those encamped in order to ensure the safety of those who may be marginalized or abused by such dynamics. In the camps for Kosovar refugees, gypsies (or Romas) often were attacked by ethnic Albanians, who were in the majority. In African camps with a strong male hierarchy, relief workers have attempted to be culturally sensitive by giving food to dominant males to distribute. Relief workers observed, however, that malnutrition among women, children, and the elderly was far more prevalent when males controlled food distribution.

If a camp becomes militarized, more food is channeled to males of fighting age; food is used not only as a recruitment tool but also as a form of exchange for sexual favors and for small arms. In such environments, relief workers often become hostages and fear for their own safety. Only in recent years have the headquarters of IGOs and NGOs reluctantly agreed to cease humanitarian operations and withdraw their assistance to protect their own personnel. Refugee camps in the former Zaire offer the clearest example of a worst-case scenario for relief workers.

The situation in the refugee camps in Zaire from April 1994 to early 1996 is the epitome of refugee camp disaster. More than 1 million Rwandan refugees and tens of thousands of militiamen and former Hutu civil servants lived in forty camps, many within a few miles of the border. Hutu militiamen, rearmed by outside sources, made nightly forays into Rwanda to challenge the Tutsi-led government and reclaim territory. Within the camps, the militias terrorized or murdered those who did not acquiesce to their demand for new recruits. NGOs such as CARE and MSF, with reputations for staying in the most desperate situations, left in 1995. Alain Destexhe, former secretary-general of the international office of MSF, explained the painful decision to withdraw the French and Belgian branches of his organization: "We can't be a party to slaughter in Rwanda. International aid has allowed the militias to reorganize, stockpile food and recruit and train new members. Agencies like ours are caught in a lose-lose situation; either continue being reluctant accomplices of genocidal warmongers or withdraw from the camps, leaving the refugee population to the mercy of their jailers."[8] Even local humanitarians who volunteered to assist in the collection and burial of refugees struck by cholera were attacked: Thirty Zairean Boy Scouts who collected the dead in the Katale Camp were tied up and slaughtered.[9] The annual cost to the UNHCR for maintaining the camps in Zaire and providing food, water, and medical supplies was approximately $300 million (or one-quarter of its annual budget).

Relief workers must also keep local, settled populations from posing as refugees and IDPs in order to receive emergency food packages and other goods. Although local populations may be only a step away from absolute poverty and need, limited relief supplies require that only those in the most desperate situation qualify for assistance. In Afghanistan, local populations mingled with IDPs as they queued up to receive their daily rations: cooking oil, rice, tea, wheat flour, some kerosene, and twelve liters of water per day per person. UNICEF also provided vitamin A supplements to children under age 5. Tools were distributed to families to construct dwellings on allotted plots. A similar situation occurred in Ethiopia: The Ethiopian Red Cross had established a food distribution center for those who were categorized as completely destitute—that is, at least 24 percent of the population. Ethiopians who owned a donkey or a goat—items critical for self-sufficiency once the crisis passed—would sell or kill their livestock to obtain emergency assistance.[10]

In areas receiving relief and development assistance, relief workers must be careful not to diminish the motivation of the noncombatant population by doing too much for them and must try not to alter long-standing traditions. In Afghanistan, for example, water is carried from areas beneath the mountains to various villages via *karezes*, or underground canals. *Karezes* have vertical shafts spaced at equal distances. They must be kept free of debris so that the underground water system does not become clogged or tainted. Traditionally, every spring each village—sometimes composed of different tribes—would work together to clean the *karezes*.

Because fighting in Afghanistan had prevented the annual cleaning of the *karezes*, the United Nations began to finance projects to do the job and thereby induce refugees to return. The UNDP channeled the material resources, and the WFP dispatched food resources through its food-for-work activities, along with the necessary tools. NGOs made the local contacts and supervised the work. The project seemed to be running smoothly until one day a group of villagers stopped a U.N. team and held it captive. They argued that their *karezes* had not been cleaned, whereas all the *karezes* of villages governed by one particular tribe had been. The U.N. team explained to the villagers that an organized gathering of elders from all of the villages had determined the priority of *kareze* cleaning. Further research, however, proved that indeed all of the *karezes* that had been cleaned had belonged to one particular tribe and that all of the elders present at the meeting belonged to that tribe. Now, instead of working together, the tribes have isolated themselves from one another. And instead of coping with the problem themselves, the villages wait for external assistance to come. The result of the project is disempowered communities and additional, unwanted dependency. The history of post–Cold War relief, if written, would contain many comparable events when relief and development organizations were not knowledgeable enough regarding local culture and social relationships to prevent well-intentioned efforts from backfiring. These events also fuel the trend toward larger donations for relief work and less for development projects.

The choices that relief workers make are altered by the commencement of an international military intervention. Relief workers are often in-country long before and after an outside military presence; yet when a humanitarian operation has become militarized, the efforts of relief workers are often subsumed within political/military objectives. Conflict commonly occurs between relief workers and peacekeepers when soldiers attempt to control the movement and activities of relief personnel. Problems between relief workers and soldiers, however, have abated somewhat in recent years due to repeated interactions and joint conferences and training.

THIRD-PARTY SOLDIERS

Unless soldiers are trained in special forces or expeditionary missions, as are U.S. Marines, or in urban warfare, as are British soldiers trained in Ireland, they are not encouraged to adjust their behavior or set aside doctrinal guidelines to adapt to changes in the conflict environment. The military's unwillingness to allow soldiers in the field to adapt their behavior to volatile internal-war situations, combined with soldiers' lack of understanding of IGOs and NGOs, led to numerous problems in the early 1990s.

Soldiers in the field rely almost entirely upon orders from headquarters outside the field. Military rules of engagement guide soldiers in their interaction with other humanitarians and with belligerents. In the early 1990s, military planners assumed that humanitarian assistance could be planned and executed as a traditional political-military intervention; thus, the military prioritized activities without the participation of humanitarian relief organizations. In Somalia, the U.S. military lacked knowledge about NGO operations and locations, which resulted in its raiding NGOs' local headquarters and confiscating NGOs' firearms.

By the end of the 1990s, however, many soldiers had volunteered repeatedly for humanitarian assignments and had become familiar with relief workers. A shared humanitarian culture of sorts is emerging from the former friction between the cultures of relief workers and soldiers that had been present in other complex emergencies. And as NGO personnel involved in humanitarian operations have found a career path to the U.N. system, some retiring military personnel with experience in relief operations have moved into the NGO sector or are working for military consulting firms involved in peace operations training.

As soldiers voluntarily choose to participate in humanitarian operations due to the personal satisfaction that can be found in helping victims of war, military planners are voicing concerns about the negative consequences that such participation has on a soldier's combat skills. A British colonel working on joint U.S.-U.K. military doctrine stated in an off-the-record interview: "You have to shake people who come out of peace support operations. They are slow, patient, concerned about proportionate use of force, show consideration at the tactical level, which can have strategic effect, and attempt to negotiate. These skills are not suited for warfighting."

Third-party military forces were deployed in a variety of situations in the 1990s. In some situations, only forceful persuasion has proved effective against starvation, genocide, and mass violations of human rights. Various types of humanitarian missions in which military forces might be useful are listed in Table 4.1.

TABLE 4.1   Possible Uses of Military Force for Humanitarian Missions in Complex Emergencies

Armed Activity	Humanitarian Objectives
Military forces deliver relief supplies but do not carry weapons.	Provide food and relief to suffering civilian populations while minimizing potential for entanglement in local conflict.
Armed forces deliver relief aid, using forces only in self-defense and to protect relief supplies.	Provide relief aid, with somewhat greater security for personnel, while deterring interference by hostile groups.
Armed monitoring or enforcement of sanctions; blockade.	Pressure the offending government to modify its behavior to better protect civilians; deprive it of arms that might be used against civilians.
Armed suppression of air traffic in the offending country.	Prevent or reduce air attacks on civilians; protect delivery of relief supplies; pressure the government to modify its behavior.
Air strikes against selected military targets, such as artillery or airfields.	Prevent use of particular weapons against civilians; punish the offending combatant; demonstrate resolve to protect civilians.
Air, ground, and/or naval actions against the armed forces of one or more combatants.	Deter or reduce attacks on civilians or relief shipments; pressure the offending government or other combatants to modify behavior.
Armed forces create safe havens or "zones of peace" and defend them against local combatants.	Shelter displaced civilians until the conflict subsides.
Peacekeeping: armed forces monitor a cease-fire or peace agreement with the consent of combatants.	Protect civilians and encourage a resumption of normal life through efforts to prevent a resumption of hostilities.
Peace enforcement: military action to enforce terms not accepted by the government and/or other combatants.	Restore peaceful conditions and allow resumption of normal life; arrange a transition to a new regime more likely to respect civilian lives.

Source: U.S. Mission to the United Nations, *Global Humanitarian Emergencies, 1995* (January 1995), p. 19.

DILEMMAS AND PRINCIPLES

The previous descriptions suggest that there are problems on the ground for principled humanitarians who operate on an often unprincipled terrain.[11] Clashing interests, competition for resources, and the complex organizational structures of external actors complicate the tasks that face humanitarians deciding on a particular course of action. In the past, humanitarians often found themselves on the horns of a dilemma: That is, they were forced to choose between two alternative courses of action, each bearing potential for unintended and indirect but nonetheless unavoidable, undesirable consequences (as well as for desirable ones). In complex emergencies, multiple interests necessitate the reformulation of "either/or" questions in a way that admits a greater number of possible solutions—broadening the humanitarians' dilemma and not making their choice of action easier.

The very notion of a single actor with the necessary resources to take action when facing a fork in the road is an oversimple ideal. In reality, there are no single actors but rather a composite of institutional actors making up the international humanitarian system. Each agency has perceptions conditioned by a multitude of interests, and each has a different level of power, influence, and access to information. The alternative courses of action among which these institutions must choose can bear life-threatening consequences for the civilian populations they serve as well as for humanitarian field staff, convoy drivers, and soldiers on the front lines. All of the tools required for a well-informed, comprehensive approach to humanitarian action are not typically held by any single institutional actor; thus, there is a need for cooperation, coordination, and steadfast commitment among institutions—a tall order, given that they do not share a single, universal worldview, mandate, or set of guidelines and procedures.

Moreover, the context is always complex and politically charged. Information on which decisions are based is often incomplete or inaccurate; and by the time decisions are implemented, the problems that they were meant to address may have changed. By the time U.N. food and services arrived in Somalia, for example, the peak of the famine had passed. U.S. soldiers who volunteered to assist in the delivery of food wondered why they did not see any starving people on the streets of Mogadishu. The proverbial bottom line is that it is impossible to plot a course of action that is guaranteed to be effective throughout a conflict and free of negative repercussions.

In short, the concept of "dilemma" does not fully capture the complexity of humanitarian decisionmaking. This chapter describes the tough choices or trade-offs facing humanitarians in the field. Like policymakers (addressed in the next chapter), humanitarians must constantly make choices that are tortuous if not impossible. Fundamentally, a decision to act or to refrain from acting must take into account inevitably adverse consequences; but action, and a decision to engage or disengage, is obligatory and not discretionary. In Dante's *Inferno*, the hottest room was reserved for those who vacillated. In war zones, "punting," or avoiding a decision, is not an option. This is one reason why the past decade's tragedies have shaken humanitarians to the core. The mere mention of Bosnia, Somalia, Rwanda, Liberia, Afghanistan, Kosovo, or Sierra Leone profoundly disturbs their composure.

The experiences of humanitarians in these countries have kindled a debate about the role of principles in an unprincipled world. Until recently, the two most essential humanitarian principles—neutrality (not taking sides with warring parties) and impartiality (nondiscrimination and proportionality)—have been relatively uncontroversial.[12] The same could be said about the key operating procedure of seeking consent from belligerents. However, the developments described in the previous chapter and the choices faced by humanitarians on the ground in this chapter illustrate that today's reality is vastly different from the past, in the complete disregard for international humanitarian law by war criminals and even by child soldiers; the direct targeting of civilians and relief personnel; the use of foreign aid to fuel conflicts and war economies; and the protracted nature of many so-called emergencies that in fact last decades.

The extent to which traditional humanitarian principles can still be usefully applied depends on the context. Even "classicists" from the ICRC are becoming aware of the unacceptable results of applying neutrality, impartiality, and consent when dealing with unprincipled actors in armed conflicts. Humanitarian action has never been easy; but abiding strictly by traditional principles formerly was a better tactical guide to sustain the vast majority of impulses to rescue war victims. Although the Biafran civil war led to dissension in the ICRC's ranks and to the creation of the MSF, in the late 1960s it was possible for classicists to view this internal war as anomalous and to dismiss the claims of dissenters. But since the end of the Cold War, events like those in Biafra have become routine.

Context is as important as principles, especially when the latter clash. Thoughtful reflection has a growing role relative to visceral reaction. Although the fact is frequently overlooked, the ICRC's own fundamental principles are not immutable. Last modified in 1965, during "an orgy of rule-making," these principles are not cast in concrete but should be adapted when necessary to reflect the changing nature of war, humanitarian agencies, and donor policies.[13]

Operational principles are not moral absolutes but norms toward which to strive. They are a means to achieve particular ends, not ends in themselves. Differences among principles exist and will continue to exist—in the interpretation given them by various individuals and agencies, in the importance of some relative to others, and in the extent to which a given principle or principles will prevail in particular circumstances.

To date, more than fifty NGOs have adopted the code of conduct used by the International Federation of Red Cross and Red Crescent Societies (IFRC). An independent effort to synthesize thinking was made by researchers at Brown University's Humanitarianism and War Project in 1993. Excerpts from these two sets of guidelines are found in Boxes 4.1 and 4.2. These principles are designed to guide the political behavior of agencies working in conflict situations. As mentioned earlier, a massive effort also was made by almost 200 NGOs to formulate technical standards in the Sphere Project.

The need for case-by-case judgments has been reinforced by the cases described earlier. From sustaining vulnerable groups in the African Great Lakes (and thereby inadvertently feeding thugs and fueling the war) to moving threatened populations in Bosnia (thereby facilitating ethnic

---

BOX 4.1 Principles of Conduct for the International Red Cross and Red Crescent Movement and NGOs in Disaster Response Programs

- The humanitarian imperative comes first.
- Aid is given regardless of race, creed or nationality of the recipients and without adverse distinction of any kind. Aid priorities are calculated on the basis of need alone.
- Aid will not be used to further a particular political or religious standpoint.
- We shall endeavor not to act as instruments of government foreign policy.
- We shall respect culture and custom.
- We will attempt to build disaster response on local capacities.
- Ways shall be found to involve program beneficiaries in the management of relief aid.
- Relief aid must strive to reduce future vulnerabilities to disaster as well as meeting basic needs.
- We hold ourselves accountable to both those we seek to assist and those from whom we accept resources.
- In our information, publicity and advertising activities, we shall recognize disaster victims as dignified humans, not hopeless objects.

Source: International Federation of Red Cross and Red Crescent Societies, *World Disasters Report 1995,* ed. Nick Cater (The Netherlands: Martinus Nijhoff, 1995), p. 146.

BOX 4.2   Providence Principles of
Humanitarian Action in Armed Conflicts

- *Relieving life-threatening suffering:* Humanitarian action should be directed toward the relief of immediate, life-threatening suffering.
- *Proportionality to need:* Humanitarian action should correspond to the degree of suffering, wherever it occurs. It should affirm the view that life is as precious in one part of the globe as another.
- *Nonpartisanship:* Humanitarian action responds to human suffering because people are in need, not to advance political, sectarian, or other extraneous agendas. It should not take sides in conflicts.
- *Independence:* In order to fulfill their mission, humanitarian organizations should be free of interference from home or host political authorities. Humanitarian space is essential for effective action.
- *Accountability:* Humanitarian organizations should report fully on their activities to sponsors and beneficiaries. Humanitarianism should be transparent.
- *Appropriateness:* Humanitarian action should be tailored to local circumstances and aim to enhance, not supplant, locally available resources.
- *Contextualization:* Effective humanitarian action should encompass a comprehensive view of overall needs and of the impact of interventions. Encouraging respect for human rights and addressing the underlying causes of conflicts are essential elements.
- *Subsidiarity of sovereignty:* Where humanitarianism and sovereignty clash, sovereignty should defer to the relief of life-threatening suffering.

Source: Larry Minear and Thomas G. Weiss, *Humanitarian Action in Times of War: A Handbook for Practitioners* (Boulder: Lynne Rienner, 1993), p. 19.

---

cleansing), operational situations in the 1990s have been tortuous—for victims as well as their humanitarian benefactors.

Because morally wrenching contexts are now the rule rather than the exception, it is increasingly difficult for humanitarians to occupy unequivocally the high moral ground; a pedestal is a precarious perch. Michael Ignatieff anguishes that "almost everyone who tries . . . has a bad conscience; no one is quite sure whether our engagement makes things better or worse."[14] Joanna Macrae states, "The idea that it is easy to distinguish the bad guy from the good woman and child is no longer sustainable."[15]

What is the value of principles, if problems are not uniform across war zones, and if neutrality, impartiality, and consent may be more or less pertinent depending on the type and phase of an armed conflict? The clear articulation of principles provides an emergency brake on the slippery slope of shameless opportunism. When principles bump into one another, compromise and tough trade-offs are inevitable, but those who deviate from principles should be aware of the costs. The only absolute principle is the respect for human life. Other principles are standard operating procedures reflecting empirical judgments about experience. They amount to finding ways to make things happen in individual situations.

To return to our earlier argument, scholars and practitioners frequently employ the word *dilemma* to describe painful decisionmaking; but *quandary* would undoubtedly be more apt. A dilemma involves two or more alternative courses of action with unintended but unavoidable and equally undesirable consequences, whereas a quandary involves tough choices among unattractive options. If consequences are equally unpalatable, then remaining inactive on the sidelines is an option rather than entering the scrum on the field. Although humanitarians are perplexed, they are not and should not be immobilized. The solution is not withdrawal but rather appropriate engagement. The key lies in making a good faith effort to analyze the advantages and disadvantages of various courses of action, and then to choose what often amounts to the lesser evil.

What the late Myron Wiener has called "instrumental humanitarianism" resembles just war doctrine in that it emphasizes contextual analyses and not formulas.[16] Humanitarian decisionmakers in war zones could be compared to clinical ethical review teams, whose members are on call to make painful decisions about life-and-death matters in hospitals. The sanctity of life is complicated by new technologies, but urgent decisions cannot be finessed. It is impermissible to long for another era or to pretend that the bases for decisions are unchanged. Humanitarians who cannot stand the heat generated by situational ethics should stay out of the post–Cold War humanitarian kitchen.

In sum, the dynamics of a war environment can change rapidly. Changes include the number of people involved and their motivations: There are politically motivated belligerents under the control of political and military leaders, militiamen, mercenaries, organized criminals, petty criminals, unarmed noncombatants, armed noncombatants, refugees of all ages and physical conditions, organized relief workers operating under the ICRC Code of Conduct, independent relief organizations, and rogue relief workers. If the conflict is attractive to the mass media, there are also journalists and camera crews as well as visiting celebrities and political hopefuls. If there is political interest, there may also be third-party intervenors in the form of peacekeepers and police.

The choices and challenges facing actors in the field are deeply affected by the policies and decisionmaking of those sitting in the national capitals of donor countries and within the various organizations of the U.N. system. The Kosovo crisis demonstrated that the institutional hardware is available for providing succor and security to noncombatants. The political frameworks are in place; the security mechanisms to support political will are ready; and the humanitarian relief infrastructure, although still in need of better coordination and consistent logistical support by the military, is able to provide for most needs of noncombatants. The current problems of humanitarian intervention are not so much related to the structure of existing humanitarian institutions as they are to policymaking. The next chapter explores the policy of humanitarian operations.

FIVE

□ □ □

Policies of Humanitarian Intervention

Policy sits above conscience.
—William Shakespeare, *Timon of Athens*, III, ii

Successful humanitarian intervention requires appropriate and effective policies supported by sufficient infrastructure and resources. A policy is a plan, adopted by a government or organization, which is designed to influence and determine subsequent decisions, actions, and other matters. Policy regarding humanitarian intervention takes a variety of forms, such as government directives, U.N. Security Council mandates, humanitarian agencies' mission statements, and military doctrine and rules of engagement. Let us examine each of these briefly.

Governments exercise political control and direction over the domestic affairs of their citizens, and they conduct foreign affairs. Criminal governmental behavior—for example, the illegal occupation by Iraq of Kuwait, or Baghdad's efforts to starve and repress its minority Kurdish and Shi'ite populations—reflects governmental policies that may lead to outside intervention legitimated by international law. Governmental policies based on respect for international law may or may not lead governments to commit resources to intervention in a complex emergency.

Mandates contained within U.N. Security Council resolutions provide blueprints for humanitarian interventions. They describe the contours of functions and responsibilities of peacekeepers and other third-party intervenors in a particular crisis at a particular point in time. They also provide guidelines for determining the number and type of personnel required to attain a specific goal.

Mission statements of U.N. humanitarian agencies are in essence policies that describe the boundaries of those agencies' duties and responsibilities.

For instance, UNHCR's mission statement explicitly limits its responsibility to the category of forcibly displaced persons legally recognized as refugees; but it also has extended its services to other categories of displaced persons when asked to do so. UNICEF's mission statement explicitly limits its responsibility to children and mothers. The Office of the Coordination of Humanitarian Affairs is responsible for ensuring that the gaps among operational agencies' mission statements or policy guidelines do not result in underserved populations or ignorance of a necessary task or geographic region.

Military doctrine and rules of engagement are also forms of policy. Military doctrine is a body of principles, codified in military manuals, that provide guidelines for how military personnel are to operate in a particular environment—for example, doctrines that govern peace support operations. Rules of engagement are specifically geared to a particular intervention at a particular point in time and describe exactly how military personnel should behave with respect to a variety of encounters with belligerents and others.

Government policies, Security Council mandates, agency mission statements, and military doctrine and rules of engagement are common foci of debates about what is wrong with humanitarian intervention. This chapter identifies the various policy debates in the humanitarian sphere and explores the main challenges of implementing existing policy in the midst of a complex emergency. The next chapter explores similar concerns regarding policy formation and implementation challenges, but with specific reference to international peace and security.

The humanitarian sphere of the United Nations is responsible for providing emergency relief and long-term assistance through its operational agencies. As its Web site announces, "A central component of United Nations policy is to ensure that emergency relief contributes to recovery and longer-term development in the affected area. Economic and social development remains the best protection against disaster—whether natural or, as is increasingly the case, man-made."[1] As innocuous as this policy statement appears, closer examination reveals a core debate in the humanitarian sphere between those who believe that emergency relief should be treated as an end in itself and those who wish to incorporate emergency relief into a more comprehensive intervention package. Mere descriptions of mission statements also conceal points of conflict, either in the conceptualization of what is required or in the difficulties inherent in implementing them.

For example, UNHCR's mandate is to safeguard the rights and well-being of refugees, although it is called on frequently to aid IDPs, which now outnumber refugees by two to one. UNHCR is to protect refugees' right to asylum and voluntary return home, and to seek to reduce situations of forced displacement by working with states and encouraging respect for human rights and fundamental freedoms. An operational policy of UNHCR is its commitment to the principle of participation by consulting refugees on decisions that affect their lives. Problems encountered by UNHCR in fulfilling its mandate include, but are not limited to, difficulty in obtaining accurate data regarding refugees; states' refusal of entry to asylum-seekers; forced, involuntary repatriation; hierarchies of authority and violence in camps; and the dilemma between needing an abusive government to agree to an agency's presence and a population of suffering noncombatants who need the agency to publicize the government's human rights abuses.

We have gone into some depth about UNHCR in order to illustrate why policies are important for individual actors in the humanitarian sphere. Although the policies and practices of UNHCR and other humanitarian agencies appear benevolent, they frequently have unintended negative consequences for noncombatant populations and for international operations more generally. The more common critiques assert that:

- Combatants' abuse of relief assets fuels war.
- Emergency relief creates recipient dependency.
- Human rights protection suffers from a strict food-security focus.
- Long-term development efforts are diminished by a short-term emergency focus.

The more common operational challenges include:

- Forced displacement creates urgent needs for asylum, temporary refugee hosting, IDP camps, or safe havens, all of which are confronted by political obstacles.
- There are two humanitarian policies, one for Africa and one for the rest of the world.

These six critiques are treated in the following sections of this chapter.

RELIEF FUELS WAR

Combatants steal or extort relief assets for a number of reasons: to sell or trade them in exchange for other war assets, such as guns or land mines; to feed combatants and provide them with medical supplies; to prevent food and medical supplies from reaching a specific noncombatant population;

to attract displaced populations to a particular area, where they will be killed; to attract new conscripts, including children; and to use in exchange for sexual favors. In addition to humanitarian goods, combatants may receive cash for providing protection to relief workers or relief warehouses and for allowing access to certain roads, airfields, or ports. Combatants may also intentionally create noncombatant displacement and acute impoverishment in order to lure relief agencies and their assets to a conflict environment, as was the case with Liberian warlords. Relief agencies often have implicitly or explicitly cut deals and accepted that a portion of their relief assets will be diverted to combatants—a kind of "tax" or "cost of doing business" in war zones.

In sum, the criticism is that relief becomes a tool of war that contributes to a protracted war-based economy and interferes with the politics and stability of a country and region. Two sides of the policy debate emerge. Humanitarians argue that although relief assets are used by combatants, no one can determine the proportion by which relief assets contribute to the prolongation of combat compared to the contributions made by other "intervenors." The latter group include states that violate sanctions to support a warring party of choice; illegal gun- and drug runners; and private companies that contract with a warring party for resource extraction while the conflict is in progress. Although a zone of armed conflict may not appear to be a good investment, potential returns can be dramatic, and investments can be recovered in as few as 6 months. Among the examples of private enterprise are diamond firms that contracted with the Zairean rebel Laurent Kabila before his overthrow of President Mobutu, and U.S. and Argentine oil companies bidding for a pipeline-construction contract with various Afghani rebel factions.

On the other side of the debate are those who demand that no third-party humanitarians be allowed within a war environment. The Organization of African Unity, for example, has requested that governments, IGOs, and NGOs provide relief assets directly to the regional organization or state government during a crisis so that the assets will be used in a politically conscious manner and will strengthen the capacity of the state under siege to assist its own population. Alex de Waal, a noted African specialist, also argues for the absence of third-party humanitarians, but on different grounds. He suggests that the provision of humanitarian assistance prevents a population from reaching a point of sufficient desperation and dissatisfaction with its own government that a revolution erupts and changes the relationship between governments and civil society. If funds are to be provided, they should be sent to grassroots groups that are capable of mobilizing and leading such a revolution. Whereas the OAU emphasizes the need for state capacity building, de Waal is interested in furthering justice and a new kind of African state.[2]

EMERGENCY RELIEF CREATES RECIPIENT DEPENDENCY

Two criticisms are posed with increasing frequency against emergency relief that is provided too soon and for too long. First, it creates dependency among recipients to the detriment of natural coping mechanisms and feelings of empowerment. And second, it encourages local groups that are not displaced or in dire need to abandon their productive activities in an attempt to acquire the same goods and services provided to the displaced.

Generally, displaced people and other victims of violence will first resort to basic survival strategies, including social networks, that they have employed in past crises in which outside relief was not an option. This is especially true in countries that experience chronic drought and famine. That said, if an environment is infused with hundreds of NGOs whose success in donors' terms is judged by how many relief assets are delivered to a crisis population, it is difficult for the displaced, as well as others who have not moved, to avoid what is called the "dependency trap."

Three policy opinions circulate within the dependency debate. One side supports dependency among aid recipients; another defends it as an unfortunate yet unavoidable possibility; and another deems it unnecessary and avoidable through empowerment strategies.

Dependency can be considered good from the perspective of those concerned about the return of displaced peoples to their homes once a conflict abates. The argument follows the logic that if refugees or IDPs are dependent upon relief inputs, then refugees and IDPs can be indirectly induced to repatriate by turning off the relief inputs in one area and turning them on in the location preferred by the donors or states. Some might argue that international law is thus violated twice—first, by combatants who are responsible for the forced displacement; and second, by third-party intervenors who are responsible for forced repatriation.

Those who deem dependency an unfortunate yet unavoidable possibility argue that the assertion that humanitarian aid retards natural coping mechanisms is flawed in that noncombatants may be unable to employ natural coping mechanisms due to the stress inherent in exposure to violence. Combat stress reactions (CSR) tend to depress the immune system (a relationship that varies according to the duration of stress). Victims become more vulnerable to disease and infection as stress decreases the number of white cells and quantity of natural antibodies in the blood. Humanitarian personnel are challenged by a population whose internal coping mechanisms for warding off disease and other health concerns are already depleted. Policies that assume that those who are internally vulnerable have sufficient energy and mental clarity to direct their own responses are considered inhumane.

Defenders of emergency relief as an end in itself also present a compelling argument: that many of those in need of emergency assistance are trapped within a global economic system that will perpetuate emergency relief. Mark Duffield, a scholar working for years in the humanitarian arena, argues that certain developing countries will remain economically marginalized because of the global economic system, thereby producing perpetual internal resource wars with accompanying human suffering.[3] For noncombatants in war zones and for many suffering from chronic famine, humanitarian assistance may be as good as it gets. In this scenario, humanitarian aid can be seen as a structural component of the global economic system—a form of long-term international welfare.

Time and energy constraints are also an issue in whether one should expect relief personnel to be sensitive to dependency concerns and to strive to provide beneficiaries with feelings of empowerment. As one U.S. aid official remarked about the exigencies of mass starvation in Somalia, "We're rightly indifferent to people's cultural needs and to appropriateness issues."[4] In short, some aid officials see the criticisms about dependency as pure foolishness in the eye of the storm, a luxury that hard-nosed and dedicated aid workers cannot afford if lives are to be saved and external resources used effectively.

Many humanitarian agencies currently attempt to ameliorate the dependency trap in a number of ways: by developing intimate knowledge about a recipient population's natural coping mechanisms so that appropriate relief plans can be made; by coordinating responses among all NGOs so that a particular beneficiary population is not overwhelmed with assistance; by assisting field personnel in determining the "displaced" status of those who present themselves for assistance; and by discontinuing emergency relief as soon as possible. Others would argue vehemently that all too often in implementing the minimum strategies for ameliorating dependency, the humanitarian system still conceptualizes recipients as victims or objects of assistance. They would argue that the process of delivering humanitarian assistance must not take priority over the objective of making civilians self-sustaining as soon as possible and imbuing them with a sense of empowerment.

Empowerment strategies include efforts to enhance participation by relief recipients in decisionmaking about their own plight. This may also mean hiring more recipients—a practice that is supported by the argument that a humanitarian system functions best when its presence is least obvious, when the local population and institutions are clearly engaged in working toward a stable future without an overwhelming presence of expatriate personnel.

Attempts to empower local institutions and people must be tailored to the social, economic, and political constructs of a society rather than applied in one-size-fits-all packages of relief and development aid. Traditional hierarchies of power cannot be dismissed as channels for relief distribution simply because they do not conform to "modern" constructs. The viewpoint that tribal relations are primitive and must be eradicated through the adoption of a democratic political system is inappropriate in many instances. Moreover, it stands in the way of designing a relief-to-development strategy for vulnerable groups—a strategy that can be incorporated easily into existing institutions that provide meaning, in addition to physical sustenance, to people's lives. Local institutions tend to be bypassed because they are little understood, not because they would be ineffective.

A failed state presents grounds for highly intrusive outside intervention, such as the recent international trusteeships in Timor and Kosovo. Societies that have imploded certainly present exceptional operational challenges. But even in cases like that of Somalia, where there is no Western-type institution of societal leadership, there may be a local consensus on leadership in some other form. As has been pointed out by several analysts, those who hold a monopoly on force and are in a position to exercise unabashed violence on their own people are too readily acknowledged by Western institutions to be the rightful heirs to leadership. One could even argue that the requirement to have recognized and recognizable counterparts in such a situation as Bosnia in the early 1990s led to a recognition of warring parties in ways that strengthened the hands of manipulative local politicians.[5]

Empowerment proponents also argue that humanitarians do not take the time to recruit or train local people because of expatriate cultural biases against locals. If there is a problem of "can-do" expatriates from a developed country treating locals as if they were incapable of contributing anything of value to expatriates' projects, then problems of exclusion can only get worse. The majority of staff members of the international humanitarian system are Western, and most of those whom they are assisting are not. Increasingly, those populations requiring considerable humanitarian relief are Muslim.

Critiques of empowerment policies focus on potentially wasteful and unreasonable delays in the delivery of humanitarian aid because of the recruitment and training of locals; the dearth of qualified people, particularly in failed states where many professionals have been executed or have gone into exile; and the inherently political nature of "empowering" (that is, the choice of a particular faction to be empowered). Critics also argue that expatriate relief organizations contribute to "brain drain" in a country by luring local professionals away from government and the private sector with relatively high salaries. Local wages and benefits are usually more modest than those offered by well-heeled, Western-financed aid

A local woman distributes food to women and children at a refugee feeding center run by a French NGO, Action Internationale Contre la Faim, which is partially
financed by UNICEF. UNICEF/Betty Press.

projects; and nowhere is this risk more prevalent than in war-torn countries. When staff are hired away from local institutions, they may never
return, or alternatively, the local economy may become overly dependent
upon infusions of assistance and foreign exchange from Western-based
salaries.

The criticism that empowerment is a political process is also valid.
Whom should the humanitarian agencies include in joint agency-recipient
discussions? For instance, if the culture being assisted does not recognize
the human rights of women, can the international humanitarian system be
true to international law if it respects local mores?

Women in camps for refugees and the internally displaced are frequently ignored if there are cultural constructions of gender roles and
concepts of authority that subordinate women (for instance, in
Afghanistan), even though women and their children constitute the majority of people in such encampments. An efficiency argument can be
made in support of organizations that override these cultural norms.
Studies have found that when women are given a role in food distribution, there is a more equitable distribution throughout the community
than if males are given the responsibility. The UNHCR's Guidelines on

the Protection of Refugee Women, adopted in 1991, specify that women should be considered the first point of control for distribution of food and other goods. Ignoring in practice what is known in theory has contributed to high death rates and levels of malnutrition among refugee and internally displaced populations and the leakage of aid to illegal markets.[6] Empowering populations may mean ignoring tradition or being intolerant of local culture for the sake of effectiveness as well as justice.

Empowerment policies contain additional ethical and operational ambiguities. For example, the care of children presents the international humanitarian system with a painful choice: choosing between taking full responsibility for providing food and shelter for the young versus giving resources to a community with the hope that the interests of this most vulnerable group will be met. Relief agencies are quick to respond to the needs of children and adolescents in crises—a stratum of society that usually accounts for some 50 to 65 percent of forcibly displaced populations. Orphanages and temporary care facilities are erected immediately after a crisis explodes, if not before. Among people who have spent their lifetimes in absolute poverty, the advent of a heightened state of emergency can lead some households to turn over the care of their young immediately and for prolonged periods.

The quandary is either to establish orphanages and camps that address the needs of children separate from their families or to empower families and communities with the hope that the children will benefit. If the international humanitarian system takes full responsibility for the care of children, it can disconnect the community from its own obligations, thereby contributing to the increasing fragmentation of community and family life. Moreover, some countries in crisis have cultures whose values subordinate the nourishment of children and women to the needs of males, even though children and pregnant or lactating women have greater nutritional needs. If the humanitarian system does not continue to support the needs of children directly, their suffering may remain acute or even increase.

RELIEF VERSUS PROTECTION

Governments in war-torn countries have primary responsibility for two critical humanitarian functions: providing emergency relief and protecting basic human rights within their borders. During complex emergencies, a government may be unable or unwilling to fulfill its obligations, or it may be selective as to which population subgroups are to be targeted for assistance and which are to be targeted for abuse or neglect. In the absence of a government's fulfillment of obligations to its citizens, actors in the international humanitarian system may respond to one or both humanitarian challenges. The central problem is that a host government or warring party may withdraw consent for humanitarian actors to have access to and deliver food and other goods to physically vulnerable populations if it is being criticized openly for gross violations of human rights. However, if the violations are not exposed, there is no incentive for the host government or warring party to discontinue its inhumane practices and violations of international humanitarian law. And there is no future for a durable peace and reconciliation without the exposure and punishment of such human rights abuses.

Humanitarian agencies traditionally have argued that it is beyond their mission statements and mandates to expose human rights abuses and that doing so would jeopardize the safety of their field personnel. In the past, relief workers have been the targets of harassments such as administrative refusal to renew visas or work permits; physical searches or beatings; and even death (as in the case of six expatriate ICRC staff members in Chechnya in 1998). If relief organizations cannot perform their tasks—that is, prove to their donors that they have successfully supplied food and other goods to victims—their funding may be slashed. Therefore, to obtain access to physically vulnerable populations and to maintain organizational credibility and survival, relief organizations may be willing to look the other way or remain silent when individual human rights are being violated.

Human rights groups have argued that less humanitarian aid would be needed if more attention were given to belligerents' blatant violations. Public opinion could be stirred sufficiently to motivate powerful governments to exert more political, and possibly military, pressure on combatants to reach a cease-fire than they would have otherwise. Inattention to systematized violations of human rights aimed at particular groups increases the personalization of a war and thereby its prolongation. Inattention to the kidnapping, torture, and killing of targeted individuals, such as intellectuals and community organizers, also deprives a community of the leadership, charisma, and talent sorely needed for postconflict reconstruction.

The tension between relief and human rights in the NGO community also exists within the U.N. system, although the human rights arm of the United Nations only recently began openly and consistently to express its views. Prior to 1992, the U.N. Commission on Human Rights kept private all investigations of states' human rights violations. The commission met only six weeks a year and never convened for an emergency session to address urgent situations of massive human rights violations. August 1992 was the first time that an emergency session was convened, at the request of the United States, to address documented atrocities in the Balkans. In Somalia, even before large-scale humanitarian operations began, NGOs and individuals repeatedly communicated human rights abuses to the Commission on Human Rights. The commission, however, never issued a public resolution or published a report. In Iraq, the commission was aware of the government's gassing of the Kurdish population between 1988 and 1989 but did nothing.

Following the 1993 World Conference on Human Rights in Vienna, a U.N. High Commissioner on Human Rights was appointed; and since that time, special investigators have been assigned to particular crises. To date, however, publicizing human rights violations has taken a back seat to relief and peace processes—a situation that has frustrated U.N. personnel with a professional duty to ensure that violations of human rights are curtailed and punished. At her departure as chief justice of the international tribunal for the former Yugoslavia, Gabrielle Kirk McDonald lashed out at the U.N. Security Council for its complacency toward prominent suspects of war crimes, such as Serbian president Slobodan Milosevic and former Bosnian Serb leader Radovan Karadzic, and its lack of vigor in seeking their arrest: "The Security Council established the tribunal. It's our parent, and parents have responsibilities. You don't give birth to a child and then leave the child to fend for itself."[7] To date, the tribunal has indicted 91 people for war crimes, genocide, or crimes against humanity during the recent wars in Croatia, Bosnia, and Kosovo. An unknown number have been indicted secretly. Eight have been convicted; 32 are in custody, awaiting trial.

A tradition of ignoring human rights abuses exists among members of the Security Council as well as heads of governmental, intergovernmental, and nongovernmental organizations that wish to sidestep human rights confrontation with states, move ahead whenever possible with negotiations, and be seen as impartial partners once cease-fires are in effect. Human rights fall victim to this ill-founded evenhandedness. By acting as if the most, and sometimes only, essential undertaking is the delivery of assistance, members of the international humanitarian system, and particularly the U.N. system, in many instances ignore opportunities for documenting and denouncing abuses. The treatment of human rights protection as a nonessential luxury has led Human Rights Watch to lament the "lost agenda" of the United Nations—that is, the organization's abnegation of its ability to make a difference in human rights emergencies in the former Yugoslavia, Cambodia, Somalia, and the Persian Gulf.[8]

The argument for allowing the politics of making peace to take priority over the pursuit of justice is clear, yet not readily defensible: If there are a number of factions fighting, it is strategically important to strengthen the legitimacy of certain faction leaders so that those leaders are able to "deliver" their armed followers at the negotiating table. Given this scenario, no matter how atrocious the actions by belligerents toward civilians, politics dictates that war crime charges be dropped even in the face of international law and moral reasoning.

The policy preferences of those who seek silence over action with regard to human rights violations, however, can be altered by public demand. This happened in El Salvador, where the Truth Commission was incorporated into the peace negotiations. Peasants who obtained experience in organizing their collective voice of dissent and desire for political participation through the humanitarian efforts of church groups demanded a role in the peace process. Although grassroots organizations were denied a seat at the negotiating table, the people's determination to contribute to their own healing led ultimately to the establishment of the Truth Commission. The commission was designed to investigate the atrocities committed against opposition politicians, communities of peasants, and church leaders such as Archbishop Oscar Romero, who had been murdered.

Public opinion often plays a role in forcing actors to uphold human rights responsibilities and international humanitarian law—the shaming of IFOR and the pressures on El Salvador's peace process are indicative. Concerned global citizens and war victims do not see a dilemma between humanitarian assistance and human rights protection. Both are possible; both should be sought.

The tensions between willing citizens and unwilling states trickle down to the United Nations, where it emerges in the form of unclear yet all-encompassing mandates, insufficient funding, and tentative responses. The United Nations has stumbled into broad humanitarian and human rights action—or perhaps more correctly, has been pushed into it by states that are themselves pushed by democratic societies imbued with the humanitarian impulse. The human rights rhetoric that permeates international declarations has yet to be matched by political will and institutional mechanisms capable of altering belligerents' behavior toward noncombatants. The human rights mechanisms in the United Nations are still weak in authority and finances—not even 2 percent of the regular budget is devoted to human rights.

Rhetoric without funding and authority prevents the international humanitarian system from responding to gross human rights violations in their early stages. To date, none of the cases in which militarized humanitarian intervention was initiated began with an early response to known mass violations of human rights. The pattern has been to ignore human rights abuses; fund emergency relief for those fleeing the abuses; and initiate a robust militarized response only after hundreds or thousands have been killed—if ever. This pattern negates the value of additional development of early warning systems or preventive deployment strategies. In any case, the current international system remains reticent to implement such strategies.

Yet, some lessons have been learned in the past decade, and change is under way within some agencies. Secretary-General Kofi Annan is the first U.N. CEO who has spoken frequently and openly about "mainstreaming human rights"—that is, including them as part of normal U.N. organizational activities. In a much-discussed opening speech to the 54th Session of the General Assembly in September 1999, he said: "The State is now widely understood to be the servant of its people, and not vice versa. At the same time, individual sovereignty—and by this I mean the human rights and fundamental freedoms of each and every individual as enshrined in our Charter—has been enhanced by a renewed consciousness of the right of every individual to control his or her destiny."

Furthermore, intergovernmental and nongovernmental organizations are calling into question the balance between relief and human rights protection. Although many workers still see the introduction of the political issue of human rights as potentially diversionary and counterproductive, others are responding to criticisms that they cannot refuse to act when confronted by human rights violations in the front lines. In light of the "well-fed dead" reality of war zones like Bosnia and Rwanda, some aid officials have conceded the uselessness of sustaining life only to have it subsequently taken away by repressive authorities. Assistance, framed in isolation from protection, can produce myopic humanitarian action. Agencies are struggling today with this reality. Three researchers report that the solution is "to view assistance and protection as complementary rather than competitive. . . . The solution is not to deny the tension, but rather to manage it skillfully."[9]

SHORT-TERM RELIEF VERSUS LONG-TERM DEVELOPMENT

Victims of war need both emergency aid during acute stages of fighting and assistance in reconstructing their lives and communities after violence has abated. The dilemma is that funds are increasingly in short supply for all forms of humanitarian action, and available funds generally are not fungible; in other words, because of agency mandates or donor preferences, emergency funds cannot be used for anything but emergency aid. Funds for reconstruction and development, in turn, cannot be used for emergencies. The UNDP had millions of dollars available for development work in Somalia that could not be used for emergency aid during the height of the famine. Since the end of the Cold War, a trend has emerged: Emergency aid is on the rise, and postconflict reconstruction

Somali citizens welcome the arrival of U.S. soldiers at Mogadishu. U.N. Photo/ 159819.

and development assistance has not kept pace with the demand. Gayle Smith, a noted researcher on development issues, has asserted: "Emblematic of this trend is Somalia: The U.S. contribution to the relief effort under Operation Restore Hope—some $1.6 billion—was five times greater than total U.S. development assistance to Somalia over the last three decades; U.S. government figures also show that this same amount is equivalent to two years of U.S. development assistance for all of sub-Saharan Africa."[10] Some U.N. agencies have altered their funding activities. As mentioned earlier, most World Food Programme resources in the past were directed to development and food-for-work programs; now 80 percent of WFP food resources are devoted to emergency assistance.

The policy debates are complicated. As explained at the outset of this chapter, U.N. policy is aimed at ensuring that emergency relief contributes to recovery and long-term development in an affected area. In sum, the United Nations is seeking to perfect the so-called relief-to-development continuum.

The concept of a continuum from relief to development is straightforward. Its underlying premise is the concomitant necessity for emergency inputs to serve longer-term objectives, or at a minimum, to do no harm to local coping capacities. The problems that constrain choices along the relief-to-development continuum are that resources are limited; donors prefer "loud" emergencies (that is, those resulting from war); relief agencies emphasize delivery of assistance rather than locals' empowerment; and the media focus on outsiders helping "victims" rather than insiders taking charge of their own future. The concept of a continuum is misleading because it is overly simplistic and mechanistic—there are no distinct points in time when emergency relief has stopped and rehabilitation, reconstruction, and development have begun. Getting beyond a philosophical commitment to do no harm and to maximize local participation requires conceiving a more organic framework of such external assistance and how it fits into a local system that has complex feedback loops.

Again, the need for conceptualization and applied research is obvious. The continuum was innovative in its own time in enlarging the perspectives and time frames used by relief workers and decisionmakers. Everyone now recognizes the need for aid practitioners to capitalize on the development potential of emergency relief. Nonetheless, the notion was too static and mechanistic. In Ian Smillie's words: "In the 1990s, the continuum concept gave way to more holistic thinking. As a result, relief and development are no longer viewed as self-contained and mutually exclusive. Linkages can and must be made if reconstruction and development are to be sustainable and recurring relief avoided."[11]

There is a bias in the international humanitarian system toward responding vigorously to loud emergencies, which are generally recognizable by the abundant media attention that they receive. These emergencies and the media's coverage of them drown out the more feeble and less dramatic calls to address the "silent" emergencies of malnutrition and preventable diseases, which could be treated by a well-planned mobilization of far fewer resources. For example, the international humanitarian system and the media reacted vigorously to the half million deaths of Somali children under age 5 in 1992. But the deaths due to poverty of 13 to 14 million children around the world (between 35,000 and 40,000 per day, according to UNICEF estimates) during that same period went relatively unnoticed. In the age of channel surfing, the drama of loud emergencies holds the attention of the world far better than a lengthy documentary of human suffering that could be prevented by development.

Those concerned only with emergency relief feel strongly that emergency relief should be an end in itself—the focus on immediate care cannot be compromised by trying to figure out how such care fits into the development agenda. Those most concerned with long-term development are deemed too eager to pronounce the emergency over and to transfer the funds to development projects.

Development agencies are indeed desperate for funds to prevent the recurrence of social, political, and economic tension. Once a conflict has been politically and militarily resolved and a "loud" emergency has

Danziger, © *Christian Science Monitor.*

quieted in terms of the attention of external governments and the media, emergency funding often dries up. Victory is declared, somewhat prematurely, as donors and journalists move on to the next crisis.[12] Unless they are citizens of donor countries' geostrategic allies, which typically receive development aid immediately following a cease-fire, most refugees and displaced persons return home with few or no prospects for remaking their lives. They are confronted by a host of basic survival problems caused by the destruction of housing, factories, schools, hospitals, roads, and crops; the theft of personal property and cash savings; and a physically and psychologically damaged community. At the same time, reconstruction efforts necessarily include the transformation of the security environment; strengthening of local administrative capacities; reconstruction of political processes, of the economy, and of the local social fabric; troop demobilization; and war crimes trials. Demobilizing soldiers frequently need an incentive—whether in the form of cash, in-kind items, or workable land—to disarm and agree to pursue lawful means to economic gain. Disarmament and demobilization measures failed in Somalia because U.N. appeals for contributions to "reward" belligerents for turning in their weapons failed. Disarmament was successful in Central America in part because incentives were available. In Nicaragua, for instance, some $44 million was provided for demobilization efforts.

Ethical dilemmas and operational challenges emerge from the dearth of funding and from the preferences of donors for emergency relief rather than reconstruction and development. Logically, if the humanitarian system knows that reconstruction and development funds will not be available during the postconflict period, efforts to relieve acute suffering should incorporate actions to empower locals in a manner complementary to longer-term objectives. Operationally, this is difficult because the entities that deliver emergency relief and those that assist in reconstruction and development frequently are different and do not communicate with each other.

Professionally, relief and development agencies—or the emergency personnel from UNICEF as distinct from its development staff—are asking different types of questions, leading them to believe there cannot be one common strategy. Institutions or individuals who address complex emergencies with the provision of emergency relief in mind are asking: How do I relieve these manifestations of human suffering? What are the most urgent requirements for food, medicine, sanitation, and protection? For those involved in development, the questions asked may include: What are the root causes of this crisis? How do we address the social, political, and economic factors that have contributed to the destabilization of this society?

Danziger, © *Christian Science Monitor*.

Operational considerations of rehabilitative and developmental work are distinct from those of relief operations. There are, for instance, increased costs associated with providing the additional calories needed by workers rebuilding infrastructure; the cost of tools and seeds for a subsequent harvest; salaries to local personnel; and the costs of housing and feeding expatriate staff (development programs are generally much less costly in this regard than relief operations). Cost calculations are justified on a number of other grounds. How vulnerable was the civilian population prior to the onset of conflict? How resilient was that population: Was it in a state of permanent emergency, or had it developed substantial coping mechanisms? Was it empowered one day and disempowered the next? What societal behavior results from overwhelming attention from the international humanitarian system one day and its virtually complete withdrawal the next?

The conceptual divide between emergency relief and rehabilitative or developmental work manifests itself in the field in the isolated behavior of relief versus development humanitarians, to the detriment of both. Humanitarian action in Iraq following the Gulf War provides an example. Non-emergency U.N. agencies worked on reconstruction and development programs without interfacing sufficiently with agencies providing emergency relief or with other development groups. The International Labor Organization was conducting studies and launching appeals for employment counseling and job retraining programs as early as November 1990; the U.N. Environment Programme was analyzing future environmental impacts of the war; and the International Maritime Organization was concentrating entirely on coordinating international aid for oil-slick cleanup.[13] No effort was made to tie these projects together, to look at the possible negative impacts that one project might have on another, or to aggregate resources and approach the humanitarian and development projects in a comprehensive fashion so that gaps in short- and long-term needs might be diminished.

Given the constraints and unpredictability of funding, the international humanitarian system is faced with an ethical question as well: Is it more prudent to refrain from delivering emergency relief to the extremely vulnerable populations that have only a minimal chance of remaining "stable" so as to benefit candidates that have a reasonable chance for reconstruction and development and for breaking the cycle of active and dormant conflict? Distinctions among victims on the basis of who can survive the acute emergency situation and recover may seem inhumane; indeed, that is why the choice between emergency aid and development is an ethical as well as an operational dilemma, and why it is the subject of intense policy debate.

Those most in need of emergency relief when a crisis hits are generally those who were marginally surviving at the outset; armed conflict exposes and depletes coping mechanisms traditionally employed to sustain what were already impoverished lives. Given limited resources, we can either save more lives now and not address the probability of future symptoms of distress based upon the same underlying problems, or we can save fewer lives now with the hope that the local population will be empowered enough through reconstruction and development efforts to ward off any future need for external humanitarian assistance or be trained sufficiently to handle future crises itself.

The tension between offering relief to the most destitute and ignoring those who need more development assistance is not missed by potential beneficiaries of assistance. The Ethiopian Red Cross Society established food distribution centers for those who qualified as completely destitute—approximately 24 percent of the population. Those who owned one donkey, ox, or camel, when told they were not poor enough to receive assistance, said that they would sell what little they had in order to become eligible for aid. There are no easy answers for a country in which millions of people are at risk of starvation and resources are limited.[14]

In cases where there is a clear state authority and conflict is localized rather than widespread, simultaneous relief and development activities have produced rather ironic consequences. Angola provides one such example. The two-decades-long war between the Movimento Popular de Libertação de Angola (Popular Movement for the Liberation of Angola) government and Jonas Savimbi's União Nacional para la Independência Total de Angola (National Union for the Total Independence of Angola) led to large-scale starvation in some areas at the same time as other areas were left relatively untouched by food insecurity. By 1994, when the peace process seemed to be back on track, in areas originally affected by starvation there was little malnutrition to be found.

However, in the urban slums and coastal cities where starvation had not formerly been an issue, the population was subjected to IMF conditionality and World Bank structural adjustment, which involved the removal of several social safety nets that had formerly helped to protect these populations. As a result, although malnutrition decreased in the area provided with emergency relief, severe malnutrition increased substantially in the area unaffected by war but subjected to a stringent new "development" policy.[15] This juxtaposition of simultaneous and largely autonomous outside aid efforts highlights the reality that the government of Angola had as little control over the actions of the Washington-based financial institutions (whose approval was necessary to secure loans) as over international NGOs (whose help was essential to provide for the

A local teacher works with students using a "school-in-a-box" provided by UN-ESCO and UNICEF as part of a Teacher's Emergency Package. UNICEF/Betty Press.

welfare of the population). Again, the multifaceted potency of multiple dilemmas along the continuum from relief to rehabilitation to development is striking.

ASYLUM, TEMPORARY REFUGE, CAMPS, AND SAFE HAVENS

Forced displacement has become a common objective or tactic of war. Instead of being a lamentable side-effect, forced displacement (and its most extreme form, ethnic cleansing) has become central to the stated objectives of many belligerents. Mass expulsions call into motion the policies and personnel of relief, development, and human rights organizations; they also create concern among neighboring states and the political organs of international and regional security regimes, such as the U.N. Security Council and NATO. As the population of concern increases for agencies such as UNHCR, so too do policies that increase states' asylum restrictions, general unwillingness to temporarily host refugees, and resistance to intervene militarily. In 1998 alone, UNHCR's total population of concern was approximately 21.5 million people: 11.5 million refugees, 1.3 million asylum-seekers whose asylum applications were pending, 5 million IDPs unable to return home, 2.4 million returned refugees and IDPs who would remain of concern for an additional two years, and 1.4 million various others.[16]

Permanent asylum, temporary refugee hosting, IDP camps, and protected safe havens are the common forms of refuge for those seeking assistance and protection. Government asylum policies have become increasingly restrictive in recent years in terms of procedures and quotas. Although asylum-seekers may be accepted as a class (as are Cubans in the United States) or broadly rejected (as are Haitians in the United States), asylum cases are generally determined on an individual basis.

Each asylum-seeker is responsible for the burden of proof upon which his or her application for admission to a conflict-free country is based— according to the language of the 1951 convention—upon the "credible" fear of persecution if returned to their native country. The precise meaning of *credible* is largely determined by the prospective host country, allowing that country's political concerns, domestic and foreign, to be brought to bear upon the applications of asylum-seekers. Thus, subjective judgments determine how many refugees are able to meet the criteria detailed in the 1967 Protocol to the 1951 Convention Relating to the Status of Refugees.

The asylum process in most states also relies on outdated bureaucratic processes that tend to lengthen the amount of time asylum-seekers remain vulnerable. The asylum process, unlike immigration laws, was designed to meet individual, not group, requests for protection. Because cases are reviewed on an individual basis in most developed and developing countries, backlogs of asylum applications are mounting. By the time Haitian refugees began to arrive on U.S. shores after the military overthrow of the democratically elected Aristide government, the Justice Department's Immigration and Naturalization Service (INS) already had a backlog of almost 400,000 applications.[17] Their treatment was quite unlike that of asylum-seekers from El Salvador and Guatemala in the mid- to late 1980s, who were permitted immediate entry and granted work permits while awaiting final determination of their asylum status. Haitian refugees were sent to safe havens in third countries, such as Grenada and Antigua, or were quickly sent back to Haiti.

Alternatives to asylum include the negotiation of agreements among several countries to share the burden of massive population movements of people in crisis so that one country does not bear the entire economic, social, and political brunt. Additional alternatives to accepting asylum-seekers are to fully guarantee safety within designated safe areas or to financially compensate, in advance, third countries willing to host "guests" for a determinate amount of time. States are not obligated to grant refugees sanctuary if they can identify another country that is willing to accept them. And states that have signed the 1967 Protocol to the 1951 Convention are only informally required to provide a camp environment until the fear of persecution has subsided.

Temporary hosting of refugees, most often in neighboring states, provides advantages such as modest transportation costs to the host country and eventually home. But refugee agencies also are confronted with tremendous obstacles to ensuring that a host country does not expel the refugees prematurely and without prior notice. It is also a challenge for agencies to ensure that refugees are not abused by their host countries or by warring parties while in the refugee camps, which are often located in underdeveloped countries plagued by economic and political instability similar to that in the refugees' homelands. As mentioned in the previous chapter with particular regard to the African Great Lakes region, refugee camps are vulnerable to infiltration by soldiers or militiamen seeking a place to rest, rearm, and recruit. The militarization of a camp environment contributes to attacks on the camps by opposing parties, forced conscription of young men and boys, and sexual and other violence against women and girls, particularly if they have been separated from their social networks during their migration away from the conflict. Host countries also have contributed in such ways to the pain and suffering of refugees.

Although countries may be amenable to accepting refugees or willing to do so under duress, host-country behavior should be carefully monitored to prevent abuse and manipulation of aid agencies. The presence of UNHCR operations caring for refugees as well as other war casualties may lead political authorities to manipulate the civil or military components of a humanitarian operation to promote political, economic, military, or criminal interests of their own, thereby narrowing the opportunities to provide relief to the suffering—and on occasion, even adding to their pain. It is obvious that negotiations must continue in the country in conflict to bring about a political and military agreement. What may be less obvious is that diplomacy must be ongoing also in refugee host countries, to maintain an environment conducive to meeting the needs of the refugees.

Although refugees are legally protected from *refoulement*, or forced return, the 1951 convention does allow for involuntary repatriation of refugees if their presence negatively affects the security of the host country. There are few instances where a refugee presence does *not* produce negative consequences for the social, political, and economic stability of the hosts. The Rwandan refugee presence in the former Zaire did more than introduce physical violence to the country. One Zairean official spelled out the nefarious impact: "The refugees are of different cultural ethics and behavior. Carrying weapons and killing are quite common among them; the same goes for stealing and squatting on other people's property. The refugee population has overwhelmed Zairean resources, destroyed our environment, introduced uncontrolled inflation into our market and abused our hospitality. We want them out of here soon."[18] In developed countries of asylum, refugees have been blamed for unemployment increases and a subsequent rise in nationalist sentiments. Guatemalan refugees in southern Mexico, for example, have been blamed for inciting revolt among the indigenous population. With few exceptions, refugees become the scapegoats for many ills of the host government. Mozambican refugees in Zimbabwe were an exception: Zimbabwean tobacco farmers became so dependent upon the abundant and cheap labor of Mozambican refugees that some resorted to locking the refugees up at night to prevent them from participating in UNHCR's repatriation efforts.

When a government reverses its policy of providing temporary asylum, humanitarian agencies are thrown into turmoil, and myriad responses can result. Kenya's refugee camps in 1995 provide an example. By July 1995, Kenya had become unwilling to continue hosting the more than 50,000 Somali refugees who had crossed the border three years earlier. The refugees' overextended stay was disrupting tourism, claimed the Kenyan government; the UNHCR was advised to close the camps and begin refugee repatriation. The UNHCR communicated Kenya's concerns to Somali elders, who rejected the repatriation proposal and arranged a press conference to appeal to the international community. As the Kenyan government, Somali elders, the UNHCR, and the media wrestled with camp closings and repatriation issues, groups such as the International Federation of Red Cross and Red Crescent Societies continued working on major construction projects in and around the camps. Roads were being repaired. New police measures were being implemented to reduce theft. Libraries and a football field were being constructed. And efforts were being made to increase school enrollment. Along with development projects, relief efforts were also still in effect: Food and charcoal were being distributed, and clinics were treating cholera, malaria, respiratory ailments, and skin infections.[19]

The simultaneous closing and reconstruction of camps seems counterintuitive at best, even to amateur analysts; yet such action does take place. The UNHCR was confronting two of its policy mandates simultaneously: negotiating with a country of asylum so that refugees could remain, and convincing refugees to repatriate. The IFRC was involved in providing relief and fostering development to the point of creating incentives for the refugees to stay. After three years of assistance, the refugees were still completely dependent on the international humanitarian system for their basic needs. And the media had to decide between airing a short, attention-getting humanitarian story about suffering Somalis being forced to repatriate by a heartless Kenyan government or a more lengthy, less sensational story about the dilemmas of humanitarian operations.

The construction of IDP camps or safe havens within the country in conflict may come about as a conscious policy resulting from fleeing noncombatants' being blocked at their borders by the neighboring country's military or forcefully expelled from a refugee camp, or resulting from noncombatants' own decision to remain within their country of origin. The differences between an IDP camp and a safe haven are the degree of protection and the freedom of movement provided. IDP camps receive minimal protection, whereas safe havens, at least in theory, are protected by third-party intervening forces. The creation of a safe area in which noncombatants remain in their homes and are encircled by protectors also provokes legal and ethical debates: Does the creation of safe areas violate the right to asylum and the right to freedom of movement?

IDP camps are preferable if a functioning government is willing to protect its own citizens or if members of the international humanitarian system volunteer in sufficient numbers to assist. But governments involved in civil wars often lack the will and the means to assist; and international organizations often do not have sufficient resources or protective forces to adequately meet the demands of running an IDP camp.

Challenges associated with caring for IDPs as well as for people remaining in safe havens include calculating how much food is needed (and how much food will probably be siphoned off) and how to protect the wide variety of assistance personnel (for example, convoy truck drivers, medics, and food distributors), media, and peacekeepers from the violence of a war that may intensify rather than diminish over time. Humanitarian assistance and protection are both extremely expensive in an environment of conflict. On the debit side of the humanitarian ledger are life insurance costs for relief workers; transportation costs, including the charter fee for trucks and airplanes and the "taxes," or extortion fees, paid to belligerents in exchange for access routes; costs associated with the theft and replacement of food and medical supplies; and costs to the legitimacy of and respect for the United Nations and the Security Council.

IDP camps also have a postconflict impact on the noncombatant population. Once a peace settlement has gone into effect and refugees who fled the violence have begun to return to their communities (if they can), resentment toward the returnees on the part of those who remained behind and suffered greatly for doing so must be addressed. This is particularly

A woman hangs her laundry at a camp for some of the estimated 25,000 persons displaced by the fall of the safe haven at Srebrenica. The barbed wire is to keep people from straying into mined areas. UNICEF/Roger Lemoyne.

awkward if returning refugees and IDPs are actually better off than war victims who remained in their home country.

Safe havens are preferable if external governments and their armed forces have a long-term commitment to the protection of the group in need of succor and protection. But donor governments frequently vacillate in their commitments, and IGOs are stymied by the inability of their member states to reach a consensus and back their words with concrete commitments. The *Economist* referred to "the confetti of resolutions" on the former Yugoslavia; and the fall of the safe havens in Bosnia is the most striking example of safe-haven policy failure. At the same time, successful safe havens have been constructed and maintained multilaterally (e.g., those in northern Iraq) and unilaterally by governments with an interest in the area (e.g., those established by the French for fleeing Hutus, once the Rwandan Patriotic Front was strong enough to pursue those deemed responsible for the slaughter of thousands of Tutsis). Although the French have been criticized for their obvious bias toward the Hutus, Opération Turquoise did act as an effective barrier to further human tragedy in the short run and to further refugee movements.

AFRICA: A SPECIAL CASE

The most alarming trend in donor funding is the overwhelming under-funding of Africa-based humanitarian programs. African countries present unique funding problems given their relative inability to attract the interests of donors, partly because donor fatigue has set in after years of political instability and ineffective economic development on that continent, and partly because of unspoken racism. Few major powers recognize immediate security concerns when humanitarian crises erupt in Africa. Nonetheless, the multitude of African refugees who are constantly on the move are also carrying with them the AIDS virus, a resurgence of malaria, environmental destruction, and a generation of traumatized and often orphaned children whose future burden it is to rebuild a war-torn and impoverished continent. An inkling of the magnitude of the problem can be gleaned from President Clinton's words to the General Assembly in September 1999: "Over the next 10 years in Africa, AIDS is expected to kill more people and orphan more children than all the wars of the 20th century combined." Throughout conflict-riddled Africa, the rights of children are being violated, and violence against women is soaring.

Policymakers tend to be more concerned with issues that will have an impact on their careers and the current administration's popularity rather than on "longer-term" developments (defined as the next election or public opinion survey). Funds to address Africa's problems are frequently unavailable. By mid-October 1999, UNHCR had received more than 90 percent of the funds it needed for 800,000 Kosovo refugees; but it had raised barely 60 percent of the money needed for more than 6 million refugees in Africa. In the Kosovo crisis, refugees received fresh fruit, cheeses, and canned meats; were inspected for lice regularly; had access to the Internet; and had their babies bathed at special mother/child centers. In Angola, the World Food Programme and aid donors were forced to focus almost exclusively on providing food to the nearly 11 million Angolans who are dependent on food aid. Of the $67 million requested from donors, only $25 million has been pledged.[20]

When Africa surfaces in the public consciousness, it is associated with unspeakable horrors: the machete massacre of at least 500,000 Rwandans in 1994, the kidnappings and murders of Western tourists and relief workers, rebels in Sierra Leone amputating the limbs of whole families, and the rampant spread of the AIDS virus. Isolationists would argue that the best remedy for what ails Africa is to allow the continent to work out its own problems without an infusion of third-party intervenors or resources. This assumes that Africa is in a period of disequilibrium and will stabilize, according to the world system's definition of stability, at some later point in time. For humanitarians and nonisolationists, Africa's problems are symptoms of what ails the world system and are not entirely of Africa's own making. The provision of assistance and protection to Africans, therefore, is not the responsibility of Africa alone.

"African solutions to African problems" is doubly problematic. First, such an approach can lead to the erosion of universal standards—as illustrated by Nigeria's dubious actions in Liberia as well as by the involvement of numerous African states in the Congo's current chaos. Second, this approach provides a comforting rationalization for the Western world, allowing it to avoid mobilizing the resources required to permanently put to rest many of the continent's armed conflicts.

CONCLUSION

The tortuous calculations and the unclear mathematics of decision-making at headquarters are fraught with the same moral ambiguities as the efforts in the field described in Chapter 4. Within the humanitarian sphere, we have seen that policy analysts as well as decisionmakers themselves must face the inevitable, unintended consequences of humanitarian action. The painful facts, as eloquently testified by events in the 1990s, are that relief can fuel conflict and foster dependency; that human rights can be shortchanged in bargaining for access to victims; that long-term development can suffer as a result of emergency assistance; that forced displacement brings in its wake a host of related obstacles; and that Africa seems to be a lost cause.

What, then, is to be done? The short answer is that we should make a valiant effort to weigh the evidence, anticipate the consequences, and act. Returning to our argument about instrumental humanitarian decisions in the field in the preceding chapter: Remaining on the sidelines is not an option. The solution is not to throw in the towel but rather to respond to the challenge with appropriate action. The key lies in making a good-faith effort to analyze the advantages and disadvantages of various courses of action, and then to choose the option that will provide the greatest benefit and cause the least harm.

For instance, it would have been preferable for NATO to have had a Security Council authorization for Kosovo; but this was not possible, due to Russian and Chinese vetoes of the proposal. In explaining the desirability of taking action in Kosovo even without U.N. authorization, President Clinton argued in his address to the General Assembly in September 1999: "Had we chosen to do nothing in the face of this brutality, I do not believe that we would have strengthened the United Nations. Instead we would have risked discrediting everything it stands for." Clinton concluded, "In the real world, principles often collide, and tough choices must be made."

Undoubtedly, some of the toughest policy choices, with the most telling implications for humanitarian action in the past decade, concern international peace and security. These choices are the subject of the next and final chapter.

SIX

□ □ □

Policies of Militarized Humanitarian Intervention

War is not neat. It's not tidy. It's a mess.
—Admiral William Crowe, 1990

Humanitarian assistance alone cannot provide adequate protection to noncombatants who are specifically targeted by belligerents. Deployment of multinational military forces may be required to protect humanitarian activities, facilitate the delivery of emergency assistance, and insulate and protect a given geographical area or people from the effects of armed conflict and violence. As Sadako Ogata, the U.N. High Commissioner for Refugees, has argued:

> The threat of force, and the will to use it, becomes indispensable where consensual arrangements have no chance of success. Enforcement is a critical issue. It may complicate the arduous efforts of conflict mediators. It may undermine neutrality and engender risks for impartial humanitarian action, but are strict neutrality and effective protection not often incompatible? Humanitarian responses should serve first of all the protection of people.[1]

A military intervention, if it occurs, is the product of political negotiations among the Security Council's five permanent members (P-5), member states of regional security organizations such as NATO or the Organization of African Unity (OAU), states participating in a "coalition of the willing," or a single state's political and military elites. After a decision is reached to intervene, a second political process begins to ensure a commitment from United Nations member states to provide necessary resources and personnel. Success in the first political process does not ensure success in the second. For example, in 1994 the Security Council unanimously decided that 5,500 peacekeepers were urgently needed in

Rwanda; it took six months for the member states to provide troops, even though 19 governments had pledged to keep some 30,000 troops on a stand-by basis for U.N. peacekeeping.

Unlike humanitarian agencies that respond to humanitarian crises with standard, predictable policy responses, the U.N. Security Council, regional organizations, and individual states determine on a case-by-case basis whether there will be a militarized intervention and what the character of that intervention will be. This chapter explores factors that determine whether an intervention is approved and the challenges of implementing policies. It also describes changes in the character of humanitarian interventions during the first post–Cold War decade, the 1990s.

THE DECISION TO INTERVENE

U.N. Charter provisions on the maintenance of international peace and security are the basis of peacekeeping and enforcement operations through the U.N. Security Council (UNSC). The UNSC is the primary forum and authority for discussing the political aspects of a potential intervention. Through its resolutions the council establishes a peace support operation, designs its mandates (including all required revisions and extensions thereto), and authorizes the deployment of troops as well as any subsequent increase or reduction in troop strength as the situation demands.

Security Council Decisionmaking

Game theory and liberal institutionalism provide two theoretical frameworks for understanding Security Council decisionmaking. Game theory maintains that the P-5 members are rational, power-seeking actors with complete and perfect information, who are involved in a process of negotiation with other members. In the words of P. Terrence Hopmann, the members are in a "situation of interdependent decisionmaking, where each must make decisions and where the outcome for the parties is not exclusively under their own control, but is a result of their joint decisions."[2] Decisions to mandate a particular peace operation must not contradict the perceived interests of each member. Using the concept of "nested games," one can show how a P-5 member may use the threat of its veto of a peace operation desired by others to achieve its gains in another arena—for example, in World Trade Organization (WTO) negotiations. The behavior of China on the Security Council provides the most transparent example of a bargaining party exchanging votes for payoffs. In November 1990—one day after China abstained on Resolution 678, which authorized the use of force against Iraq—the Bush administration invited the Chinese foreign minister to Washington. This was the first high-level exchange since the Tiananmen Square massacre. Four days later, Washington helpfully abstained on a World Bank vote allocating, for the first time since Tiananmen, an international development loan to China for purposes other than "basic human needs."[3] In contrast, NATO's sidestepping of U.N. approval in the Kosovo crisis diminished the ability of China as well as Russia, which rejected NATO intervention, to veto intervention or to gain in another arena in exchange for an abstaining vote.

A primary criticism of the game theory model for Security Council decisionmaking is that it is contextually insensitive to the influence of institutional rules, procedures, and norms that assist in redefining or expanding interests and stimulating new ideas. Game theory focuses primarily upon given preferences and perceptions without asking about their origins.

In contrast, liberal institutionalism argues that environment and organizational structures mediate between narrowly defined interests and behavior and can influence and even transform actors' conceptions of what constitutes vital interests. A hypothesis generated by such a model would maintain that if each permanent member has no substantial reason to reject a U.N. intervention, then the decision to issue a mandate may be governed by a feeling of obligation to the more idealized notion of collective responsibility outlined in the U.N. Charter.

A link between game theory and institutionalism is the dependency of actors on information concerning the conflict (the reduction of uncertainty) and the probabilities of successfully meeting the objectives outlined in a proposed mandate (the measure of risk and cost). Whether one explains Security Council deliberations as negotiations among autonomous, rational actors pursuing individual national interests or as a collective response by institutionally conditioned representatives of a public good called "international peace and security," the sources and the credibility of information, as well as the privilege given certain data over others, influence both the issue of a mandate and its content.

The case of Rwanda illustrates the need for future investigation into information pathways and processing. Shortly before the genocide began, the U.N. secretariat received varied information from two sources: The U.N. Special Representative of the Secretary-General (SRSG) to Rwanda cabled that there was tension in Kigali. On the same day, the commanding officer of the United Nations Assistance Mission for Rwanda (UNAMIR) sent a cable describing a reign of terror permeating the city. The secretary-general accepted the first interpretation of activities, and the wave of genocide commenced less than one month later.[4] One possible explanation for the primacy given one cable over the other is cognitive bias: That is, decisionmakers tend to look for information that supports what they would like to see happen, in view of their personal and professional interests.

The procedures by which humanitarian crises are placed on the agenda of the Security Council also partially explain why certain crises are not addressed immediately or are never addressed. The Security Council can manipulate the presentation of events: The provisional agenda for the Security Council's consideration is drawn up by the secretary-general and approved by the president of the council. Titles of items on the agenda can be altered so as to be less objectionable to particular P-5 members and potentially less demanding of Security Council action. As described by Sydney Bailey, the most noted authority on U.N. Security Council procedures: "In addition to proposals to vary the wording of items, which are usually adopted without a vote, the Council has voted on motions to include an item in, or delete an item from, the agenda; to include an item in the agenda but to postpone consideration; to add an item not included in the Provisional Agenda; to confirm or change the order of items; to combine two or more items; and to adopt or reject the Provisional Agenda as a whole."[5]

Regional Organizations and Coalitions of the Willing

As will be discussed later in this chapter, the Security Council became more reluctant to authorize new U.N. peace support operations as the 1990s drew to a close. Usually under the auspices of the United Nations, regional organizations (such as NATO and the OAU security group) and ad hoc coalitions of individual states with an interest in a conflict's outcome (also referred to as "coalitions of the willing") became the operational commanders and financiers for peace support operations requiring force.

Distinctions must be noted between U.N. peacekeeping forces and multinational forces authorized by the Security Council. U.N. peacekeeping operations are under the direct operational control of the United Nations, although each national contingent follows the command of its own national commanders. Such operations are established after there is a demonstrated commitment to peace by the warring parties. The cost of a U.N. peacekeeping operation is shared among all U.N. member states. Peace support operations conducted by a regional organization or coalition of the willing are under the operational control of a lead nation, do not require a demonstrated commitment to peace by the parties, and are undertaken at the cost of those states carrying out the operation. The Security Council may yield to other parties in the conduct of peace support operations because of its reluctance to be involved in messy, costly crises or because of dissent in the form of a veto (for example, Kosovo).

Chapter VIII of the U.N. Charter allows for regional arrangements deemed necessary to restore stability. Incentives for regional involvement are strong. The flow of refugees into neighboring countries is usually economically unsettling and can bring about or exacerbate social unrest. Wars disrupt normal patterns of trade, which might be distorted further if economic sanctions are imposed. Personal contacts among regional leaders are usually intense, if not always warm. Shortcomings of regional collective action include the fact that regional blocs of power and influence routinely require a regional hegemonic power to lead a collective response to political and social instability and to humanitarian needs.

The North Atlantic Treaty Organization has proven a viable alternative to the UNSC as a forum for initiating peace support operations, although its mission statement restricts NATO's actions to the enhancement of security and stability among its 19 members and through the Euro-Atlantic area.

Since the end of the Cold War, NATO has been restructured to adapt to peacekeeping and crisis management tasks undertaken in cooperation with countries that are not members of the alliance as well as with IGOs. Although humanitarian intervention in the former Yugoslavia has benefited from NATO's restructuring, the alliance's internal adaptation is guided primarily by the fundamental objectives of ensuring its military effectiveness, preserving the transatlantic link, and increasing security burden-sharing among NATO members. Humanitarian intervention is, in a sense, a way for NATO to fine-tune its internal adaptations and evolving command structure. NATO is striving for flexibility in its ability to generate forces to conduct a full range of alliance missions and to operate seamlessly in multinational and joint formations.

African peacekeeping increased in the latter half of the 1990s because of the growing unwillingness of external powers to expose their forces to uncontrollable violence in places like Somalia, Rwanda, and Sierra Leone. In lieu of non-African forces directly engaging in African crises, Western funding has been increased to West and Central African troop-contributing countries. The United States established the African Crisis Response Initiative (ACRI) in late 1996 to organize and train an African peacekeeping team. Congress allocated $35 million for ACRI's start-up costs. The initial training focuses on the development of soldier skills for peacekeeping, working with refugees and humanitarian organizations, and observing human rights.

Unlike NATO's peace support operations or coalitions of the willing, such as the Australian-led intervention in East Timor in late 1999, African peacekeeping suffers from the deep involvement of troop-contributing countries in the hostilities, on one side of the conflict or the other. Decisions to intervene may be based upon a contributing country's political objectives or opportunity for economic gain. Traditional humanitarian principles of impartiality or neutrality may be totally absent.

State Decisionmaking

The perspectives of traditional realists and structural institutionalists can provide interpretations of why states decide to contribute material and troops. A traditional realist approach argues that a state participates when it is in its perceived national interest to do so. The state is seen as a rational, autonomous, and unitary actor capable of behaving strategically out of self-interest, regardless of bureaucratic restraints or the preferences of civil society. In contrast, structural institutionalism argues that barriers in structures and processes may prevent or may facilitate state participation even if dominant political elites hold an opposing view. A research design following a structural-institutionalist approach would examine in a systematic manner the organization of the military, peace operations funding, the political system, the organization of the state, and the state's position in the international system.[6] The organization of a state's military is a critical factor. Is the military conscripted, and are there special forces trained for low-conflict environments? Is there interservice competition? Do promotion procedures provide an incentive to the military for involvement in peace operations? Are existing military doctrine and training conducive to peace operations? To what extent do military elites influence or control foreign policy?

Organization in a national capital identifies which agency will bear the cost of participation, and decides whether the reimbursement from the United Nations adequately offsets the cost of participation. Organization of the state identifies the internal state apparatus responsible for peacekeeping and decisionmaking, and for the operationalization of executive strategies. Organization of the political system identifies the influence exerted on state decisionmaking by the structure of representation, electoral practices, networks of organized political parties, and NGOs' advising and pressuring of governments to support peace operations.

PHASES OF INTERVENTION

Decisions to intervene tend to follow a series of relatively predictable phases—from neutral, purely humanitarian operations guided primarily by the mission statements and mandates of U.N. agencies, through Chapter VI efforts at resolution by peaceful means, and if necessary, the use of force under Chapter VII of the U.N. Charter.

During the first phase, certain NGOs and U.N. organizations operate within a country with the consent of its government (if one exists), providing food, shelter, water, and medicine to victims of natural disasters, growing political instability, and forced displacement of communities. When violence escalates, other NGOs and U.N. agencies are called upon by their constituents and governing bodies to deploy relief personnel to the area. Attempts at the pacific settlement of disputes, as outlined in Chapter VI of the U.N. Charter, may run in tandem with humanitarian action. Consent by the government to the presence of humanitarian personnel generally has been negotiated, although often heavily conditioned. If a cease-fire or other agreement has been negotiated, U.N. peacekeepers also may be deployed to the area to monitor compliance.

However, if consent to assist the most vulnerable is not forthcoming or is so heavily conditioned that humanitarian assistance cannot be administered without tilting the political balance in favor of one of the belligerents, humanitarians then consider whether to withdraw or limit operations as the Security Council contemplates more forceful measures. If the lives of humanitarian personnel and peacekeepers are targeted, the Security Council may move from Chapter VI to Chapter VII. A stream of decisionmaking takes place at various levels and within various institutions as violence escalates and populations are put at greater risk or begin migrating to unstable neighboring areas or countries. Development NGOs must decide when to ask for relief assistance; relief personnel must decide when to ask for diplomatic and peacekeeping assistance; and the Security Council must determine how and at what point it becomes necessary to move toward force and away from traditional diplomacy, impartiality, and political neutrality. Additional questions follow: What tools of Chapter VII should be employed—such as economic, communications, and diplomatic sanctions and the use of force by land, sea, and air—and how will they affect relief efforts and personnel? Should the level of force be proportional to the force exerted by the warring parties upon noncombatants? Or is it better to dismiss caution and overwhelm belligerents?

Economic sanctions and overwhelming air campaigns, used as tools of intervention, have been widely criticized by humanitarians. Chapter VII allows for economic sanctions against the accused. The logic of economic sanctions is that they create pain and suffering in the lowest strata of society, which within time will percolate upward to the governing authority and bring about policy changes or perhaps a change in regime. Economic sanctions often are applied in knee-jerk reaction, regardless of the fact that authoritarian regimes are not accountable to civil society and are not affected by the pain and suffering of noncombatants. Indeed, there is little evidence to suggest that civilian pain leads to political gain. In the words of Boutros Boutros-Ghali: "Sanctions, as is generally recognized, are a blunt instrument. They raise the ethical question of whether suffering inflicted on vulnerable groups in the target country is a legitimate means of exerting pressure on political leaders whose behaviour is unlikely to be affected by the plight of their subjects."[7] Moreover, repressive governments may even be strengthened by sanctions because they can mobilize local support to counteract targeting by outsiders—a kind of "martyr" or "rally-around-the-flag" effect that plucks the most shrill nationalist chords. To counter the effects of economic sanctions on the most vulnerable populations, humanitarian agencies are then called upon to increase assistance. The effects of sanctions and humanitarian assistance in many ways cancel each other out, and at a high price. Economic sanctions—in Iraq and Haiti, for example—hurt most those whom the international community was supposedly trying to help (women, children, the sick, and the elderly) and left targeted regimes and elites ensconced in power.[8]

The diplomacy and subsequent military action approved by the Security Council were decisive in reversing Iraqi aggression against Kuwait and Iraq's own Kurdish population. But the combination of previous and ongoing economic sanctions against Iraq from 1989 and into the twenty-first century has yielded immense suffering among Iraqis. U.N. Security Council Resolution 661 was the first of numerous calls for economic sanctions against Iraq. Although food and medicine earmarked for humanitarian efforts were exempted, the process by which shipments must be inspected before entry into Iraq created a critical lag in the delivery of relief supplies and aggravated human suffering.

Economic sanctions also create hardships for nondisplaced locals whose livelihood is hindered or completely eliminated by the consequences of sanctions. For example, sanctions against Serbia in the Bosnian crisis affected the ability of host families caring for roughly 95 percent of incoming refugees from Bosnia and Croatia to support themselves. One study concluded that "90 percent of the resident Serbian population . . . was unable to meet basic food needs."[9] By the time the Dayton Accords were signed in 1995, Serbia had received some 550,000 refugees, including 250,000 Bosnian Serbs who had fled the war in Bosnia-Herzegovina in 1992 and 300,000 Croat Serbs who had escaped the conflict in Croatia in 1991 and 1995. Thousands more Kosovar Serbs and gypsies became the responsibility of the Yugoslav government in 1999.

Air campaigns are similarly indiscriminate and therefore tend to be ineffective. Overwhelming air bombardments, such as those on Baghdad in 1991 and on Belgrade in 1999, are undertaken because they present a relatively low risk of mortality in comparison with peacekeeping forces.

An Iraqi boy stands in front of a destroyed building in Baghdad following U.S. surgical strikes.
UNICEF/John Isaac.

"Surgical strikes" is the term frequently used to describe the military's intent to directly target and hit military-related sites during militarized humanitarian missions. During the Gulf Crisis, the term was used widely by
the media as television screens showed real-time film footage of U.S. mis-
siles going through the front doors of the Iraqi military command. However, the visuals misled the public into believing that massive high-tech
weaponry was infallible and could discriminate between combatants and
noncombatants. The bombing of a Baghdad air raid shelter and the subsequent deaths of hundreds of Iraqi women and children who had sought
safety there was not given much coverage by the media. However, the
NATO air campaign against Serbia in 1999 confirmed to many that coer-

cive diplomacy in the form of an overwhelming air campaign may be the only alternative to halting massive violations of human rights. This campaign was described by many as the first "humanitarian war."[10]

The case studies in Chapter 3 provide examples in which there was ambiguity within and between mandates over when to move from diplomacy to force. From the beginning of Chapter VII action in the Bosnian crisis, proportionality of force was the strategy. Its ineffectiveness was obvious and left uncorrected until the Croatian offensive and NATO attacks in August 1995. Within four months of the use of overwhelming force by a Croatian-Bosnian alliance and NATO air strikes, a peace agreement was signed. Many argue that the years of diplomatic negotiations produced nothing but borrowed time for war criminals and unnecessary loss of life. As one close collaborator of the U.N. secretary-general put it, "It is extremely difficult to make war and peace with the same people on the same territory at the same time."[11]

A distinction must be made, however, between the use of force and the display of force, Somalia being a striking example of the latter. The display of force in that country was overwhelming, particularly initially; but the use of force was at first constrained and later underwhelming (total withdrawal), when it became clear that 25,000 soldiers could not capture one warlord and that outside soldiers would have to be casualties in order to bring about stability in the failed state. "Mission creep" is a catchphrase used by the military to describe unwanted divergence from an operation's original mandate. Critics of military performance and fecklessness argue that the armed forces do not understand the difference between mission creep and flexibility. Cynics argue that military reluctance to incur casualties—the so-called Somalia syndrome—has led to "mission cringe."

At present, movement from Chapter VI to Chapter VII—and frequently, back again—often introduces contradictory actions that can cancel each other out or even inflate the degree of suffering among noncombatants. Mandates and strategies are further complicated when Chapter VI and Chapter VII actions are used simultaneously (as in the former Yugoslavia) or alternated (as in Rwanda). Chapter VI is theoretically impartial and neutral; Chapter VII makes a highly political statement regarding which belligerent is at fault and must be brought back into line by concentrated and coercive actions of the international community— first by sanctions, and if sanctions are ineffective, then by military force. Humanitarian practitioners also have failed to integrate into their operational philosophies the basic incompatibility between their traditional operational principles (impartiality and neutrality) and the requirements of working in a war zone where Chapter VII actions are in effect. Chapter VII is anything but impartial and neutral. It is the only instance in the

UNPROFOR peacekeepers monitor a checkpoint patrolled by Bosnian and Croatian police. U.N. Photo/J. Isaac.

world organization's constitution in which finger-pointing is condoned and blame is attached to decisions. To try to preserve a traditional humanitarian stance within a Chapter VII operation is to force what is definitely a square peg into a round hole.

Mandate ambiguity is understandable, given that the Security Council's P-5 members attempt to negotiate a resolution that is politically agreeable among themselves, and not necessarily one that is operationally or tactically feasible. This is one reason why P-5 discussions regarding an intervention are held behind closed doors and are not recorded.

Undeniably, there is an inherent contradiction in the Security Council's acting as manager of international security. Ongoing strains between legitimacy and efficiency reflect a general tension between absolute duties and relative interests. The paradox is that to find legitimacy, "military intervention must be based on universal principles, while its implementation depends on a particular constellation of power and interests."[12]

In sum, powerful state interests are negotiated during discussions of whether to intervene. The compromises and constraints woven into the decision emerge in the mandate's architecture. The resulting ambiguity in mandate, in turn, is reflected in confusion in the field and ineffective protection of noncombatants. Mandate ambiguity is less likely to be found in operations led by a single state or regional organization with strong objectives. The protection of Kurds in northern Iraq, an effort led by the United States in Operation Provide Comfort; the stabilization of the crisis in Rwanda, led by France in Opération Turquoise; and NATO's bombing of Serbia in 1999 are three examples of clear intent, coordinated implementation, and commitment of adequate military means. In northern Iraq and Kosovo, in particular, the willingness to maintain a secure environment for the Kurds and Kosovars, respectively, was present and remains today with NATO air power poised to respond in both cases as it has in the past.

RECENT TRENDS IN MILITARIZED HUMANITARIAN INTERVENTION

An upsurge in the frequency of U.N. peace support operations immediately followed the end of the Cold War (three operations commenced within a two-month period in 1992); peaked in 1993, in terms of the number of peacekeepers deployed (78,744), and in 1994, in terms of U.N. peacekeeping expenditures ($3.5 billion). By the decade's end, the operational command and execution of peace support operations had shifted more toward regional organizations—a shift that is supported by Article VIII of the U.N. Charter and by U.N. critics who charge that the United Nations is not operationally or politically capable of mounting an unambiguous, consistent, and successful intervention campaign. A comparison of U.N. peacekeeping troop contributions between 1993 and 1999 illustrates the diminished U.N. military presence (see Chapter 1, Figure 1.1).[13]

The decline in U.N.-led militarized operations is attributable to real and perceived failures during the early to mid-1990s. Operational planners relied on Security Council mandates and state policymakers to provide a conceptual framework for understanding the material and personnel requirements for a peace support operation. The humanitarian interventions of the early 1990s took place largely without conceptual guidance, clear and feasible mandates, flexible rules of engagement, or explicit definitions of the conditions under which missions would be terminated. In the absence of conceptual mooring and the presence of increasingly violent and complicated conflicts, operational institutions and personnel struggled with designing practical plans for constantly changing environments of which they had very little knowledge and experience; coordinating among multinational contingents, key humanitarian agencies and relief personnel; and resolving command and control issues.

Along with political elites, military commanders from major powers have lost confidence in the ability of the United Nations to lead a multinational effort in a potentially volatile environment. As the success of recent

NATO actions has demonstrated, alternative force structures, such as NATO or a coalition of interested states, may be preferable, leaving U.N.-led force structures to conduct only those operations with a low risk of escalation in violence. The most consistent recommendation from peace-keeping observers is that the United Nations concentrate on improving its real capabilities—essentially, activities closer to Chapter VI than to Chapter VII. It should focus its energy on developing "peace packages" comprising peacemaking, peacekeeping, and peace-building activities in the context of nonviolent, consent-based operations. Some believe that the United Nations should attempt to regain the trust of states by building a portfolio of successes in low-risk environments. In this scenario, the organization would reinforce existing low-risk instruments for peace, such as observer missions. All of these recommendations, of course, are based on relatively untested assumptions about what ails the U.N. system and begin with the belief that there is a strong association between structural problems at U.N. headquarters and performance in the field.

Field-level problems highlight the inadequacies of political decisions and planning strategies. Common implementation problems of the early to mid-1990s can be found in military after-action reports and in case studies that emphasize a host of tactical issues.

In northern Iraq, implementation efforts were constrained by the hostility of the Iraqi government toward the Kurds, the isolated terrain, the weakness of the United Nations, and the absence of alternatives for the Kurds, who could neither return home nor remain permanently in camps. Additional constraints were the pace of U.N. mobilization, the narrowness of NGO mandates, and the difficulty of protecting relief personnel. Although the United Nations could improve its procurement and deployment mechanisms and supply greater protection to NGOs in the field, it can do little to ensure the long-term viability of the politically fragmented Kurdish population. There can be no exit strategy from the safe havens in northern Iraq.

After-action reports from the crisis in Somalia highlight the first experiences of U.S. military forces in true cooperation with nonstate actors. The U.S. military did not understand U.N., NGO, or ICRC mandates, due to its lack of formal training in civilian resources and organizational mandates. As time passed and experience accumulated in military-NGO cooperation, learning occurred.

Positive and negative experiences of military and humanitarian collaboration in Rwanda were reported by various NGOs and U.N. agencies. There were three joint military-humanitarian phases: the multilateral peacekeeping forces of UNAMIR during the worst wave of genocide; the French unilateral security action and the U.S. Support Hope humanitarian action; and the national military contingents involved in humanitarian activities under UNHCR invitation and direction. The designated functions of military units during the Rwandan crisis were to provide a secure environment for humanitarian activities, to assist humanitarians, and to carry out various relief activities on their own.

Because UNAMIR troops did not have the mandate to use force except in self-defense, they were unable to provide a secure environment for victims and humanitarian personnel—a task in which military contingents supposedly have a comparative advantage. Only French troops in Opération Turquoise proved capable of fostering a secure environment, but not without heavy criticism from French NGOs that viewed the military's show of force as undermining their ability to deal with all victims impartially. Even after the humanitarian emergency had stabilized, more humanitarian organizations had arrived on the scene, and troop operations had wound down, some NGOs maintained their distance from military units performing strictly humanitarian activities. Dutch NGOs, such as MSF-Holland, which were thankful for Dutch military transport to Goma, nevertheless maintained the view that the presence of the military compromised their organizations' humanitarian mandate. Many others, however, praised the professional working relationship between the military and humanitarians. Irish soldiers made the task easier by wearing T-shirts and carrying no weapons while assisting NGOs; the Irish government, unlike wealthier countries, also provided its military personnel at no cost to the relief organizations. The cost of UNAMIR was $162 million. The official figure for Opération Turquoise is about $200 million, and that for Operation Support Hope, about $135 million, although unofficial tallies are much higher—some, four or five times greater.[14]

The positive aspects of military-humanitarian collaboration in Rwanda included the military's financial, technical, and logistical capacity; its "can-do" approach; its ability to attract media and public attention to human tragedy; and its focus on evaluation of performance once tasks were completed. On the negative side, military units were less willing than humanitarians to take risks (the Japanese troops, for example, refused to work inside refugee camps for security reasons, and some U.S. troops were not allowed to leave the Kigali airport); contingency planning did not occur until the last moment; and the timetable of military involvement was problematic (humanitarian personnel were reluctant to form working relationships with military units not scheduled to remain in the area for long). Perhaps the clearest lesson concerned physical protection: Here, unilateral action was more effective than action under U.N. command and control.

The failures of past interventions have made the international humanitarian system more cautious. The chronology of events, and the tools used by international humanitarian actors in the crisis in East Timor in

Danziger, © *Christian Science Monitor.*

late 1999 may be indicative of a new pattern of crisis escalation and third-party interventions that could continue in the twenty-first century.

Indonesia used its military might to integrate East Timor as an Indonesian province in 1975. With the diplomatic help of the United Nations, on May 5, 1999, Indonesia and Portugal (a former administrator of East Timor) agreed to allow the East Timorese to vote on whether to accept special autonomy within Indonesia or to seek complete independence. The "popular consultation" with the East Timorese required, first, the registration of voters, followed by the actual vote. On August 30, 1999, some 98 percent of registered voters went to the polls and decided by a margin of 21.5 percent to 78.5 percent to seek complete independence. Following is a chronology of the massive humanitarian and human rights abuses conducted by pro-autonomy militias against the pro-independence population and the corresponding responses by the international humanitarian system.

In 1975, Indonesian troops landed in East Timor and declared it the 27th province of Indonesia. The U.N. Security Council and General Assembly call for Indonesia to withdraw and to respect East Timor's territorial integrity and the inalienable right of its people to self-determination. From 1975 to 1999, the East Timorese independence movement received no assistance from the international system except for informal consultations in which diplomatic pressure was the only tool of persuasion. Not until April 1998 did the U.N. Commission on Human Rights publicly note its deep concern over reports of human rights violations in East Timor. In December 1998, the U.N. secretary-general issued a public statement underlining the need for stability and peace in the territory.

Indonesian president Bacharuddin Habibie indicated in a public statement in January 1999 that his government might be prepared to consider independence for East Timor. Diplomatic talks among the parties followed in New York. Indonesia accepted sole responsibility for the protection of East Timorese throughout the process leading to a popular consultation. The May 5 agreements, which called for a popular consultation, were followed two days later by Security Council Resolution 1236, which stressed the Indonesian government's responsibility for ensuring the safety and security of international staff and observers. Resolution 1246 of June established the U.N. Administrative Mission in East Timor (UNAMET), an international group of 900 U.N. staff members, including 270 unarmed civilian police, who would carry out duties related to the popular consultation. UNAMET also employed 4,000 locals during its stay.

From January to August 30, 1999, intimidation and violence against pro-independence supporters increased dramatically. Indonesian military, police, and militia forces became engaged in a campaign of terror. A pattern of massive involuntary displacement began. Reports of killings in pro-independence villages increased. Serious militia attacks occurred on the UNAMET regional office and a humanitarian convoy accompanied by a UNAMET humanitarian affairs officer and a local representative of the UNHCR.

The only international responses to clear indications of humanitarian and human rights abuses were statements by the Security Council, demanding an immediate halt to the violence; by the U.N. secretary-general, who made public the continued challenge to security by armed civilian groups most probably trained by the Indonesian military, and the urgent problem of internal displacement; and by humanitarian and human rights agencies, asking the Indonesian authorities to make good on their pledge to investigate attacks and bring justice to those responsible. UNAMET's call for the removal of Indonesian army officers who were associated with militia activities could not be backed by force.

One week before the popular vote, the Security Council was briefed on the unsettling security situation in East Timor. However, the Security Council and the West were preoccupied with Kosovo, and the council's only response was to issue a statement expressing strong concern. The unarmed UNAMET civilian police requested additional security measures and received verbal assurances from Indonesia that it would protect voters.

On voting day, seven polling stations were temporarily shut down due to violence, and a local U.N. staff member was fatally stabbed. Two days after the vote, militia members attacked pro-independence supporters outside the UNAMET compound. UNAMET headquarters soon became a refuge for frightened journalists and several hundred IDPs. The response of the Security Council and the secretary-general was to produce statements urging the Indonesian authorities to exercise their responsibility to the people. The murders of more local UNAMET staff members followed.

When the votes were tallied and independence was declared to be the people's choice, a militia rampage began. The U.N. High Commissioner of Human Rights begged the Security Council to deploy international or regional forces. The secretary-general initiated high-level talks with governments that might have an interest in mounting and supporting an international force and with the Indonesian government to obtain the latter's consent to an international presence.

While talks were in progress, militiamen attacked the compound of the International Committee of the Red Cross. The U.N. began its withdrawal of UNAMET personnel, in whose defense the secretary-general remarked that the "situation has clearly got far beyond what a small mission, which was sent to organize the popular vote and never equipped or mandated to enforce law and order, can possibly be expected to cope with."[15]

By the time President Habibie agreed to accept international assistance to restore peace and security in East Timor (September 12, 1999) and the Security Council voted to set up a multinational force acting under Chapter VII of the U.N. Charter (Resolution 1264, September 15, 1999) to be led by Australia, the humanitarian disaster in East Timor was of catastrophic proportions. Nearly two-thirds of the population had fled their homes and were dependent upon humanitarian assistance. The estimate of funds needed to care for the IDPs over a six-month period was $135.5 million; the World Food Programme estimated that 740,000 East Timorese would require food aid for that period. Before the escalation in violence following the vote, the UNHCR had organized aid convoys only for an estimated 60,000 IDPs. The threat of malaria also was of great concern as the rainy season was soon to commence and there was a lack of medical supplies and personnel due to the intimidation of relief workers by militia forces and common criminals. IDPs who had fled to the countryside could not be reached due to lack of security.

The limits of U.N. protection are clear in this case. The United Nations has no standing military force or assets. It cannot deploy troops or equipment

East Timorese families find shelter in Assunta Church, in Kupang, West Timor. According to government sources, an estimated 230,000 East Timorese had been displaced to West Timor by the end of September 1999. UN/UNHCR/F. Pagetti.

rapidly. Months may pass before the secretary-general can persuade governments to contribute personnel and material. No government was willing to offer troops for an early U.N. intervention, especially without the consent of Indonesia, which ironically and tragically was responsible for the emergency. The U.N. budget is extremely limited and requires a coalition of the willing to assume responsibility for their own costs in exchange for the freedom to exercise control within another government's territory under the authority and legitimacy of the United Nations. While the U.N. secretary-general and member states work the phones, humanitarian and human rights personnel must work the field without any meaningful form of protection for themselves or those who they are trying to assist.

Given the above scenario, vulnerable populations are completely dependent upon their own forms of self-defense for protection and upon the international humanitarian system for food, health care, and shelter. Justice comes only after the conflict is over, if at all. In the case of East Timor, the Commission on Human Rights has requested that the secretary-general establish a committee to investigate human rights violations throughout the territory.

In the early 1990s, it was widely thought that the media could influence the Security Council and member states to act quickly and responsibly. Those heady days of optimism are past, although the media remains a factor in accelerating certain decisionmaking processes, as discussed in Chapter 2. In the early 1990s, some thought that a U.N. standing army could be created that would respond to humanitarian crises before the numbers of refugees, IDPs, dead, and dying mounted, and that the further development of early warning systems would increase the speed with which a protection force could be deployed. These ideas appear to be mistaken. To all indications, there is already an abundance of early warnings, and no one is caught off guard by the outbreak of humanitarian and human rights catastrophes; yet the speed of organized responses has not accelerated.

It has become increasingly clear that protection is extremely problematic in most humanitarian crises. If the international system of states cannot effectively provide protection to vulnerable populations suffering from extreme humanitarian and human rights abuses, then NGOs, commonly referred to as members of international civil society, must work harder before protection becomes necessary.

The challenge, thus, is what has commonly been referred to as "development education." This is a task of NGOs that is distinct from their assistance and protection efforts in war zones but that may in fact be more critical in the long run, helping alter attitudes and preferences in order to attack silent emergencies. This book is focused almost exclusively on the targets of operational NGOs (the victims of war); but the targets of educational and advocacy NGOs (their contributors, the public, and national decisionmakers) are just as important. Educational NGOs seek primarily to influence citizens, whose voices are then registered through public opinion and bear fruit in the form of additional resources for NGOs' activities as well as for new policies, better decisions, and on occasion, enhanced international regimes. Educational NGOs often play a leading role in promoting the various "days," "years," and "decades" that the U.N. system regularly proclaims. Nongovernmental organizations can reinforce the norms promoted by intergovernmental organizations through public education campaigns, which in turn can help hold states accountable to their international commitments.

Western operational NGOs are under growing pressure from their Third World partners to educate contributors and Western publics about the origins of poverty and violence. Without such efforts, one commentator remarked that "conventional NGO project activities are manifestly 'finger-in-the-dike' responses to problems that require nothing short of worldwide and whole-hearted government commitment to combat."[16] Operational activities are supported by the education of populations and the mobilization of public opinion in favor of more equitable global distribution of power and resources.

Nongovernmental organizations focusing exclusively on education in their own countries without overseas activities within at least some internal conflicts are not numerous, but they exist. The most effective educators are those with credibility, knowledge, and convictions gained from substantial operational experience or from firsthand experience with war-torn societies. Examples are Oxfam and Save the Children, whose efforts in development education are linked to the origins of poverty and injustice as well as to specific campaigns for dealing with the victims of wars like those in Bosnia and Somalia. Many NGOs have moved away from an exclusive concern with projects and toward a focus on preventing the need for relief projects in the first place through the promotion of structural change and avoidance of violent conflict. The shift is toward educating the public about its attitudes and the necessity for systemic change, and away from a preoccupation with relief. Two observers summarize the logic behind this shift, in the context of their negative views about the World Bank and the IMF: "Many of the causes of under-development lie in the political and economic structures of an unequal world . . . and in the misguided policies of governments and the multilateral institutions (such as the World Bank and IMF) which they control. It is extremely difficult, if not impossible, to address these issues in the context of the traditional NGO project."[17]

Linked to education are the related activities of NGOs working primarily in the corridors of governments and intergovernmental organizations, where international responses to internal conflicts are shaped. These advocates pursue discussions with national delegates and staff members of international secretariats in order to influence international public policy. "Lobbying" is perhaps an accurate image but an inaccurate description, because by definition *lobbying* applies only to efforts to influence legislators. In seeking to inform or alter the policies of governments as well as of governmental, intergovernmental, and nongovernmental agencies, advocacy NGOs seek to influence a wide variety of policymakers and not simply parliamentarians. Prominent examples in the humanitarian arena in the United States include the Lawyers' Committee for Human Rights, Refugees International, and the U.S. Committee for Refugees. In spite of the pertinence of advocacy NGOs, they are not numerous and have the greatest difficulty in raising funds.

A great deal of NGO advocacy in the past has been directed *against* the official policies of governments and U.N. organizations. Recently, however, many nongovernmental organizations have moved toward institutionalizing a full-fledged partnership with U.N. member states. Historically, NGOs have had some responsibility for the implementation of treaties drafted mainly by representatives of states. But now these NGOs aspire to more direct involvement in the drafting of language and in the political processes resulting in treaties. When governments or international institutions are trying to shape their responses to humanitarian emergencies in war zones, NGO views can be influential, as responses in northern Iraq, Somalia, Rwanda, Haiti, Bosnia, Kosovo, and Timor suggest. Both through formal statements in U.N. forums and informational negotiations with international civil servants and members of national delegations, advocacy NGOs seek to ensure that their views and those of their constituencies are reflected in international texts and decisions. Some offer research and drafting skills and provide scientific or polling data to support their positions. Firsthand reports and testimonies from NGO field staff also are powerful tools for influencing parliamentary committees.

CONCLUSION

Complex emergencies will continue because no viable and politically acceptable solutions have been found to deal with resource scarcity, political manipulations, and adaptive measures (of which conflict is one) of economically marginalized societies incapable of competing in the world market. Moreover, decreases in private investment and development assistance leave international crisis management as the sole predictable source of external material inputs and worldwide attention—providing marginalized groups an incentive to initiate or perpetuate civil wars and other internal conflicts. Conflicts may also continue because they are profitable for certain merchants and justify the maintenance of troop levels and military budgets. There have been dramatic increases in sales of weapons from developed to developing or politically unstable countries since 1989 (for example, 41 percent of 1993 U.S. arms exports went to nondemocratic regimes). Some countries justify their military expenditures by the need to develop and train for peacekeeping responses. In such an environment, the economic immigrants who are refused visas and work permits today may very well be tomorrow's refugees who are refused asylum.

Long-term development assistance, although it may appear to be the answer to many ills, is not a panacea for humanitarian problems. Although more often than not economically satisfied countries have buffers to prevent them from imploding, not all geographic areas are good candidates for sustainable development; in some locales, the environment is

The positive impact of humanitarian action is reflected in the eyes of this Central American child.
U.N. Photo.

not sufficiently life-sustaining. Many people are affected by chronic
famine resulting from the infertility of the soil and inhospitable climatic
conditions, and the investment of funds in unsustainable land is inappropriate.

In some developing countries, remittances sent home by relatives
working abroad are as important a source of foreign exchange as is foreign aid. As immigration laws tighten in response to domestic factors
such as limited resources, social unrest, and nationalist sentiments, remittances drop and survival mechanisms kick in, including violence and
crime. Demands for international humanitarian assistance are therefore
expected to rise. The breakdown of states and increase in humanitarian

need are also rooted in privatization trends. Weak states can no longer depend upon state-to-state cooperation as a source of legitimacy. Legitimacy now frequently rests on a state's ability to provide social services. Without social services, local military forces become the preferred vehicle for confiscation and redistribution of resources.

In sum, actors following and affecting world politics know that crises will appear, whether they are prepared to address them or not. Meanwhile, changes may be occurring that will shape future possibilities for intervention. A hint at possibly desirable changes arose during the opening ceremony of the final U.N. General Assembly of the twentieth century. One of the U.N. secretary-general's more pleasurable ceremonial tasks is to open this assembly; but the secretary-general's September 1999 speech was anything but routine. The focus was on globalization and humanitarian intervention; but the latter touched a raw nerve, especially among representatives of developing countries. Secretary-General Kofi Annan's predecessor, Boutros Boutros-Ghali, had been indirect in pointing out, "The time of absolute and exclusive sovereignty, however, has passed; its theory was never matched by reality."[18] Annan's language was far more direct and concrete, as he announced, "States bent on criminal behaviour [should] know that frontiers are not the absolute defence . . . , that massive and systematic violations of human rights—wherever they may take place—should not be allowed to stand."[19]

Moreover, Annan expressed the heretical view that effectively addressing abuses is more important than U.N. aggrandizement. Although he did not endorse the use of force by NATO without Security Council authorization, he stressed the importance of not standing idly by when faced with the kind of atrocities that Serbs were committing in Kosovo. In addressing "those for whom the greatest threat to the future of international order is the use of force in the absence of a Security Council mandate," the secretary-general brought up the events in Rwanda. If there had been a coalition of the willing that did not receive a council imprimatur, "should such a coalition have stood aside and allowed the horror to unfold?" In posing this rhetorical question, Annan clearly was speaking not as a bureaucrat protecting his organizational turf at all costs but as an idealist.

Why does the topic of this book, humanitarian intervention, remain so controversial? The secretary-general's speech raised hackles because a revolution is taking place in the justification for intervention: A lower threshold for the entry of international military forces into intranational conflicts is gaining wider acceptance, although it has not yet been canonized.

The past decade has witnessed a dramatic increase in the weight assigned humanitarian values as acceptable justification for diplomatic and

military action. "In the 1990s," wrote Adam Roberts, "humanitarian issues have played a historically unprecedented role in international politics."[20] On the dramatic example of the military campaign in Kosovo,
Michael Ignatieff noted that "its legitimacy [depends] on what fifty years
of human rights has done to our moral instincts, weakening the presumption in favor of state sovereignty, strengthening the presumption in favor
of intervention when massacre and deportation become state policy."[21]

There is a persistent tendency in the discourse of international relations
to juxtapose ideals with Reälpolitik. Despite the dramatic growth in the
numbers and significance of transnational actors, the principal locus of
political decisions in response to the push and pull of humanitarian values is still the state. There is no compelling evidence that the state's role
has been transcended within international relations in general or humanitarian affairs in particular. The point is not to establish a "space of victim-
hood"[22] against the state but rather to get state authorities to take seri-
ously their obligations to the individuals living within their jurisdiction.
This book ultimately does not challenge the concept that states act on the
basis of power and material interests, but it does show the extent to
which humanitarian values have shaped perceptions of state interests
among intervening states.

There is no escape from moral reasoning in international politics; but
David Rieff was correct when he wrote, "Our moral ambitions have been
revealed as being larger than our political, military, or even cognitive
means."[23] Greater attention to humanitarian values from policymakers
and practitioners has not of course brought utopia, but it has made the
world a somewhat more livable place. It is inconceivable, for instance,
that a responsible Western leader could have made the same argument
about Kosovo that Neville Chamberlain made about Czechoslovakia. Although vigorous action was too slow in East Timor, at least the outcry
over Indonesia's military and militia atrocities was immediate; and
enough arms were twisted in Djakarta to permit the deployment of the
Australia-led force, which was followed by the first full-fledged experi-
ment with U.N. trusteeship.

Humanitarian values have become more central to the definition of
vital interests as well as more central to the worries of thugs and war
criminals. Notwithstanding the remarkably mixed record of humanitarian intervention in the 1990s, the eternal policy challenge in an eternally
imperfect world is to reduce the discrepancy between rhetoric and reality.
The humanitarian glass is nine-tenths empty, but perhaps readers of this
volume will live to see the day when it will be half full.

□ □ □

Discussion Questions

CHAPTER ONE

1. According to international law, do states have a duty to intervene in wars where human atrocities are evident?

2. If international law is to be respected, do humanitarians have an obligation to address local mores that ignore the rights of certain groups, such as women?

3. When is state sovereignty sacrosanct?

4. Can humanitarians be apolitical in a war zone?

5. How do you foresee the future evolution of the humanitarian idea?

CHAPTERS TWO AND THREE

1. What are the difficulties encountered in the coordination of a collective response to humanitarian needs in a war zone? Which problems are rooted in a particular organizational structure, and which ones exist across organizational structures?

2. Are the problems outlined in the previous question surmountable? If so, how?

3. What elements should be added to a design for an international humanitarian system that "works" from the perspective of the victims of war?

4. Is there an international humanitarian community? system? regime?

5. Which of the case studies seemed most and least successful in terms of minimizing life-threatening suffering? Why?

6. To what extent do racism, geographical proximity, and geopolitics play a role in humanitarian intervention?

CHAPTER FOUR

1. Do you find our explanation credible of why violations of international humanitarian and human rights law are increasing? Can you think of other factors explaining this increase?

2. Should human rights protection be included in an emergency relief effort? Can a single organization effectively satisfy both the provision of food and the protection of rights?

3. Should humanitarians arm themselves? Should noncombatants be allowed to carry weapons?

4. Is triage operationally or ethically acceptable?

5. Should rape be considered a war crime on a par with other war-related atrocities? Does it matter whether the perpetrator was a soldier in uniform operating under the orders of his military commander or was a common criminal?

CHAPTERS FIVE AND SIX

1. Which of the humanitarian arguments presented at the beginning of this chapter seems most logical, and why?

2. Why does the international humanitarian system respond more quickly and generously to loud emergencies than to silent ones?

3. Would it be preferable to cordon off a war until the belligerents are exhausted and then to devote all humanitarian resources to the alleviation of abject poverty, instead of intervening while war is still raging?

4. What is the most pressing policy issue facing humanitarians?

5. How can states and aid agencies respond more effectively to large and sudden movements of displaced people?

6. Who should determine when it is safe for refugees to be repatriated?

7. What policies would support distressed communities so that the period of their dependency on external assistance is short and the social, economic, and political recoveries are longer-lasting?

8. Can the humanitarian sphere be treated separately from international peace and security?

9. Is "political humanitarianism" an oxymoron or a necessity?

Notes

PREFACE

1. Joseph S. Nye, Jr., "The New National Interest," *Foreign Affairs* 78, no. 4 (July/August 1999), p. 30.

INTRODUCTION

1. World Health Organization, *The World Health Report, 1999* (Geneva: World Health Organization, 1999), Annex Table 1.

2. Steven Kull, "What the Public Knows That Washington Doesn't," *Foreign Policy* (Winter 1995–1996):102–115.

3. James F. Hoge, Jr., "Editor's Note," *Foreign Affairs* 73, no. 6 (November-December 1994):v. For a wide-ranging collection of essays, see Paul A. Winters, ed., *Interventionism: Current Controversies* (San Diego: Greenhaven Press, 1995).

4. Alex de Waal and Rakiya Omaar, "Can Military Intervention Be Humanitarian?" *Middle East Report*, nos. 187–188 (March-April/May-June 1994):7.

5. This term was first used by Thomas G. Weiss and Kurt M. Campbell, "Military Humanitarianism," *Survival* 33, no. 5 (September-October 1991):451–465.

6. See Malcolm N. Shaw, *International Law*, 3d ed. (Cambridge: Cambridge University Press, 1991).

7. Adam Roberts, "Humanitarian War: Military Intervention and Human Rights," *International Affairs* 69 (1993):429–449.

8. For these and other gruesome statistics, see United Nations High Commissioner for Refugees, *The State of the World's Refugees, 1997–98: A Humanitarian Agenda*(New York: Oxford University Press, 1997).

9. Commission on Global Governance, *Our Global Neighbourhood* (Oxford: Oxford University Press, 1995), p. 90.

CHAPTER ONE

1. Immanuel Kant, *Perpetual Peace*, ed. Lewis White Beck (New York: Liberal Arts Press, 1957).

2. For a more detailed understanding of realism and neorealism, respectively, see Niccolo Machiavelli, *The Prince*, trans. and ed. Harvey C. Mansfield, Jr.

186 ☐ Notes

(Chicago: University of Chicago Press, 1985); and Kenneth Waltz, *Man, the State, and War* (New York: Columbia University Press, 1959).

3. John Ruggie, "Continuity and Transformation in the World Polity: Toward a Neorealist Synthesis," in Robert O. Keohane, ed., *Neorealism and Its Critics* (New York: Columbia University Press, 1986), pp. 131–157; and John Ruggie, ed., *Multilateralism Matters* (New York: Columbia University Press, 1993).

4. See Robert Keohane and Joseph S. Nye, Jr., *Power and Interdependence* (Boston: Little, Brown, 1977), p. 19.

5. Jean-Jacques Rousseau, *Selections* (New York: Perennial Library, 1986), p. 162.

6. See Joseph Wronka, *Human Rights and Social Policy in the 21st Century* (Lanham, Md.: University Press of America, 1992).

7. Hersch Lauterpacht, *International Law and Human Rights* (London: Stevens and Son, 1950), p. 84, quoted in Wronka, *Human Rights and Social Policy,* p. 49.

8. Thomas Buergenthal, *International Human Rights Law* (St. Paul: West, 1988), p. 3.

9. See Gil Loescher, *Beyond Charity: International Cooperation and the Global Refugee Crisis* (New York: Oxford University Press, 1994).

10. See Ephraim Isaac, "Humanitarianism Across Religions and Cultures," in Thomas G. Weiss and Larry Minear, eds., *Humanitarianism Across Borders: Sustaining Civilians in Times of War* (Boulder: Lynne Rienner, 1993), pp. 16–21.

11. See Benedict Anderson, *Imagined Communities* (London: Verso, 1983).

12. See Craig Murphy, *International Organizations and Industrial Change* (Oxford: Polity Press, 1994).

13. The League of Nations' institutional life span technically stretched from January 1920 to April 1946, although it had been pronounced dead in 1935 and again in 1939 and was mothballed during World War II.

14. José E. Alvarez, "The 'Right to Be Left Alone' and the General Assembly," in *Article 2(7) Revisited,* Reports and Papers 1994, no. 5 (Providence, R.I.: Academic Council on the United Nations System, 1994), p. 9.

15. See Felice Gaer, "Human Rights NGOs Confront Governments at the UN," *Third World Quarterly* 16, no. 3 (September 1995):389–404. For an extended discussion of this issue, see Jack Donnelly, *International Human Rights* (Boulder: Westview Press, 1994).

16. See *The Geneva Conventions of August 12, 1949,* and *Protocols Additional to the Geneva Conventions of 12 August 1949* (Geneva: International Committee of the Red Cross, 1989).

17. Anthony Parsons, *From Cold War to Hot Peace* (London: Michael Joseph, 1995), p. viii.

18. For a discussion of the range of such conflicts, see Ted Robert Gurr and Barbara Harff, *Ethnic Conflict in World Politics* (Boulder: Westview Press, 1994; Michael E. Brown, ed., *Ethnic Conflict and International Security* (Princeton: Princeton University Press, 1993); and a special issue of *Daedalus* 122, no. 3 (Summer 1993), entitled *Reconstructing Nations and States.*

19. Boutros Boutros-Ghali, *An Agenda for Peace* (New York: United Nations, 1992), par. 59.

20. United Nations Press Releases, GA/AB/3227; GA/AB/3287; and GA/SPD/167.

21. Boutros Boutros-Ghali, *Supplement to an Agenda for Peace: Position Paper of the Secretary-General on the Occasion of the Fiftieth Anniversary of the United Nations* (New York: United Nations, 1995), pars. 4, 77.

22. Ibid., par. 6.

23. International Peace Academy, *The OAU and Conflict Management in Africa* (New York: International Peace Academy, 1993), p. 2.

24. Francis M. Deng, "Sovereignty, Responsibility, and Accountability: A Framework of Protection, Assistance, and Development for the Internally Displaced" (Washington, D.C.: Brookings Institution, 1995), p. 58.

25. Rakiya Omaar and Alex de Waal, *Humanitarianism Unbound?* Discussion Paper 5 (London: African Rights, November 1994), p. 5.

26. International Committee of the Red Cross, *Respect for International Humanitarian Law: ICRC Review of Five Years of Activity (1987–1991)* (Geneva: ICRC, 1991), p. 4.

CHAPTER TWO

1. *Crosslines* 3, no. 4 (December 1995–January 1996).

2. For further analysis, see Marion J. Levy, Jr., "Armed Force Organizations," in Henry Bienen, ed., *The Military and Modernizations* (Chicago: Aldine-Atherton, 1971), pp. 41–78.

3. See Laura Miller and Charles Moskos, "Humanitarians or Warriors? Race, Gender, and Combat Status in Operation Restore Hope," *Armed Forces and Society* 21, no. 4 (Summer 1995):624, 631.

4. Gayle Young, "Countries Train Together in Egypt," at www.cnn.com, November 14, 1995.

5. Refugee Policy Group, *Somalia: Lives Lost, Lives Saved* (Washington, D.C.: Refugee Policy Group, November 1994), p. 27.

6. National Intelligence Council, *Global Humanitarian Emergencies: Trends and Projections, 1999–2000* (Washington, D.C.: National Intelligence Council, 1999), p. 24.

7. U.S. Permanent Mission to the United Nations, *Global Humanitarian Emergencies, 1995* (New York: U.S. Permanent Mission to the United Nations, January 1995), pp. 14–15.

8. UNDP, *Human Development Report 1999* (Oxford: Oxford University Press, 1999), p. 192.

9. Jim Clancy and Jackie Shymanski, "Snow . . . Fog . . . Grumbling Troops," www.cnn.com, December 16, 1995.

10. See UNHCR, *Concept Paper: Humanitarian Emergencies and Refugees* (Geneva: UNHCR, April 3, 1995).

11. See Edward C. Luck, *Mixed Messages: American Politics and International Organizations, 1919–1999* (Washington, D.C.: Brookings Institution Press, 1999).

12. U.S. Permanent Mission, *Global Humanitarian Emergencies*, p. 14.

13. *UNDHA Humanitarian Bulletin* 95/2 (October 31, 1995).

14. Graham Allison, "Conceptual Models of the Cuban Missile Crisis," *American Political Science Review* 63, no. 3 (September 1969):689–718. See also Graham Allison and Philip Zelikow, *Essence of Decision: Explaining the Cuban Missile Crisis* (New York: Longman, 1999).

15. Eric Schmitt, "Troop Move Pits White House Against Pentagon," *New York Times*, June 7, 1995, A19.

16. Quoted in Miller and Moskos, "Humanitarians or Warriors?" p. 624.

17. Erskine Childers, with Brian Urquhart, *Renewing the United Nations* (Uppsala: Dag Hammarskjöld Foundation, 1994), pp. 28–29.

18. Patricia Weiss-Fagen, *After the Conflict: A Review of Selected Sources on Rebuilding War-Torn Societies* (Geneva: U.N. Research Institute for Social Development, May 1995), p. 2.

19. For a discussion of this history, see Thomas G. Weiss, "Humanitarian Shell Games: Whither UN Reform?" *Security Dialogue* 29, no. 1 (March 1998):9–24.

20. Peter Macalister-Smith, *International Humanitarian Assistance: Disaster Relief Actions in International Law and Organization* (Dordrecht, Netherlands: Nijhoff, 1985), p. 37.

21. Hugo Slim and Angela Penrose, "U.N. Reform in a Changing World: Responding to Complex Emergencies," in Joanna Macrae and Anthony Zwi, eds., *War and Hunger* (London: Zed Books, 1994), p. 198.

22. See Gayle E. Smith, "Relief Operations and Military Strategy," in Thomas G. Weiss and Larry Minear, eds., *Humanitarianism Across Borders: Sustaining Civilians in Times of War* (Boulder: Lynne Rienner, 1993), pp. 97–116.

23. Sphere Project, *Humanitarian Charter and Minimum Standards in Disaster Response* (Geneva: Sphere Project, 1998).

24. See James P. Ingram, "The Future Architecture for International Humanitarian Assistance," in Weiss and Minear, eds., *Humanitarianism Across Borders*, pp. 171–193.

25. For a discussion, see Thomas G. Weiss, "Principles, Politics, and Humanitarian Action," *Ethics & International Affairs* 13 (1999):1–22.

26. See Bernard Kouchner and Mario Bettati, *Le devoir d'ingérence* (Paris: Denoël, 1987); Bernard Kouchner, *Le malheur des autres* (Paris: Odile Jacob, 1991); and Mario Bettati, "Intervention, ingérence ou assistance?" *Revue Trimestrielle des Droits de l'Homme*, no. 19 (July 1994):308–358.

27. Charles Tilly, *From Mobilization to Revolution* (Reading, Mass.: Addison-Wesley, 1978), p. 5.

CHAPTER THREE

1. Lars Schoultz, "U.S.–Latin American Relations," in Joel Krieger, ed., *The Oxford Companion to Politics of the World* (New York: Oxford University Press, 1993), p. 948.

2. Cristina Eguizábal, David Lewis, Larry Minear, Peter Sollis, and Thomas G. Weiss, *Humanitarian Challenges in Central America: Learning the Lessons of Recent Armed Conflicts*, Occasional Paper no. 14 (Providence, R.I.: Brown University, Thomas J. Watson Jr. Institute for International Studies, 1993), pp. 35–36.

3. Ibid., p. 56.

4. Molly Moore, "For Hurricane's Victims, No End to Disaster," *Washington Post*, August 1, 1999, A1.

5. For an in-depth analysis of military costs and benefits of this operation as well as those in Somalia, Bosnia, Haiti, and Rwanda, see Thomas G. Weiss,

Military-Civilian Interactions: Intervening in Humanitarian Crises (Boulder: Rowman & Littlefield, 1999).

6. Larry Minear, U.B.P. Chelliah, Jeff Crisp, John Mackinlay, and Thomas G. Weiss, *United Nations Coordination of the International Humanitarian Response to the Gulf Crisis, 1990–92*, Occasional Paper no. 13 (Providence, R.I.: Brown University, Thomas J. Watson Jr. Institute for International Studies, 1992), p. 1.

7. Ibid., p. 17.

8. Jeffrey Clark, "Debacle in Somalia: Failure of the Collective Response," in Lori Fisler Damrosch, ed., *Enforcing Restraint: Collective Intervention in Internal Conflicts* (New York: Council on Foreign Relations Press, 1993), pp. 205–239.

9. Enrico Augelli and Craig N. Murphy, "Lessons of Somalia for Future Multilateral Humanitarian Assistance Operations," *Global Governance* 1, no. 3 (September–December 1995):341–368.

10. Mohamed Sahnoun, *Somalia: The Missed Opportunities* (Washington, D.C.: U.S. Institute of Peace, 1994).

11. Clark, "Debacle in Somalia," pp. 220, 229.

12. Lawrence Freedman, "Why the West Failed," *Foreign Policy* 97 (Winter 1994–1995):59.

13. Quoted in Stanley Meiser, "U.N. Relief Hopes Turn to Despair," *Washington Post*, October 25, 1993, A1.

14. Quoted in Roger Cohen, "Allied Resolve to Bolster U.N. Peacekeeping in Bosnia; US Weighs a Combat Role," *New York Times*, May 30, 1995, A1.

15. Quoted in Barbara Crossette, "At the U.N., Thoughts About Bosnia but No Action," *New York Times*, December 9, 1994, A12.

16. Quoted in Larry Minear, Jeffrey Clark, Roberta Cohen, Dennis Gallagher, Iain Guest, and Thomas G. Weiss, *Humanitarian Action in the Former Yugoslavia: The U.N.'s Role, 1991–1993*, Occasional Paper no. 18 (Providence, R.I.: Brown University, Thomas J. Watson Jr. Institute for International Studies, 1994), p. 1.

17. Ivo H. Daalder, "Emerging Answers," *Brookings Review* 17, no. 3 (Summer 1999):22–25.

18. Adam Roberts, "NATO's 'Humanitarian War' over Kosovo," *Survival* 41, no. 3 (Summer 1999):102–123; and Charles Krauthammer, "The Short Unhappy History of Humanitarian War," *National Interest* 57 (Fall 1999):5–8.

19. David M. Durant, "WebWatch," *Library Journal* 124, no. 14 (1999):134, 136.

20. Physicians for Human Rights, *War Crimes in Kosovo: A Population-Based Assessment* (New York: Physicians for Human Rights, 1999).

21. See also James Hooper, "Kosovo: America's Balkan Problem," *Current History* 98 (April 1999):159–164; and *Security Dialogue* 30, no. 3 (September 1999).

22. "Economic, Humanitarian and Ecological Consequences of NATO Aggression Against Yugoslavia," *Yugoslavia Survey* 41 (1999):9–26.

23. "The Washington Summit and the Kosovo Crisis," Special Summit Edition of *NATO Review*, no. 2 (Summer 1999).

24. Federal Institute of Public Health, *Health Statistical Year Book 1996 of FR Yugoslavia* (Belgrade, 1997).

25. See Carolyn Hamilton and Nathalie Man, *Report of the Children and Armed Conflict Unit: The Impact of Armed Conflict on Children in Kosovo* (London: Children's Legal Centre, 1999).

26. See *RNIS 27: Report on the Nutrition Situation of Refugees and Displaced Populations* (RNIS) (New York: United Nations ACC/Sub-Committee on Nutrition, July 1999).

27. *Washington Post*, July 30, 1999, A25.

28. See Shashi Tharoor, "The Future of Civil Conflict," *World Policy Journal* 17, no. 1 (Spring 1999):1–12.

29. "Kosovo Refugees Receiving Useless Drugs," *Washington Post*, July 1, 1999, A22.

30. Colum Lynch, "U.N. Refugee Chief Says Rich Nations Favor Kosovo Over African Aid," *Washington Post*, July 27, 1999, A20.

31. See *RNIS 27*.

32. "Rwanda Appeals for Halt of Arms Flow to Rebels," *New York Times*, May 31, 1995, A6.

33. See Holly J. Burkhalter, "The Question of Genocide: The Clinton Administration and Rwanda," *World Policy Journal* 9, no. 4 (Winter 1994–1995):45.

34. Ibid.

35. Antonio Donini and Norah Niland, *Rwanda: Lessons Learned: A Report on the Coordination of Humanitarian Activities* (Geneva: U.N. Department of Humanitarian Affairs, 1994), pp. 11, 2–3.

36. Ibid., p. 8.

37. "Tribunal Readies Case in Rwandan Massacres," available at www.cnn.com, November 14, 1995.

38. Jose E. Alvarez, "Crimes of State/Crimes of Hate: Lessons from Rwanda," *Yale Journal of International Law* 24 (1999):364–483.

39. See Jim Whitman and David Pocock, eds., *After Rwanda: The Coordination of United Nations Humanitarian Assistance* (London: Macmillan, 1996); *The International Response to Conflict and Genocide: Lessons from the Rwanda Experience* (Copenhagen: Joint Evaluation of Emergency Assistance to Rwanda, 1997); and Raimo Väyrynen, "More Questions than Answers: Dilemmas of Humanitarian Action," *Peace & Change* 24, no. 2 (1999):172–196.

40. See Glynne Evans, *Responding to Crises in the African Great Lakes*, Adelphi Paper 311 (Oxford: Oxford University Press, 1998); and Linda Melvern, "Genocide Behind the Thin Blue Line," *Security Dialogue* 28 (1997):333–346.

41. John Prendergast and David Smock, "Postgenocidal Reconciliation: Building Peace in Rwanda and Burundi," *United States Institute of Peace Special Report*, September 1999, p. 2.

42. Tamara Jones, "Coming to the Aid of the Displaced People of Kosovo," *Washington Post Magazine*, July 4, 1999, p. 20.

43. Gordon Adam, "A Dramatic Treatment . . . ," *Crosslines* 3, no. 2 (April-May 1995):42.

CHAPTER FOUR

1. See Louise Doswald-Beck, "Implementation of International Humanitarian Law in Future Wars," *Naval War College Review* 52 (1999), no. 1:24–52.

2. Cindy Collins, "Humanitarian Implications of Small Arms and Light Weapons Proliferation," internal paper prepared for the U.N. Office for the Coordination of Humanitarian Affairs, July 1998.

3. "Targeting the Helpers . . . ," Editor's Desk, *Refugee Magazine* 114 (1999).

4. GA 52/38J of 8 January 1998.

5. A detailed discussion can be found in Thomas G. Weiss, "Whither International Efforts for Internally Displaced Persons?" *Journal of Peace Research* 36, no. 3 (1999):363–373.

6. Quoted in Human Rights Watch, *Stoking the Fires* (New York: Human Rights Watch, 1997), p. 30.

7. International Committee of the Red Cross, *Human Rights & Humanitarian Organization* (Geneva: ICRC, 1999); and Mark Frohardt, Diane Paul, and Larry Minear, *Protecting Human Rights: The Challenge to Humanitarian Organizations*, Watson Institute Occasional Paper no. 35 (Providence, R.I.: Brown University, Thomas J. Watson Jr. Institute for International Studies, 1999).

8. Alain Destexhe, "A Border Without Doctors," *New York Times*, February 9, 1995, A7.

9. Ian Smillie, *The Alms Bazaar: Altruism Under Fire—Non-Profit Organizations and International Development* (London: Intermediate Technology Publications, 1995), p. 111.

10. International Federation of Red Cross and Red Crescent Societies, *World Disasters Report 1995* (Geneva: IFRC, 1995), p. 42.

11. This discussion is a shortened version of Thomas G. Weiss, "Principles, Politics, and Humanitarian Action," *Ethics & International Affairs* 13 (1999):1–22.

12. Neutrality and impartiality are emphasized because of their centrality to the humanitarian ethos and because they give rise to so much controversy. The emphasis on consent is justified because nonintervention in domestic affairs is the glue of international relations; and consent guides virtually all U.N. actions, with the exception of Chapter VII coercion. See Marion Harroff-Tavel, "Neutrality and Impartiality: The Importance of These Principles for the International Red Cross and Red Crescent Movement and the Difficulties Involved in Applying Them," *International Review of the Red Cross*, no. 273 (November-December 1989):536–552, quote at p. 536. See also Yves Sandoz, "The International Committee of the Red Cross and the Law of Armed Conflict Today," *International Peacekeeping* 4, no. 4 (Winter 1997):86–99.

13. David P. Forsythe, *Humanitarian Politics: The International Committee of the Red Cross* (Baltimore: Johns Hopkins University Press, 1977), p. 28.

14. Michael Ignatieff, *The Warrior's Honor: Ethnic War and the Modern Conscience* (New York: Henry Holt & Company, 1997), p. 5.

15. Joanna Macrae, "The Death of Humanitarianism? An Anatomy of the Attack," *Disasters* 22 (December 1998):316.

16. Myron Wiener, "The Clash of Norms: Dilemmas in Refugee Policies," *Journal of Refugee Studies* 11, no. 4 (1998):1–21. See also Dan Smith, "Interventionist Dilemmas and Justice," in Anthony McDermott, ed., *Humanitarian Force* (Oslo: International Peace Research Institute, 1997), pp. 13–39, especially pp. 29–31.

CHAPTER FIVE

1. United Nations, www.un.org/ha/general.htm, July 1, 1999.
2. Alex de Waal, *Famine Crimes: Politics and the Disaster Relief Industry in Africa* (London: James Currey, 1997).
3. Mark Duffield, *Aid Policy and Post-Modern Conflict: A Critical Review,* Occasional Paper no. 19 (Birmingham, U.K.: University of Birmingham, 1998); and "NGO Relief in War Zones: Toward an Analysis of the New Aid Paradigm," in Thomas G. Weiss, ed., *Beyond UN Subcontracting: Task-Sharing with Regional Security Arrangements and Service-Providing NGOs* (London: Macmillan, 1998), pp. 139–159.
4. Larry Minear and Thomas G. Weiss, *Humanitarian Action in Times of War: A Handbook for Practitioners* (Boulder: Lynne Rienner, 1993), p. 33.
5. Amir Pasic and Thomas G. Weiss, "The Limits of Non-State Politics in the Former Yugoslavia," *Security Dialogue* 7, no. 1 (Autumn 1997):194–228.
6. Roberta Cohen, "Put Refugee Women in Charge of Food Distribution," *Hunger 1996, Countries in Crisis: Sixth Annual Report on the State of World Hunger* (Silver Spring, Md.: Bread for the World Institute, 1996), p. 35.
7. "Department War Crimes Tribunal Chief Assails U.N. Inaction," *Washington Post,* November 9, 1999, A26.
8. Human Rights Watch, *The Lost Agenda: Human Rights and U.N. Field Operations* (New York: Human Rights Watch, 1993).
9. Mark Frohardt, Diane Paul, and Larry Minear, *Protecting Human Rights: The Challenge to Humanitarian Organizations,* Occasional Paper no. 35 (Providence, R.I.: Brown University, Thomas J. Watson Jr. Institute for International Studies, 1999), p. viii.
10. Gayle E. Smith, "Emerging from Crisis: From Relief to Development," *Humanitarian Monitor,* no. 2 (February 1995):28.
11. Ian Smillie, *Relief and Development: The Struggle for Synergy,* Occasional Paper no. 33 (Providence, R.I.: Brown University, Thomas J. Watson Jr. Institute for International Studies, 1998), p. xiii.
12. There is a growing literature on this topic. See the series of essays in Robert I. Rotberg and Thomas G. Weiss, eds., *From Massacres to Genocide: The Media, Public Policy, and Humanitarian Crises* (Washington, D.C.: Brookings Institution, 1996); and in Larry Minear, Colin Scott, and Thomas G. Weiss, *The News Media, Civil Wars, and Humanitarian Action* (Boulder: Lynne Rienner, 1996).
13. Larry Minear, U.B.P. Chelliah, Jeff Crisp, John Mackinlay, and Thomas G. Weiss, *United Nations Coordination of the International Humanitarian Response to the Gulf Crisis, 1990–1992,* Occasional Paper no. 13 (Providence, R.I.: Brown University, Thomas J. Watson Jr. Institute for International Studies, 1992), pp. 15–16.
14. International Federation of Red Cross and Red Crescent Societies, *World Disasters Report 1995* (Geneva: IFRC, 1995), p. 42.
15. John Seaman, "Relief, Rehabilitation, and Development," *IDS Bulletin* 25, no. 4 (October 1994):34–35.
16. UNHCR, "1998 Refugee Statistics," available at www.unhcr.ch, July 28, 1999.
17. "America's Least-Wanted," *Economist* 332, no. 7872 (July 16, 1994):23–24.

18. Quoted in United Nations High Commissioner for Refugees, *The State of the World's Refugees, 1995* (New York: Oxford University Press, 1995), p. 37.

19. IFRC Situation Report no. 5, available at www.ifrc.org (July 27, 1995).

20. "Angola Facing War and Hunger," *Economist* 351, no. 8121 (May 29, 1999):41.

CHAPTER SIX

1. Sadako Ogata, "Statement to a Conference on Humanitarian Response and the Prevention of Deadly Conflict, Convened By the Carnegie Commission on the Prevention of Deadly Conflict and UNHCR," Geneva, February 1997.

2. P. Terrence Hopmann, *The Negotiation Process and the Resolution of International Conflict* (Columbia, S.C.: University of South Carolina Press, 1996), p. 26.

3. Bruce Russet, Barry O'Neill, and James Sutterlin, "Breaking the Security Council Restructuring Logjam," *Global Governance* 2, no. 1 (1996):65–80.

4. Joint Evaluation of Emergency Assistance to Rwanda, *The International Response to Conflict and Genocide: Lessons from the Rwanda Experience* (Copenhagen: Steering Committee of the Joint Evaluation of Emergency Assistance to Rwanda, March 1996).

5. Sydney D. Bailey, *The Procedure of the UN Security Council* (Oxford: Clarendon Press, 1988), p. 51.

6. Cindy Collins and Thomas G. Weiss, *An Overview and Assessment of 1989–1996 Peace Operations Publications*, Occasional Paper no. 28 (Providence, R.I.: Brown University, Thomas J. Watson Jr. Institute for International Studies, 1997), pp. 78–79.

7. Boutros Boutros-Ghali, *Supplement to an Agenda for Peace: Position Paper of the Secretary-General on the Occasion of the Fiftieth Anniversary of the United Nations* (New York: United Nations, 1995), par. 70.

8. See Thomas G. Weiss, David Cortright, George A. Lopez, and Larry Minear, eds., *Political Gain and Civilian Pain: The Humanitarian Impact of Economic Sanctions* (Boulder: Rowman & Littlefield, 1997).

9. Larry Minear, Jeffrey Clark, Roberta Cohen, Dennis Gallaghan, and Thomas G. Weiss, *Humanitarian Action in the Former Yugoslavia: The U.N.'s Role, 1991–1993*, Occasional Paper no. 18 (Providence, R.I.: Brown University, Thomas J. Watson Jr. Institute for International Studies, 1994), p. 13.

10. Adam Roberts, "NATO's 'Humanitarian War' over Kosovo," *Survival* 41, no. 3 (1999):102–123.

11. Shashi Tharoor, "The Changing Face of Peace-Keeping and Peace-Enforcement," speech presented at the International Institute for Strategic Studies meeting in Vienna, Austria, September 9, 1995, p. 10.

12. Pierre Hassner, "Beyond Nationalism and Internationalism," *Survival* 35, no. 2 (Summer 1993):61.

13. Council for a Livable World, "U.N. Peacekeeping," available at www.clw.org/pub/clw/un/troops0499.htm, April 1, 1999.

14. Larry Minear and Philippe Guillot, *Soldiers to the Rescue: Humanitarian Lessons from Rwanda* (Paris: OECD, 1996).

15. United Nations, "East Timor," available at www.un.org/peace/etimor, August 4, 1999.

16. John Clark, "Policy Influence, Lobbying, and Advocacy," in Michael Edwards and David Hulme, eds., *Making a Difference: NGOs and Development in a Changing World* (London: Earthscan, 1992), p. 199.

17. Michael Edwards and David Hulme, "Introduction," in ibid., p. 20.

18. Boutros Boutros-Ghali, *An Agenda for Peace* (New York: United Nations, 1992), para. 17.

19. Secretary-General's Speech to the 54th Session of the General Assembly, September 20, 1999.

20. Adam Roberts, "The Role of Humanitarian Issues in International Politics in the 1990s," *International Review of the Red Cross* 81, no. 833 (March 1999):19.

21. Michael Ignatieff, "Human Rights: The Midlife Crisis," *New York Review of Books* 46, no. 9 (20 May 1999):58.

22. François Debrix, "Deterritorialised Territories, Borderless Borders: The New Geography of International Medical Assistance," *Third World Quarterly* 19, no. 5 (1998):827–846.

23. David Rieff, "A New Age of Liberal Imperialism?" *World Policy Journal* 16, no. 2 (Summer 1999):3.

□ □ □

Additional Reading and
Related Web Locations

ADDITIONAL READING

American Academy of Arts and Sciences. *Reconstructing Nations and States.* Special issue of *Daedalus* 122, no. 3 (1993).

Amnesty International. *Peace Keeping and Human Rights.* IOR 40/01/94. London: Amnesty International, January 1994.

Anderson, Mary B. *Do No Harm: Supporting Local Capacities for Peace Through Aid.* Cambridge, Mass.: Collaborative for Development Action, 1996.

Anderson, Mary B., and Peter J. Woodrow. *Rising from the Ashes: Development Strategies in Times of Disaster.* Boulder: Westview Press, 1989.

Appleyard, Reginald. *International Migration: Challenges for the Nineties.* Geneva: International Organization for Migration, 1991.

Benthall, Jonathan. *Disasters, Relief, and the Media.* London: Tauris, 1993.

Boutros-Ghali, Boutros. *An Agenda for Peace 1995.* New York: United Nations, 1995.

Brown, Michael E., ed. *Ethnic Conflict and International Security.* Princeton: Princeton University Press, 1993.

_____. *International Implications of Internal Conflict.* Cambridge, Mass.: MIT Press, 1996.

Cahill, Kevin M., M.D., ed. *A Framework for Survival: Health, Human Rights, and Humanitarian Assistance in Conflicts and Disasters.* New York: Basic Books, 1993.

Chopra, Jarat. *Peace-Maintenance: The Evolution of International Political Authority.* London: Routledge, 1999.

Chr. Michelsen Institute. *Humanitarian Assistance and Conflict.* Bergen, Norway: Chr. Michelsen Institute, 1997.

Claude, Richard P., and Burns H. Weston, eds. *Human Rights in the International Community.* Rev. 2d ed. Philadelphia: University of Pennsylvania Press, 1992.

Cohen, Roberta, and Francis M. Deng. *The Forsaken People: Case Studies of the Internally Displaced.* Washington, D.C.: Brookings Institution, 1998.

Cohen, Roberta, and Francis M. Deng, eds. *Masses in Flight: The Global Crisis of Internal Displacement.* Washington, D.C.: Brookings Institution, 1998.

Cohn, Ilene, and Guy S. Goodwin-Gill. *The Role of Children in Armed Conflict.* Oxford: Clarendon Press, 1994.

Collins, Cindy, and Thomas G. Weiss. *An Overview and Assessment of 1989–1996 Peace Operations Publications.* Occasional Paper no. 28. Providence, R.I.: Watson Institute, 1997.

Commission on Global Governance. *Our Global Neighbourhood.* Oxford: Oxford University Press, 1995.

Cortright, David, and George A. Lopez, eds. *Economic Sanctions: Panacea or Peace-building in a Post–Cold War World.* Boulder: Westview Press, 1995.

Cranna, Michael, ed. *The True Costs of Conflict: Seven Recent Wars and Their Effects on Society.* New York: Free Press, 1994.

Crocker, Chester A., Fen Osler Hampson, and Pamela Aall, eds. *Managing Global Chaos: Sources of and Responses to International Conflict.* Washington, D.C.: U.S. Institute of Peace, 1996.

Cuny, Frederick. *Disasters and Development.* New York: Oxford University Press, 1984.

Cuny, Frederick, Barry N. Stein, and Pat Reed, eds. *Repatriation During Conflict in Africa and Asia.* Dallas: Center for the Study of Societies in Crisis, 1992.

Damrosch, Lori Fisler, ed. *Enforcing Restraint: Collective Intervention in Internal Conflicts.* New York: Council on Foreign Relations, 1993.

Damrosch, Lori Fisler, and David J. Scheffer. *Law and Force in the New International Order.* Boulder: Westview Press, 1991.

Deng, Francis M. *Protecting the Dispossessed: A Challenge for the International Community.* Washington, D.C.: Brookings Institution, 1993.

Deng, Francis M., and Larry Minear. *The Challenges of Famine Relief.* Washington, D.C.: Brookings Institution, 1992.

de Waal, Alex. *Famine Crimes: Politics and the Disaster Relief Industry in Africa.* London: James Currey, 1997.

Diehl, Paul. *International Peacekeeping.* Baltimore: Johns Hopkins University Press, 1993.

Donnelly, Jack. *Human Rights and International Relations.* Boulder: Westview Press, 1993.

Duffield, Mark, and John Prendergast. *Without Troops and Tanks: Humanitarian Intervention in Ethiopia and Eritrea.* Trenton, N.J.: Red Sea Press, 1994.

Dunne, Tim, and Nicholas J. Wheeler, eds. *Human Rights in Global Politics.* Cambridge: Cambridge University Press, 1999.

Durch, William J., ed. *U.N. Peacekeeping, American Policy, and the Uncivil Wars of the 1990s.* New York: St. Martin's Press, 1996.

———. *The Evolution of U.N. Peacekeeping: Case Studies and Comparative Analysis.* New York: St. Martin's Press, 1993.

Edwards, Michael, and David Hulme, eds. *Beyond the Magic Bullet: NGO Performance and Accountability in the Post–Cold War World.* West Hartford, Conn.: Kumarian Press, 1996.

The Emperor's New Clothes: Charting the Erosion of Humanitarian Principles. Special issue of *Disasters* 22, no. 4 (December 1998).

Famsbotham, Oliver, and Tom Woodhouse. *Humanitarian Intervention in Contemporary Conflict.* Cambridge: Polity Press, 1996.

Ferris, Elizabeth G., ed. *The Challenge to Intervene: A New Role for the United Nations?* Uppsala: Life and Peace Institute, 1992.

Field, John Osgood, ed. *The Challenge of Famine: Recent Experience, Lessons Learned.* West Hartford, Conn.: Kumarian Press, 1993.

Forsythe, David P. *Human Rights and Peace: International and National Dimensions.* Lincoln: University of Nebraska Press, 1992.

_____. *Humanitarian Politics.* Baltimore: Johns Hopkins University Press, 1977.

_____. *The Internationalization of Human Rights.* Lexington, Mass.: Lexington Books for the Free Press, 1991.

Girardet, Ed, ed. *Somalia, Rwanda, and Beyond: The Role of the Informational Media in Wars and Humanitarian Crises.* Dublin: Crosslines Global Report, 1995.

Gordenker, Leon, and Thomas G. Weiss, eds. *Soldiers, Peacekeepers, and Disasters.* London: Macmillan, 1991.

Gottlieb, Gidon. *Nation Against State: New Approaches to Ethnic Conflicts and the Decline of Sovereignty.* New York: Council on Foreign Relations, 1993.

Gowing, Nik. *Media Coverage: Help or Hindrance in Conflict Prevention?* New York: Carnegie Commission, September 1997.

_____. *Real-Time Television Coverage of Armed Conflicts and Diplomatic Crises: Does It Pressure or Distort Foreign Policy Decisions?* Cambridge, Mass.: Harvard University Press, 1994.

Gurr, Ted Robert, and Barbara Harff. *Ethnic Conflict in World Politics.* Boulder: Westview Press, 1994.

Gutman, Roy, and David Rieff, eds. *Crimes of War: What the Public Should Know.* New York: Norton, 1999.

Halperin, Morton H., and David J. Scheffer. *Self-Determination in the New World Order.* Washington, D.C.: Carnegie Endowment, 1992.

Hampton, Janie. *Internally Displaced People: A Global Survey.* London: Earthscan, 1998.

Hannum, Hurst. *Autonomy, Sovereignty, and Self-Determination.* Philadelphia: University of Pennsylvania Press, 1990.

Harriss, John, ed. *The Politics of Humanitarian Intervention.* London: Pinter, 1995.

Henkin, Alice H., ed. *Honoring Human Rights and Keeping the Peace.* Washington, D.C.: Aspen Institute, 1995.

Henkin, Louis, and John Lawrence Grove, eds. *Human Rights: An Agenda for the Next Century.* Washington, D.C.: American Society of International Law, 1995.

Hoffman, Stanley. *Duties Beyond Borders: On the Limits and Possibilities of Ethnic International Politics.* Syracuse, N.Y.: Syracuse University Press, 1981.

_____. *The Ethics and Politics of Humanitarian Intervention.* Notre Dame, Ind.: University of Notre Dame Press, 1996.

Human Rights Watch. *The Lost Agenda: Human Rights and U.N. Field Operations.* New York: Human Rights Watch, 1993.

_____. *Stoking the Fires.* New York: Human Rights Watch, 1997.

Hutchinson, John F. *Champions of Charity: War and the Rise of the Red Cross.* Boulder: Westview, 1996.

Ignatieff, Michael. *The Warrior's Honor: Ethnic War and the Modern Conscience.* New York: Henry Holt & Co., 1997.

Independent Commission on International Humanitarian Issues. *The Dynamics of Displacement.* London: Zed Books, 1987.

_____. *Famine: A Man-Made Disaster?* New York: Random House, 1985.

_____. *Modern War: The Humanitarian Challenge.* London: Zed Books, 1986.
_____. *Winning the Human Race?* London: Zed Books, 1998.
International Committee of the Red Cross. *Geneva Conventions of August 12, 1949 and Protocols Additional to the Geneva Conventions of 12 August 1949.* Geneva: ICRC, 1989.
International Federation of Red Cross and Red Crescent Societies, *World Disasters Report 2000.* Oxford: Oxford University Press, 2000.
The International Response to Conflict and Genocide: Lessons from the Rwanda Experience. Copenhagen: Joint Evaluation of Emergency Assistance to Rwanda, 1997. 5 volumes.
Johnstone, Ian. *Aftermath of the Gulf War: An Assessment of UN Action.* Boulder: Lynne Rienner, 1994.
Kalshoven, Frits, ed. *Assisting the Victims of Armed Conflict and Other Disasters.* Dordrecht, Netherlands: Nijhoff, 1989.
Keen, David. *The Economic Functions of Violence in Civil Wars.* Adelphi Paper no. 320. Oxford: Oxford University Press, 1998.
Kent, Randolph. *Anatomy of Disaster Relief: The International Network in Action.* London: Pinter, 1987.
King, Charles. *Ending Civil Wars.* Adelphi Paper no. 308. Oxford: Oxford University Press, 1998.
Lake, Anthony, ed. *After the Wars: Reconstruction in Afghanistan, Indochina, Central America, Southern Africa, and the Horn of Africa.* Washington, D.C.: Overseas Development Council, 1990.
Larkin, Mary Ann, Frederick Cuny, and Barry Stein, eds. *Repatriating Under Conflict in Central America.* Washington, D.C.: Georgetown University and CIPRA, 1991.
Loescher, Gil. *Beyond Charity: Interventional Cooperation and the Global Refugee Crisis.* New York: Oxford University Press, 1994.
Louise, Christopher. *The Social Impacts of Light Weapons Availability and Proliferation.* Discussion Paper no. 59. Geneva: United Nations Research Institute for Social Development/International Alert, March 1995.
Luck, Edward C. *Mixed Messages: American Politics and International Organizations, 1919–1999.* Washington, D.C.: Brookings Institution, 1999.
Lyons, Gene M., and Michael Mastanduno, eds. *Beyond Westphalia? National Sovereignty and International Intervention.* Baltimore: Johns Hopkins University Press, 1995.
MacAlister-Smith, Peter. *International Humanitarian Assistance: Disaster Relief Organizations in International Law and Organization.* Dordrecht, Netherlands: Nijhoff, 1985.
Macrae, Joanna, and Anthony Zwi, eds. *War and Hunger: Rethinking International Responses to Complex Emergencies.* London: Zed Books, 1994.
Makinda, Samuel. *Seeking Peace from Chaos: Humanitarian Intervention in Somalia.* Boulder: Lynne Rienner, 1992.
Maren, Michael. *The Road to Hell: The Ravaging Effects of Foreign Aid and International Charity.* New York: Free Press, 1997.
Martin, Lisa. *Coercive Cooperation: Explaining Multilateral Economic Sanctions.* Princeton: Princeton University Press, 1992.

Mayall, James, ed. *The New Interventionism: United Nations Experience in Cambodia, Former Yugoslavia, and Somalia.* New York: Cambridge University Press, 1996.

McDermott, Anthony, ed. *Humanitarian Force.* Oslo: International Peace Research Institute, 1997.

Minear, Larry, and Philippe Guillot. *Soldiers to the Rescue: Humanitarian Lessons from Rwanda.* Paris: Organisation for Economic Co-operation and Development, 1996.

Minear, Larry, Colin Scott, and Thomas G. Weiss. *The News Media, Civil Wars, and Humanitarian Action.* Boulder: Lynne Rienner, 1996.

Minear, Larry, and Thomas G. Weiss. *Humanitarian Action in Times of War: A Handbook for Practitioners.* Boulder: Lynne Rienner, 1993.

_____. *Humanitarian Politics.* New York: Foreign Policy Association, 1995.

_____. *Mercy Under Fire: War and the Global Humanitarian Community.* Boulder: Westview Press, 1995.

Moore, Jonathan, ed. *Hard Choices: Moral Dilemmas in Humanitarian Intervention.* Boulder: Rowman & Littlefield, 1998.

Moynihan, Daniel Patrick. *Pandaemonium: Ethnicity in International Politics.* New York: Oxford University Press, 1993.

Natsios, Andrew S. *U.S. Foreign Policy and the Four Horsemen of the Apocalypse: Humanitarian Relief in Complex Emergencies.* Westport, Conn.: Praeger, 1997.

Norwegian Refugee Council. *The Protection of Internally Displaced Persons by NRC.* Oslo: NRC, January 1994.

Omaar, Rakiya, and Alex de Waal. *Somalia: Death, Destruction, and Despair.* London: African Rights, 1994.

_____. *Humanitarianism Unbound? Current Dilemmas Facing Multi-Mandate Relief Operations in Political Exercises.* Discussion Paper no. 5. London: African Rights, November 1994.

Pieterse, Jan Nederveen, ed. *World Orders in the Making: the Case of Humanitarian Intervention.* London: Macmillan, 1998.

Ramcharan, B. G. *The International Law and Practice of Early Warning and Preventive Diplomacy: The Emerging Global Watch.* Dordrecht, Netherlands: Nijhoff, 1991.

Reed, Laura W., and Carl Kaysen, eds. *Emerging Norms of Justified Intervention.* Cambridge, Mass.: American Academy of Arts and Sciences, 1993.

Rieff, David. *Slaughterhouse: Bosnia and the Failure of the West.* New York: Simon and Schuster, 1995.

Roberts, Adam. *Humanitarian Action in War: Aid, Protection, and Impartiality in a Policy Vacuum.* Adelphi Paper no. 305. Oxford: Oxford University Press, 1996.

Roberts, Adam, and Benedict Kingsbury, eds. *United Nations, Divided World: The U.N.'s Role in International Relations.* 2d ed. Oxford: Clarendon Press, 1994.

Rodley, Nigel, ed. *To Loose the Bands of Wickedness.* London: Brassey, 1992.

Rosenau, James N. *The United Nations in a Turbulent World.* Boulder: Lynne Rienner, 1992.

Rotberg, Robert I., and Thomas G. Weiss, eds. *From Massacres to Genocide: The Media, Public Policy, and Humanitarian Crises.* Washington, D.C.: Brookings Institution, 1996.

Sahnoun, Mohamed. *Somalia: The Missed Opportunities.* Washington, D.C.: United Nations Institute of Peace, 1994.

200 ☐ Additional Reading

Salomon, Kim. *Refugees in the Cold War: Toward a New International Refugee Regime in the Early Postwar Era.* Lund, Sweden: Lund University Press, 1991.
Sen, Amartya. *Poverty and Famines.* New York: Oxford University Press, 1981.
Shawcross, William. *The Quality of Mercy: Cambodia, the Holocaust, and Modern Conscience.* New York: Simon and Schuster, 1984.
Shearer, David. *Private Armies and Military Intervention.* Adelphi Paper no. 316. Oxford: Oxford University Press, 1998.
Shepherd, Jack. *The Politics of Starvation.* Washington, D.C.: Carnegie Endowment for International Peace, 1975.
Smillie, Ian. *The Alms Bazaar: Altruism Under Fire—Non-Profit Organizations and International Development.* London: Intermediate Technology Publications, 1995.
Sommer, John G. *Hope Restored? Humanitarian Aid in Somalia, 1990–1994.* Washington, D.C.: Refugee Policy Group, November 1994.
Strobel, Warren P. *Late-Breaking Foreign Policy: The News Media's Influence on Peace Operations.* Washington, D.C.: U.S. Institute of Peace Press, 1997.
UNDP. *Human Development Report 2000.* New York: Oxford University Press, 2000.
UNESCO. *International Dimensions of Humanitarian Law.* Dordrecht, Netherlands: Nijhoff, 1988.
UNHCR. *The State of the World's Refugees, 1997–98: A Humanitarian Agenda.* New York: Oxford University Press, 1997.
UNHCR. Division of Programmes and Operational Support. *Policy and Methodological Framework for Quick Impact Projects.* Geneva: United Nations High Commissioner for Refugees, June 30, 1994.
Väyrynen, Raimo. *The Age of Humanitarian Emergencies.* Research for Action no. 25. Helsinki: World Institute for Development Economics Research, 1996.
Weiss, Thomas G. *Military-Civilian Interactions: Intervening in Humanitarian Crises.* Boulder: Rowman & Littlefield, 1999.
Weiss, Thomas G., David Cortright, George A. Lopez, and Larry Minear, eds. *Political Gain and Civilian Pain: Humanitarian Impact of Economic Sanctions.* Boulder: Rowman & Littlefield, 1997.
Weiss, Thomas G., David P. Forsythe, and Roger A. Coate. *The United Nations and Changing World Politics.* 3d ed. Boulder: Westview Press, 2000.
Weiss, Thomas G., ed. *The United Nations and Civil Wars.* Boulder: Lynne Rienner, 1995.
Weiss, Thomas G., and Leon Gordenker, eds. *NGOs, the UN, and Global Governance.* Boulder: Lynne Rienner, 1996.
Weiss, Thomas G., and Larry Minear, eds. *Humanitarianism Across Borders: Sustaining Civilians in Times of War.* Boulder: Lynne Rienner, 1993.
Williams, Michael C. *Civil-Military Relations and Peacekeeping.* Adelphi Paper no. 321. Oxford: Oxford University Press, 1998.
Woodhouse, Tom, Robert Bruce, and Malcolm Dando, eds. *Peacekeeping and Peacemaking: Towards Effective Intervention in Post–Cold War Conflicts.* New York: St. Martin's Press, 1998.
Zartman, I. William, ed. *Elusive Peace: Negotiating an End to Civil Wars.* Washington, D.C.: Brookings Institution, 1996.

WEB LOCATIONS

ACUNS (Academic Council on the U.N. System)—www.netspace.org/acuns—Addresses current issues related to U.N. reform and activities and provides links to related Web sites of various U.N. agencies.

CNN—www.cnn.com—Offers a brief profile of current events and provides links to related Web sites with more detailed analysis of conflicts in progress, such as Croatian Radio Broadcast, which is updated daily, and the weekly Bosnian newspaper.

Hunger Web—www.netspace.org/hungerweb—Addresses a variety of issues related to hunger, provides situation updates and reference materials, and does excellent research.

International Federation of the Red Cross—www.ifrc.org—Updates the activities of international and national Red Cross organizations, offers detailed descriptions of relief activities and resource demands, and states codes of conduct.

Journal of Humanitarian Affairs—www.gsp.cam.ac.uk/jha.html—Offers in-depth articles on humanitarian issues and posts job listings. Updated monthly.

One World Organization—www.oneworld.org—Acts as server for "globally minded broadcasters and NGOs" on a variety of issues, such as conflict, aid, health, and human rights; provides links to related Web sites of NGOs, including those of CARE, Oxfam, and Amnesty International; and is updated daily.

ReliefWeb—www.reliefweb.int—Provides information useful to the humanitarian relief community, giving updates on a number of geographic areas where multiple relief organizations are present and delivering assistance. Updated daily by the U.N. Office for the Coordination of Humanitarian Affairs. The site is popular among NGOs. Also lists job postings.

USAID—www.info.usaid—A resource for country statistics on which U.S. aid policy is based. Provides links to related Web sites for the State Department, the Peace Corps, and other U.S. agencies.

United Nations—www.un.org—The United Nations recently spent a considerable sum to improve its Web site in terms of user-friendliness and up-to-date information. Viewers should read both the "Peace and Security" section, which provides information on peacekeeping, disarmament, and observer missions, and the "Humanitarian Affairs" section, which provides information on various humanitarian interventions.

Volunteers in Technical Assistance—www.vita.org—An informational resource on international development issues. Provides links to related NGO Web sites. Updated regularly.

Glossary

Anarchy carries two distinct meanings. When applied to international relations, *anarchy* refers to the absence of authoritative institutions or norms above sovereign states. In an international system of anarchy, states must employ self-help methods to survive. *Anarchy* and *chaos* are synonymous in more popular usage, in reference to general disorder.

Asylum is temporary refuge granted by a foreign state to those fleeing their country of origin because of reasonable fear of persecution or harm.

Bilateral (or foreign) aid (to be distinguished from multilateral aid) is financial, material, or technical assistance provided to one country by another. Such aid can be used to maintain the political influence of donor countries in recipient countries. Bilateral aid may be *tied,* meaning that recipient governments are required to purchase a certain percentage of goods and services from the donor government, or it may be *conditional,* meaning the recipient government is required to change certain of its current policies to receive aid. Within some quarters, the words *assistance* and *cooperation* are thought to be less demeaning than *aid.*

Chapter VI of the U.N. Charter outlines the means used for the pacific settlement of disputes. Legitimate action includes diplomatic efforts, such as good offices, mediation, and fact-finding missions.

Chapter VII of the U.N. Charter outlines coercive action in response to threats to the peace, breaches of the peace, and acts of aggression. Legitimate action includes economic and military sanctions to enforce international decisions.

A **charter** is a written instrument executed in due form that creates and defines the signatories' rights and responsibilities and the procedures for signatories' interaction. The U.N. Charter is the world organization's constitution.

A **civil war** is an intrastate armed conflict generally fought between the regime in power and its challengers. Conflicts within failed states, where there is no recognized state authority, are also described as civil wars.

The **CNN effect** is the presumed causal phenomenon, coming to light especially during the Gulf War, in which the media (CNN in particular) demonstrate their power to inform and sway public opinion, which in turn affects international responses to humanitarian emergencies. In the post–Cold War era, civil wars have almost entirely replaced international wars as the primary form of armed conflict.

The **Cold War** refers to the ideological standoff between the United States and the Soviet Union following World War II and ending with the demise of the Soviet

203

Union in 1991. The Cold War was characterized by East-West conflicts by proxy, usually in developing countries.

Comparative advantage describes the relationships among a group of actors with a common objective, each having specific and unique characteristics that they exploit collectively so as to be more effective in reaching their objective. The respective tasks of the individual actors are coordinated, or assigned in a way that recognizes the differences among them and reflects who does what best.

Compassion (or donor) fatigue is a notion used to explain a decrease in resources or interest in humanitarian activities in complex emergencies or in related development activities designed to foster growth. It implies that donors have become overwhelmed by the increase in humanitarian needs and the rise in conflicts in recent years, along with the lack of success in development efforts, and have reduced their contributions because of personal or institutional resignation to the inevitability of conflict and the inability of past efforts to produce measurable or meaningful successes.

A **complex emergency** is a crisis characterized by political, economic, and social destabilization. A complex emergency might also include natural disasters, such as famine, and massive population movements.

Consent of political authorities within a conflict area means that some humanitarian actors, such as the ICRC, will withhold assistance to suffering populations until internal political authorities agree to the presence of external humanitarian workers and the conditions under which they will operate.

A **contact group** is a coalition of states that use their collective diplomatic, and sometimes economic, power to foster or negotiate peace among belligerents in a conflict.

The **continuum from relief to rehabilitation** (short-term, transitional projects designed to facilitate the restoration of a community's social, economic, judicial, and political infrastructure) **to development** (long-term projects designed to improve living standards) is a theoretical construct that describes a gradual and comprehensive approach to addressing complex emergencies. The construct has increasingly been criticized as oversimple and mechanistic.

A **convention** is a legally binding international agreement among states on a particular matter of common concern.

A **corridor of tranquillity** is an access road used to deliver humanitarian assistance during active fighting. Theoretically, warring parties agree not to impede the transport of humanitarian aid through designated corridors of tranquillity.

A **declaration** is a nonbinding international document that embodies states' individual and collective intention to uphold the ideals contained in this joint proclamation.

Dependency is the condition of reliance upon external sources for aid or support. Dependency can be created when victims are not capable of providing for themselves, and it may linger long after the initial stages of crisis have passed, which was the original justification for short-term aid.

Distributive justice is a process in which gross disparities in ownership of and control over resources and funds are remedied through more equitable redistribution.

The **division of labor** is a classic economic theory stipulating that if an actor has a comparative advantage in performing a particular activity, then there will be an efficiency gain from allowing that actor to specialize in that task.

According to the **domino theory**, a hypothesis originating with President Dwight Eisenhower in 1954, if one country fell to communism, its fall would initiate a ripple effect in which other countries also would succumb to communism.

Donor fatigue: See **Compassion fatigue.**

Empowerment is a process by which those previously without the means to provide certain benefits (physical or psychological) for themselves are given the means and opportunities to do so.

Enforcement/coercion strategies, as outlined in Chapter VII of the U.N. Charter, are forceful means by which the international community pressures belligerents to halt their violations of international laws or norms. Synonymous with *intervention.*

Ethnic cleansing is the systematic elimination of a targeted ethnic group for political purposes. Ethnic cleansing can be carried out through genocidal acts or forced migration.

Ethnicity refers to the collection of perceived or actual identifying characteristics of a group of people, generally including language, culture, history, race, and religion.

A **failed state** is one in which there is no clearly legitimate sovereign or governing authority.

Genocide is the deliberate, planned, and systematic extermination of a national, ethnic, religious, political, or racial group.

Human rights, the rights that one has simply because one is a human being, are held equally and inalienably. They are the economic, social, and political guarantees necessary to protect individuals from the threats to human dignity and integrity commonly posed by the modern state and modern markets.

Humanitarian action covers a range of activities, such as diplomacy, emergency relief, and rehabilitation and development projects, designed to alleviate human suffering in both the short and the long term and to protect human rights.

The **humanitarian imperative** refers to an individual belief that wherever there is human suffering, the international humanitarian system must respond, regardless of political considerations.

Humanitarian intervention consists of efforts by outside parties to ensure the delivery of emergency aid, and may include efforts to protect the rights of local peoples without the consent of local political authorities.

Humanitarian space refers to the range of operational freedom humanitarian actors have in providing assistance.

Idealism is a perspective adopted by many political leaders following World War I. Idealism claims that humankind is perfectible, that war is not inevitable, and that a harmony of interests among states is possible; it is a theoretical tradition in international relations that focuses on international cooperation and international law.

Impartiality, with regard to the provision of humanitarian aid, is a standard according to which aid must be provided to all noncombatants on the basis of need.

Imperialism is a country's extension of its power, authority, and influence over other territories and peoples.

Import substitution is an economic policy whereby local production displaces or substitutes for goods that previously would have been imported.

Intergovernmental organizations (IGOs) are associations whose members are composed of states and whose functions, in theory, are to reflect the common concerns of members.

Internally displaced persons (IDPs) are those who have fled their homes as a result of a conflict but have not crossed over internationally recognized borders into another state.

International humanitarian law (or international law of armed conflicts) is the body of legal standards, procedures, and institutions governing the social intercourse of sovereign states with respect to war. The principles of humanitarian law, which are found primarily in the four Geneva Conventions of 1949 and the Additional Protocols of 1977, state that armed forces are not free to pursue their objectives by any means they consider necessary or convenient, that only military personnel and property be targeted, and that it is unlawful for an armed force to engage in any attack or operation if the anticipated suffering of either soldiers or civilians is disproportionate to the military gains that might be made. Individuals in the armed forces prefer the phrase *laws of war* over *international humanitarian law.*

International law governs relations between states and other legal persons in the international system. The sources of international law include international conventions, international custom, and general principles of the laws of states.

Intervention: See **Enforcement/coercion.**

Jus ad bellum is the humanitarian law governing the decision to resort to war, wherein self-defense is deemed the only legitimate cause for declaring war.

Jus in bello is the humanitarian law governing the conduct of war after a decision to resort to war is made, according to which states must discriminate between combatants and noncombatants and must demonstrate proportionality with regard to the means of war.

A **lead agency** is a U.N. organization designated by the secretary-general to assume a leadership position in a particular relief operation. Its functions are to coordinate relief activities among a multitude of humanitarian actors within and outside of the U.N. system and to serve as a focal point for the dissemination of information.

Liberal institutionalism is the school of thought among international relations theorists that recognizes that states are indeed the most important actors in international relations but also claims that cooperation among them is achievable through involvement in transnational institutions, where common interests merge, transparency of others' actions is revealed, and transaction costs are reduced.

Liberation theology, as it emerged in Latin America in the 1960s, is the argument that the special duty of the believing Christian is to work for the liberation of the poor and oppressed through, among other avenues, active opposition to existing power structures.

Loud and silent emergencies are two types of humanitarian crises, which tend to generate different types of international responses. Loud emergencies are evidenced by active physical violence between warring parties, and they tend to receive attention from the media and humanitarians. Silent emergencies, which can contribute to eventual loud emergencies, are best characterized by structural violence—that is, conditions arising from social, economic, and political structures that increase the vulnerability of various groupings of people to many forms of harm, such as hunger, poverty, and disease. Silent emergencies are considered less newsworthy and generally attract less attention and fewer (and weaker) attempts at intervention than do loud emergencies.

Multilateral aid (to be distinguished from bilateral aid) is financial, material, or technical assistance channeled to countries by other countries via international organizations such as U.N. agencies or the European Union.

Neutrality in the provision of humanitarian aid is a principle according to which aid must be provided regardless of the origins, beliefs, or ideology of the beneficiaries.

A **no-fly zone** is a demarcated territory determined to be off limits to antagonistic aircraft. No-fly zones require effective individual or collective security measures to enforce the integrity of the territory and its protected population.

Nongovernmental organizations (NGOs) are typically nonprofit, nonofficial organizations that are actively involved in humanitarian assistance, human rights advocacy, or socioeconomic development. NGOs can be local, national, or international in scope, and they rely on donations, grants, and/or contract fees for their operations.

A **norm** is a standard, model, or pattern of behavior to which actors adhere with a relatively high degree of predictability.

Official development assistance is aid provided by governments, through their own bilateral agencies or intergovernmental and nongovernmental organizations, with the provision that at least 25 percent is a grant and not a loan.

A **paramilitary** group is an association of combatants that operates in place of or as a supplement to a regular military force. It may be an informal and spontaneous association, or one that is officially sponsored. It is often difficult to determine who is in control of paramilitary groups.

Peace-building refers to rehabilitation strategies applied to a war-torn society once a peace agreement has been signed. Peace-building includes activities such as demobilization programs and community building.

Peacekeeping is the deployment of a U.N.-sanctioned troop presence in the field, hitherto with the consent of all the parties concerned and normally involving U.N. military and/or police personnel and frequently civilians as well. Military force is used only in self-defense and as a last resort.

Peacemaking traditionally is action to bring hostile parties to agreement, essentially through pacific means such as those foreseen in Chapter VI of the Charter of the United Nations.

Populations at risk are those dependent on outside aid to avoid malnutrition or death.

Preventive deployment refers to efforts by the international community to stabilize a region affected by progressively escalating political and military conflict. Preventive deployment requires consent of a host government and can include early posting of civilian, police, and/or military personnel to maintain order within a country, along both sides of a border in dispute, or on one side of a border.

Protection in the context of humanitarian action refers to ensuring respect for the human rights of vulnerable populations.

Realism (neorealism) is the dominant approach to international relations. It assumes that people are self-interested and seek to dominate others; that the state is a rational, unitary actor pursuing its perceived self-interest within an anarchic international system; and that cooperation among states is determined by each state's narrow and immediate interest in doing so.

Refoulement occurs when countries of asylum forcefully expel or return refugees to the frontiers of territories where their lives or freedom would be threatened. *Refoulement* is a violation of Article 33 of the Refugee Convention.

Refugees are individuals who have fearfully fled their homes as a result of political conflict and have crossed an internationally recognized border in search of asylum.

A **regime** is a set of principles, norms, rules, and decisionmaking procedures influencing state behavior (and that of other relevant international actors) in an issue area. The notion of a regime points to patterns of international governance that are not necessarily limited to a single treaty or organization.

Relief is the delivery of emergency goods and services to ameliorate hunger, pain, anxiety, and other forms of human vulnerability.

Repatriation is the sending of refugees or other economic migrants back to their countries of origin.

Resettlement consists of permanently permitting refugees to remain in a country of asylum, or establishing a new community for internally displaced persons within their own country.

A **safe haven or safe area** is an internationally protected area within a conflict zone that is reserved for the care and safeguarding of civilians who are generally dependent upon outside humanitarian assistance for day-to-day survival. The reality of safe havens has not always matched the theory.

Sanctions are economic measures, as outlined in Chapter VII of the U.N. Charter, by one or more states to force another state to comply with legal obligations or international norms. Sanctions include the cessation of economic transactions, the freezing of assets abroad, and the suspension of travel and communication links.

Sister-city programs, in the context of Central American humanitarian crises, were advocacy projects designed to educate those in developed countries with sufficient material resources and political clout to influence U.S. decisionmakers to scale back U.S. intervention in the political affairs of Central America.

Sovereignty, narrowly defined, is a state's claim to supreme political authority in a defined territory, particularly to the rights of self-determination and of noninterference by other states in its domestic affairs.

A **treaty** is a contract in writing between two or more states.

Triage is the process by which treatment of vulnerable populations at various levels of need is prioritized in situations where there are multiple demands for attention and limited human and material resources.

The **Vietnam syndrome** is the resistance to U.S. military engagement in overseas conflicts that grew out of the substantial public opposition to U.S. involvement in Vietnam, where over 50,000 Americans lost their lives. Conflict situations that stimulate the appearance of the Vietnam syndrome are those that are perceived to require substantial military ground troops in a civil war environment and in which the possibilities of protracted involvement in the conflict and of substantial U.S. deaths are high and the chances of success are low. The alternative is the "Powell Doctrine," named after the former chairman of the Joint Chiefs of Staff, Colin Powell, which calls for a clear definition of policy goals and for the use of all available firepower and moral resolution to overwhelm an enemy as quickly as possible.

Index